D0371969

THE MOST

American

THING IN

America

STUDIES IN *Theatre History* AND *Culture*

EDITED BY THOMAS POSTLEWAIT

Typical Scene at a Redpath Chautauqua.

THE MOST *American* THING IN *America* CIRCUIT *Chautauqua*

AS PERFORMANCE

CHARLOTTE M. CANNING

UNIVERSITY OF IOWA PRESS   IOWA CITY

University of Iowa Press, Iowa City 52242

Copyright © 2005 by the University of Iowa Press

Printed in the United States of America

Design by Richard Hendel

http://www.uiowa.edu/uiowapress

The University of Iowa Press is a member of Green Press
Initiative and is committed to preserving natural resources.

The publication of this book was generously supported
by the State Historical Society, Inc., and a University
Cooperative Society Subvention Grant awarded by the
University of Texas at Austin.

Printed on acid-free paper

Library of Congress Cataloging-in-Publication data

Canning, Charlotte, 1964–.

The most American thing in America: circuit Chautauqua as
performance / by Charlotte M. Canning.

p.   cm.—(Studies in theatre history and culture)

Includes bibliographical references and index.

ISBN 0-87745-941-X (cloth)

1. Chautauquas.   2. Popular culture—United States—History—
20th century.   I. Title.   II. Series.

LC6301.C4C36 2001

306'.0973—dc22   2004062088

05 06 07 08 09 C 5 4 3 2 1

For Fritz

"If these old walls could speak. . . ."

Contents

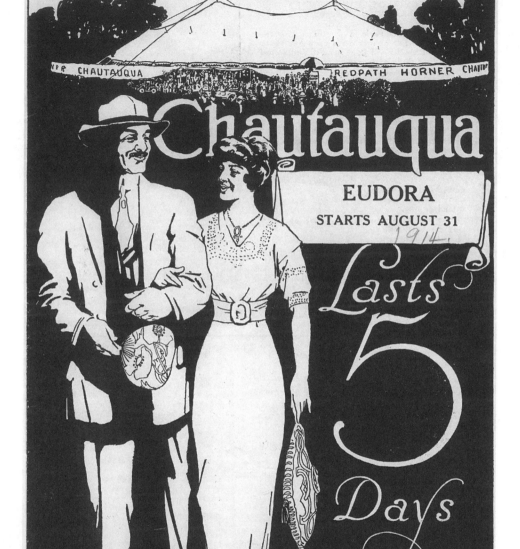

Chautauqua

EUDORA

STARTS AUGUST 31

1914

Lasts

5

Days

Acknowledgments

Ten years have passed since I presented at the Association for Theatre in Higher Education the first paper from what would turn out to be the research for this book. During that time, I have been the recipient of the generosity of many people and institutions, and I would be remiss if I did not acknowledge their largess. While I must share the credit with them for the strengths of this book, I take sole responsibility for its weaknesses; any failings are a result of my own limitations, not their lack of sagacity.

First thanks must go to Thomas Postlewait, editor of the series in which this book appears, and Holly Carver, director of the University of Iowa Press. Both of them were calm and supportive presences who never lost their sense of humor, even when it seemed that this book would never be completed. Tom Postlewait deserves special thanks all his own for his untiring willingness to read yet another draft and his unwavering belief in the project. I do not think there would be a book without him; he was truly the perfect editor for this project.

Early versions of chapters 1, 3, 4, and 5 appeared in *Performing America: Cultural Nationalism in American Theatre*, *Theatre Journal*, and *Land/Scape/Theatre*. J. Ellen Gainor, Jeffrey Mason, Loren Kruger, Susan Bennett, Una Chaudhuri, and Elinor Fuchs were the editors whose keen perceptions and challenging remarks transformed my own sense of the value of this project. What I learned from them marks every page of this book.

While editorial support is crucial, institutional support is no less important, and the University of Texas at Austin was a model setting for writing this book. Grants from the Department of Theatre and Dance, College of Fine Arts, Office of Graduate Studies, and Vice President for Research made travel, research assistants, and a leave possible. For all of that I am eternally grateful. In addition, the Center for the Study of Modernism, through Linda Henderson, invited me to present my work, and that feedback strengthened my analysis. The presentation of three of these chapters to the Humanities Institute in fall 2003, when I was a faculty fellow, allowed me to make a huge conceptual leap. Director Evan Carton's willingness to discuss the work with me and make key suggestions was the very model of what a humanities institute should provide. My colleagues in the seminar offered incisive comments of the kind every scholar deserves to receive.

Other institutions also played a central role in the creation of this book. First and foremost is the University of Iowa, especially the University Libraries Special

Collections, the site of the largest Circuit Chautauqua collection in the world. I was treated like an honored guest every time I visited, and without the knowledge, expertise, and support of successive directors Robert McCown, Richard Kolbert, and Sidney F. Huttner there would be no book. Every scholar should have the privilege of such extraordinary research colleagues. Additionally, the chance to present a paper at Iowa during the research, thanks to the Theatre Arts and American Studies departments, played an important role in the development of my thinking. Librarians at Swarthmore College, the Harry Ransom Humanities Research Center at the University of Texas at Austin, the New York Public Library for the Performing Arts, and the University of Arizona were similarly helpful. A residency at the Boulder Chautauqua in spring 2003, thanks to Nini Coleman, Ray Tuomey, and Martha Vail, allowed me to complete two chapters in the inspiring setting of an ongoing Chautauqua and provided me with a living example of the best of Chautauqua's legacy. At the same time, an invitation from the Center for the Humanities and Arts from the University of Colorado at Boulder gave me a chance to share what I was writing.

There are some colleagues, both at Texas and elsewhere, whose contributions were so valuable I cannot begin to describe them here. Their feedback, intelligence, humor, and friendship make Jill Dolan, Stacy Wolf, Lisa Moore, Madge Darlington, Joni Jones, Sharon Grady, Janet Davis, Esther Beth Sullivan, Sue-Ellen Case, Katrin Sieg, Mady Schutzman, Rebecca Schneider, and Shannon Jackson the perfect colleagues. It is the rare day when one of them doesn't make an incredible difference in my life. Without Brian Singleton, Douglas Dempster, Charles Roeckle, Lucia Gilbert, Ellen Donkin, and William Roger Louis, I could not be the scholar I am, and I thank each of them for their continuing interest in me and my work. Lynn Miller deserves a sentence all her own because it was her neo-Chautauqua performances that made me curious about Chautauqua in the first place.

The students in various graduate courses I have taught over the years have been a large part of my ability to stay with this project. Their enthusiasm and incisive questions stretched my scholarly abilities beyond what I thought were my limitations. The classes Historiography of American Theatre History, Historiography, and American Women and Popular Entertainment created a community of learners as utopian as one could hope for in the contemporary university setting. I had a similar experience with the research assistants who made time in their busy schedules for my work. I hope never to have to write a book without such incredible student colleagues.

Until his death in 1999, Richard Oram was an extraordinary resource. He patiently answered my many questions and never failed to make me laugh. I hope I have managed to capture his love for and skepticism about Circuit Chautauqua. His family is continuing the spirit of generosity Dick established and has allowed me continued access to his materials and papers.

I would be remiss if I did not mention the Weston Playhouse Theatre. For two perfect Vermont summers the company, particularly Tim Fort, Martha Bailey, Amy Fort, Malcolm Ewen, Steve Stettler, Audrey Duke, Stuart Duke, and Barbara Lloyd kept me excited about my book through their perceptive questions and support, even though I found it almost impossible to resist the lure of excellent theater, community, and friendship—the very things this book explores.

Lastly, I must acknowledge the incredible debt I owe to my family, who always acted as though it was perfectly reasonable to have someone in their midst who talked about Chautauqua nonstop for ten years. No scholar has ever had a more lively and supportive family than I have in the Cannings and Schwentkers, especially my parents, Joan and Tom Canning. My brother, Andy Canning, deserves a special mention, as he often seemed to have a greater interest in Chautauqua than I did. Harriette Kohler Smith, too, played an important role as the only living person in my family who had attended Chautauqua. No one has ever had a more loving critic than I have had in her. Fritz Schwentker is the single person without whom none of this would be possible. An inspiration in everything he does, I have dedicated this book to him to acknowledge the many and diverse rewards and pleasures of our life together. Near the end of writing this book, those rewards and pleasures multiplied exponentially when Frances Rose Canning Schwentker came into our lives. Sharing our lives with her is teaching us both on a daily basis the true meaning of happiness.

SWARTHMORE
CHAUTAUQUA

1924

Abbreviations

Arizona:
    The Loring Campbell collection, Oversize
    PN2285 .C19. Special Collections,
    University of Arizona Libraries, Tucson
Chautauqua Institution:
    Chautauqua Institution Archives,
    Chautauqua, New York
Iowa:
    Chautauqua Collection,
    University of Iowa Libraries, Iowa City
Nebraska:
    Nebraska State Historical Society, Lincoln
New York:
    Billy Rose Theatre Collection,
    New York Public Library for the
    Performing Arts, New York
Old Dartmouth:
    New Bedford Whaling Museum,
    Old Dartmouth Historical Society,
    New Bedford, Massachusetts
Swarthmore:
    Paul M. Pearson Papers,
    Friends Historical Library, Swarthmore College,
    Swarthmore, Pennsylvania
Texas, AHC:
    The Center for American History,
    University of Texas at Austin
Texas, HRC:
    Harry Ransom Humanities Research Center,
    University of Texas at Austin

THE MOST *American* THING IN *America*

Remembering the Platform

Marian Castle, reflecting back on her experiences as a booking agent and superintendent for Circuit Chautauqua during the 1920s, predicted in 1932: "But who can say that some future historian may not write: 'The circuit Chautauquas, which flourished from 1904 to 1930, should be ranked as one of the most significant indications of an awakening American culture?'"[1] Chautauqua was "culture" for Castle because it addressed how people understood their lives and what they wanted to make of that understanding. As one very poor community's committee said to her when she abashedly had to ask it to make up the ticket sales deficit, "Bring out the new contract, Miss Superintendent. . . . Even though we may not eat very rich fare this year, we got to keep on with the Chautauqua so we'll have something nice to think about, anyhow."[2] For that particular committee, and many others, Chautauqua was a place where American culture was made and remade. Those rural citizens could see their ideas, attitudes, and politics reflected back to them every summer on the Chautauqua platform, and that experience spoke to them forcefully. For roughly thirty years, during the span of time Castle mentions, Circuit Chautauqua toured the United States, performing almost solely in the nation's rural precincts. It promised to inspire cultural, community, and individual improvement through performances of various kinds. In the span of three days to a week, audiences could expect musical groups, lectures, elocutionary readers, special programming for children, and leisurely socializing with other members of the community. In order to write the history of such performances, it is important to explain why that history needs to be written in the first place.

Castle assumed that such a significant institution, which performed annually to hundreds of thousands, perhaps even millions of people and whose efficacy was proclaimed in national and even international periodicals, would never be forgotten. In fact, quite to the contrary, the entire perspective of her article assumes she is writing for a posterity curious about a much discussed and revered past. She does not doubt that there will be continuing nostalgia for Chautauqua days gone by. All of those who share their Circuit Chautauqua memories with her have the same feelings of loss she does, as well as the sense that they participated in something of lasting historical significance. In the conclusion she admits that despite her own initial skepticism about Chautauqua, she came to realize that "those of us who have really lived and worked under the big brown tents can never quite forget."[3] That nothing so defining, so affecting, could ever slip out of national memory was the consensus of those who had engaged with Circuit Chautauqua in one way or another.

Seventy-two years after Castle wrote her article, in 2004, one is hard-pressed to find significant numbers of people who have ever heard of Circuit Chautauqua. The population of those who experienced the Circuits firsthand is vanishing, and it does not seem to have entered into the American mythos. Memories of Chautauqua present themselves in unexpected ways. When I would answer the question, "What are you working on?" the second most common response (after "What's that?") was: "Oh, right, from *Zen and the Art of Motorcycle Maintenance*." Robert M. Pirsig's 1974 book, the meditative account of a man's journey across the United States by motorcycle with his son, casts itself as a "sort of Chautauqua." Pirsig believes it to be the best evocation he can imagine for something that deliberates matters of great import. "What is in mind is a sort of Chautauqua—that's the only name I can think of for it—like the traveling tent-show Chautauquas that used to move across America, this *America*, the one that we are now in, in an old-time series of popular talks intended to edify and entertain, improve the mind and bring culture and enlightenment to the ears and thoughts of the hearer. The Chautauquas were pushed aside by faster-paced radio, movies, and TV, and it seems to me that the change was not necessarily an improvement."[4] This romanticized view that something irreplaceable has been lost is probably what Castle expected to be typical. Instead, Pirsig's book stands virtually alone in recognizing the important cultural role of Chautauqua.

There are few such other examples to place beside *Zen and the Art of Motorcycle Maintenance*. One is the Chautauqua Foundation, a nonprofit organization established in 1992 to "create public awareness of Texas Rivers and of existing and potential pollution problems by involving the public in various river-related activities."[5] When asked why he named it "Chautauqua," founder Joe Kendall thought the term, which he understood to mean "combining education and entertainment," fit his enterprise exactly.[6] Chautauqua Airlines, which primarily serves the eastern United States and was founded in western New York, echoes some of Chautauqua's founding belief in its vision: "We believe that every employee, regardless of personal beliefs or world view, has been created in the image and likeness of God. We seek to become stronger from our diversity. We seek personal respect and fulfillment from our work. Most of all, we seek to recognize the dignity and potential of our Chautauqua family."[7] It takes a highly knowledgeable reader to identify the historical antecedents of either enterprise.

Chautauqua's palimpsestic traces are everywhere if you simply look hard enough. As you walk up the hill to attend the Shakespeare Festival in Ashland, Oregon, a small plaque informs you that you are in Chautauqua Park. The Angus Bowmer Theater, it turns out, was built on the very foundations of an annual Chautauqua. In San Marcos, Texas, the Chautauquan, a free local paper, serves all of Hays County, and in the same town Texas State University's main building sits on Chautauqua Hill, also the site of a former Chautauqua. In "places as different as Norman, Oklahoma and Pacific Palisades, California . . . there are streets named Chautauqua."[8] References lurk, often unremarked, in the biographies of famous men and women: journalist William Shirer, artist Grant Wood, comedian Edgar Bergen, Progressive politician Robert La Follette, and muckraker Ida Tarbell are only a few of those whose lives were shaped and molded by their Chautauqua experiences.

It does not seem too unreasonable to expect that memories of Chautauqua would be in more than the few places mentioned here, given its tremendous national influence at the end of the nineteenth century and into the twentieth. Chautauqua has not fared much better outside the popular realm, however. In his book on the New York Chautauqua—the first incarnation of Chautauqua, started thirty years before the Circuits began—historian Andrew C. Rieser remarks wryly: "I had difficulty finding critical work on the subject. Chautauqua seemed to possess an uncanny ability to evade scholarly attention." He goes on to observe: "And although some prominent academic historians had devoted whole articles or chapters to the subject, it had never received the official tincture of academic approval in the form of a dedicated, book-length, critical narrative."[9]

My experiences researching this book are remarkably similar to Rieser's. There are several memoirs by people directly involved in the Circuits. Managers

Charles Horner, Harry Harrison, and J. Roy Ellison all wrote or contributed to books about their experiences.[10] Performers, too, took the time to pen Chautauqua memoirs. Gay MacLaren, Marion Scott, Irene Briggs Da Boll, Frances Perry-Cowen, and Bob Hanscom created lively and engaging portraits of their time on the road.[11] Sometimes it was left to the children of performers to record their parents' lives and the effect Chautauqua had on those lives. Jean Handley Adams and James R. Schultz lovingly re-create a time gone by.[12] The press contemporary with Circuit Chautauqua could not write enough about the phenomenon, and thus there is an almost unlimited supply of opinion, celebration, and condemnation from that source. Importantly, as Rieser notes, few scholars have honed in on the movement itself. John E. Tapia and John S. Gentile are two of those who wrote dissertations on the subject and revised them into books.[13] Most other dissertations on the subject lie in libraries unread, except by those of us who, eager for any analysis and critique we can get of Circuit Chautauqua, request them through interlibrary loan.[14]

Theater historians do not fare much better than scholars in the larger field of history when it comes to assessing and reviewing Circuit Chautauquas. In part because of their peculiar negotiation of America's antitheatrical prejudice, Circuit Chautauquas have always been marginalized in theater and performance history. From the dominant narratives of theatrical progress and innovation, Circuit Chautauquas failed to meet conventional conditions of theater: they were not urban; they made no innovations in performance technique, stage material, or design effects; they produced no dramatic literature; and they were largely ignored by professional theater practitioners and critics. Theater historians have more or less followed the lead of those practitioners and critics. In A History of the American Theatre 1700–1950, published twenty years after the Circuits' demise, Glenn Hughes dismissed Chautauquas as "culturally pretentious" entertainment "developed to serve that segment of the population which resisted the frankly theatrical."[15] Twenty-three years after Hughes, Garff Wilson characterized Chautauquas as "merely a mechanism for presenting various established forms of theater both popular and legitimate."[16] Very few theater histories after Wilson's mention Chautauqua at all. One notable exception is Don B. Wilmith and Christopher Bigsby's impressive three-volume history of the American theater. Volume 2 devotes three paragraphs to the Circuits, an allocation of space equal to that which they give other popular entertainments.[17]

While the popular references previously cited, like Pirsig's and Kendall's, revere Chautauqua's contributions to public discourse on moral, cultural, and political issues, these contributions were not made through readings or discussion groups but instead through a series of stage performers embodying various messages from overt politics and patriotism to covert critiques and beliefs. In the Chautauqua tent, small-town America was participating in the performance of small-town America. If something was "awakening," in Castle's terms, it was because the audience understood that what they were witnessing had the potential to transform their lives. Live "performance represents one powerful way in which cultures set about the necessary business of remembering who and what they are. Performance is also one powerful way of making them into who and what they are, and even into who and what they might someday be."[18] By performing the America they wanted to exist, Chautauqua and its communities helped to make that America exist, even if only for the duration of the performance.

The task of this book is to evoke Chautauqua in such a way that those who participated in it would recognize what they knew as Chautauqua. The movement has been characterized as education, politics, reform, and community building but rarely as performance. Individual elements—music, elocution, or theater, for example—have been so labeled, but the entire experience has not been understood in that way. Yet performance offers an analytical framework that carries with it the implications of creation, transformation, accomplishment, and effect, all of which I will claim for Chautauqua.

The processes and investments of a culture are most often visible in its performances. Understanding performance requires the intersection of seemingly disassociated inquiries, encouraging a broader and more inclusive portrait. Performance is an act of embodiment that is always implicated in the social and cultural formations in which it is embedded. Concomitantly, it enacts what should or could be. In the United States, performance is a particularly useful approach to Chautauqua because performance has been practiced less as a literary form, as it has in Europe, and more as a reaction to and embodiment of national and local experiences. The performer, rather than the writer, has been a more dominant presence on the American stage, particularly up through the early twentieth century. Many spectators believed that Chautauqua "was the greatest thrill of our life in the little towns."[19] How better to understand why that was than to look at the site where both the small town and the thrill were most visible?

"'Chautauqua? What under the sun do you mean?' I asked. . . . 'What is this thing we are to see?'"[20]

Frances D. C. McCaskill, who would become a field representative for the Community Chautauqua Circuit, asked this question of a friend in 1917.

Her article charts her own two-year Circuit Chautauqua journey from igno-rance to interest to investment. She was not the first person to be puzzled by the term "Chautauqua," however, or the last. People are still asking for defini-tions and explanations of this moment in American history.

The Chautauqua Institution was founded in 1874 in western New York by a group of Methodists who wanted to extend the intellectual and critical capac-ities of those who called themselves Christians. Chautauqua's first, and most enduring, incarnation was (and is) on Lake Chautauqua near Lake Erie and the border with Pennsylvania. Those Methodists were led by John Heyl Vincent of New Jersey, later a Methodist bishop, and Lewis Miller of Akron, Ohio, an inventor and businessman. Both men wanted to offer something that would "emphasize training for teachers and the application of the best pedagogy methods for Sunday school." Miller made the proposal to Vincent, inspired by his experiences at a conventional camp meeting where he and two colleagues were sitting "at some distance from the crowd," because of their discomfort with typical camp meeting revivalism.[21]

Camp meeting revivals were a familiar part of the religious landscape in the nineteenth and early twentieth centuries, and Chautauqua cannot be defined without understanding what it was rejecting. Early American Methodism, the largest nineteenth-century denomination in the United States, was spread by circuit-riding preachers who had little formal education. "The most famous of the circuit-riding Methodist preachers, Peter Cartwright, reported that camp meetings were attended by rowdies with knives, clubs, and horsewhips deter-mined to break up the proceedings."[22] The preacher and the congregation joined forces to give back as good as they got. Later, that exuberant energy moved out of the pews and into the pulpit. Spectators became a more passive audience, and their rapt attention "released the preachers," who became more histrionic and sensationalistic in their presentation, creating "one of the most arresting aspects of the development of evangelicalism . . . the decline of the sermon from the vernacular to the vulgar."[23] This development distanced some from camp meetings because the forum was serving as a spectacular call to the emotions rather than as a reasoned petition to the intellect.

What Miller, repudiating camp meeting emotionalism, had in mind was nothing like a camp meeting "in the familiar evangelical sense, but [one that] would devote itself to Bible study, teacher-training classes, musical entertain-ment, lecturers, and recreation as well as devotional exercises," a historian observed in 1974.[24] Vincent was ultimately convinced, although he needed much reassurance that what they would organize would "enlarge the outlook of the already consecrated church member" (that is, its primary purpose would not be conversion) and that there would be no "narrowness in the programme at Chautauqua."[25] Topics for discussion, Miller assured Vincent, would be broadly selected and based on a desire for intellectual as well as spiritual development. Calling their gathering an assembly, they distinguished Chautauqua from camp meetings by limiting the number of sermons preached and proscribing evangelistic services. Nevertheless, some attendees "were indignant when they learned that exhortation and a call to sinners to repent had no place on the program."[26] Even though it lacked these familiar elements, the first Chautauqua drew between 10,000 and 15,000 people.[27] Vincent and Miller were clearly on to something.

It did not take very long for the idea to capture people's imaginations, and in less than ten years Chautauqua grew from "a summer assembly of Sunday School teachers on a camp meeting ground to a monster institution of popular education, embracing many realms of human inquiry and study, permanently built and thoroughly established in the hearts of thousands of people," a contemporary enthused.[28] A key factor in the development of that "monster" institution was the Chautauqua Literary and Scientific Circle (CLSC). The CLSC, started to provide "Chautauqua All the Year," offered a guided course "not planned for specialists, seeking full knowledge upon one subject, but for general readers."[29] Ultimately, the CLSC expanded and was transformed into the first correspondence degree program in the United States and as such, Hugh Orchard emphasized in 1923, "began to exert a powerful influence in preventing education from becoming an aristocracy among the favored few."[30] Through this program, which featured organized classes on religious and secular subjects, as well as lectures by leading public figures, Chautauqua became a place for self-improvement and informed discussion.

Overwhelmingly popular, Chautauqua quickly expanded beyond its geographical boundaries in western New York. Within two years "the seeds of Chautauqua were borne by the winds to many places . . . and these grew up . . . a hundred, even a thousand fold," as other towns and counties established Chautauquas of their own.[31] By the end of the nineteenth century, the movement stretched as far west as Kansas and as far south as Missouri. As Victoria Case and Robert Ormond Case summarized in 1948:

> The Chautauqua idea was much too good to remain uncopied. Within two years a group in Ohio . . . set up a similar assembly on a small scale at Lakeside, with a pavilion in a grove of trees . . . and the identical overlay of respectability. They engaged lecturers and announced study classes and culture, uplift and education. . . . The race was on, until by 1900 fully two hundred pavilions

had been set up . . . and thirty-one states had their own "Chautauqua" or perhaps half a dozen of them, each following as faithfully as they could the pattern set by Vincent.[32]

Mimicking the original, these independent assemblies, as they were called to distinguish them from the "Mother" Chautauqua, followed the Chautauqua ideal, defined as "education for everybody, everywhere in every department, inspired by a Christian faith."[33] No matter how sincerely adhered to and believed in by those of the independent assemblies, the ideal was becoming formulaic, and it was only a short jump from the formula to the commercial.

The Circuit Chautauquas were able to combine the basic notion of Chautauqua—education and uplift—with sound commercial practices. Most of the Circuit owners had gained their experience booking lectures and entertainment for the Lyceum circuits. Begun in 1826 in New England, the Lyceum movement had been inaugurated by Massachusetts farmer Josiah Holbrook as a "voluntary association of individuals disposed to improve each other in useful knowledge."[34] While traveling through New England and lecturing rural people about local geography, Holbrook "found the ordinary people so keen to listen and learn that he conceived the idea of a regular system of education through popular lectures maintained by the communities themselves."[35] Communities would encourage local citizens to give talks, but it was visiting experts who transformed Lyceum into a unique national event. Eventually, the movement broadened regionally, and by the 1830s there were hundreds of organizations to support lectures and discussions. While Chautauquas began and remained rural and took place in the summer, Lyceum spread beyond its rural origins to become a popular winter urban activity. Lyceum provided two important precedents for Circuit Chautauqua. It offered a circuit model that demonstrated that events could be scheduled to move around an established route with regular appearances at designated intervals, but more important, Lyceum demonstrated that people were hungry for, and would spend money on, anything that promised self-development, education, and inspiration.

One bureau in particular became identified with an efficient and businesslike approach to Lyceum and was able to translate that into the successful invention of a Chautauqua Circuit: the Redpath Lyceum Bureau, founded by James Redpath in 1868. Redpath offered a variety of lecturers on a range of subjects and was best known for his celebrity lecturers, including Mark Twain, Susan B. Anthony, and Henry Ward Beecher. Keith Vawter began working for the Redpath Bureau in the late nineteenth century; by 1900 he was managing Redpath territory west of Pittsburgh and, like other Lyceum managers, was observing the independent assemblies carefully and seeing great potential in the new summer Chautauquas. As his colleagues were doing, he occasionally helped the assemblies by booking talent for them and believed that the financial losses and other difficulties could be avoided if the same program moved in a circuit from community to community in a reasonable sequence, cutting down on expensive and disorganized travel.

The Circuit system was Vawter's inspiration; although accounts vary about the extent of the contributions of his collaborators, Charles Horner and J. Roy Ellison, it is clear that Keith Vawter was largely responsible for establishing Circuit Chautauqua.[36] By 1904 Vawter, under the Redpath auspices, was ready to offer a Circuit.[37] That first year was not particularly successful. Vawter lost over $7,000, "and that was just $7000.00 more than Mr. Vawter had to lose."[38] Vawter and others who tried Circuits between 1904 and 1908 were at the mercy of the locations of the preexisting assemblies, uneven travel distances, and railroad schedules. Talent and crews often had to backtrack with their luggage and railroad cars of equipment in order to make their commitments. "The excessive railroad jumps and ofttimes sleepless nights . . . endured . . . in making widely scattered dates . . . was [sic] really a shamefully cruel and wicked method of procedure."[39] More important, the randomness of the travel arrangements created huge financial deficits for the managers. Vawter studied these problems carefully and in 1907 launched a far more successful Circuit system that allowed him to control the locations by erecting his own tents and eliminating dependence on preexisting locations. By 1910 his Circuit system was a solid presence across the West and Midwest. Within the next ten years there would be twenty-one companies offering Circuits, chief among them the five Redpath Bureaus (Redpath-Vawter, Redpath-Horner run by Charles Horner, Redpath-Chicago with Harry Harrison as manager, Redpath-Columbus under Vernon Harrison, and Redpath–New England managed by Crawford Peffer), Alkahest Chautauqua, Coit-Alber Chautauquas, Midland Chautauquas, White and Myers Chautauqua, Lincoln Chautauquas, Standard Chautauqua, Swarthmore Chautauqua, and Ellison-White and Dominion Chautauquas (managed by J. Roy Ellison, who assisted Keith Vawter in 1904).[40] The systems were independent ventures, but the managers worked closely together, recommending personnel to each other, sharing information on towns, and avoiding each other's territory. Early on there was much competition for territory, but the International Lyceum and Chautauqua Managers Association was founded by the larger bureaus in 1914 to work as an "informal monopoly" that established standardized talent contracts, provided a forum through which to adjudicate disputes over territory, and served as a venue in which managers could meet and exchange ideas.[41]

It is difficult to estimate how many people attended Chautauquas. Figures tend to be inflated, and misinterpretations of the numbers are often repeated in article after article. For 1924, for example, it is often claimed that 40 million Americans attended Chautauqua.[42] This would mean that roughly one in three Americans were spectators.[43] Paul Pearson, manager of the Swarthmore Circuit, cited the 40 million number, but he indicated that it was an "aggregate" figure, that is, it was arrived at by "counting each person every time he attended."[44] Figures from 20 million to 40 million abound, but it seems more likely that attendance was closer to between 9 million and 20 million people during peak years.[45] The most solid numbers seem to be for the number of Chautauquas held each year; they range from 555 in 1910 to over 9,000 in 1921, although these numbers vary as well.[46] Of course, people may have been counted more than once. It is, however, safe to say that over the life of Chautauqua, millions of Americans, from coast to coast and border to border, participated in Circuit Chautauquas.

Circuit Chautauqua was and would remain to the end a rural event. By the end of World War I, Circuit Chautauqua could be found in every state in the Union, but in the beginning it was a phenomenon of the Midwest. The first three states through which Redpath-Vawter toured were Iowa, Nebraska, and Wisconsin.[47] Nine years later in 1913, the states with the heaviest concentration of Chautauquas were Iowa, Ohio, Illinois, Indiana, and Missouri. Towns tended to be small, with less than 10,000 residents, although managers always assumed that people would come from outlying areas and that the actual town population would not finally determine audience size. Circuit Chautauqua moved west in 1912 when J. Roy Ellison, who had worked with Vawter, left to found his own Circuit. He established his headquarters in Portland, Oregon, and traveled to Bozeman, Montana, to begin booking a western circuit. By 1920 Gallatin County, where Bozeman is located, had just over 15,000 people, making it a pretty typical Chautauqua site.[48] Ellison would also expand Chautauqua into Canada, booking the first Circuits in Alberta in 1917.[49] There were occasional attempts to bring Circuit Chautauqua to large cities, but they almost inevitably failed.[50]

Each Circuit was comprised of one or two more "outfits" (tent, crew, and superintendent, who served as the master of ceremonies and managed the outfit) than were used at any given time. On Charles Horner's first Circuit, for example, there were always seven outfits in operation with two in transit, each outfit needing two days to strike the tent, travel, and set up. In a kind of leapfrogging that prevented either chronological or geographical gaps in the schedule, performers could move smoothly among outfits.

In tents that seated 2,000 people, the platform was forty feet wide and twenty feet deep.[51] After 1908 the platform area was not part of the tent proper but was an addition to the tent, called the "kitchen." The kitchen placed the performance area outside the seating area, "enabling the entire audience to see all the program from any part of the tent" and allowing for dressing rooms on either side.[52] Chautauquas lasted for three to seven days, and towns were guaranteed a different program each day.[53] All the outfits in a Circuit shared the same performers and speakers. "First-day talent remained first-day all season, second-day remained second-day, and so on for the seven days. Thus all groups traveled the same routes for the first time and railroading and programming became simplified."[54] This efficient organization, coupled with the ability to determine each town's dates so that railroad travel could be structured in short hops rather than complicated backtracking, allowed Chautauqua to become, for the first time, a commercially viable and nationwide endeavor.

Both the greatest strength and the greatest weakness of the new Circuits was the booking system. At the end of the year's Chautauqua in each town, superintendents worked hard to resecure that town for the coming year. Doing this was crucial to maintaining the Circuit geographically, and managers pressured superintendents to get the local committee made up of guarantors to sign their names again. "Try hard for your contracts," a manager wrote, since without rebooking the Circuit would be harder to maintain, both because it was one less town for the coming year and because it would leave a hole in the plan. In 1920 Redpath superintendents on the Five-Day DeLuxe Circuits were ordered to check out seventeen prospective Illinois towns, as they might "fill in some of the gaps."[55] The superintendents were also coached on how to appeal to their audiences. "Some of the Superintendents address their audiences as 'people.' In the South, Ladies and Gentlemen, Friends, or Kind Folks is absolutely essential" cautioned one advisory bulletin.[56] Keeping the local committee productive and invested was a great challenge; without that committee there could be no annual Chautauqua, because the members took the financial risks and sold their neighbors on the idea.

While the new system made the success of the Circuits possible, the contract with the local communities made it a foregone conclusion. The managers of the Circuits took few financial risks, because the committee of local business and community leaders deposited a nonnegotiable guarantee of $2,000 to $3,000 against the managers' loss to be recouped in the sale of season tickets (adults for $2.00 or $3.00 and children for $1.00).[57] The contract was only a page long, yet it clearly benefited the managers, who got the first $2,500 of the gross and 50 percent after that. They also received most of the proceeds from single-ticket sales, which could be in the thousands for a popular attraction like William Jennings Bryan.[58] The management promised only a Chautauqua—they determined the dates and talent at their convenience.

Once a contract was signed, the Circuit urged the guarantors to set up a committee to manage Chautauqua in their town. Their biggest challenge was selling the season tickets to meet their guarantee. Redpath-Vawter, for example, urged complicated systems of dividing the town into wards, each of which was to be headed by a captain. Captains would then recruit people to sell tickets in the wards, with quotas for each ward to meet. Identifying the right team members was crucial; in the country, finding the key farmer was an important part of the effort. "One farmer in one of our Chautauqua communities sold fifty tickets last year and gloried in what a wonderful service he had done his neighbors by influencing them to attend the Chautauqua," Keith Vawter wrote to the committees.[59] Alkahest Chautauqua sent letters to their guarantors reminding them that "it is all right to sell your season tickets for next year during this year's session on the Chautauqua."[60] Circuit offices had to act as cheerleaders to keep committees enthusiastic. When announcing their 1921 dates, the town of Highmore, South Dakota, was reminded by White and Myers Chautauqua to "be sure to put spirit in your campaign and then spirit and 'pep' into your Chautauqua when it comes." The reason for reminding committees relentlessly of their tasks was that "they do not work very much between the visits of the representatives but their enthusiasm is always increasing as the time for the Chautauqua approaches."[61] To address this problem, advance agents were sent out to the towns for weekly visits starting a month before Chautauqua was to arrive to help towns decorate the streets and buildings, sell season subscriptions, choose an appropriate site, and place advertisements in the local paper.

Despite the excitement most people evinced about the arrival of Chautauqua, not all committees felt as the Owensboro, Kentucky, committee did in 1926: "There is no doubt in our minds that we can make this [a] very successful Chautauqua, notwithstanding the very bad conditions locally, owing to the bad crops. It will take a great deal more work on our part than we have been putting in the Chautauqua, which we are going to give this coming year."[62] This self-sacrificing attitude was rare (especially later, after World War I); most committees were outraged when they had to make up the balance of the guarantee, as was the committee in Monticello, Indiana. "You will note that the guarantors dropped from 35 in 1920 to 10 in 1921. One reason was that it had always been a financial loss to the guarantors. . . . I am fearful as to the possibility of ever getting another Chautauqua."[63] Circuits stood firm in the face of this kind of anger. "These ten businessmen signed the contract last season with their eyes open, and knowing perfectly well their obligation. . . . The job of selling Chautauqua season tickets this year is not a girls [sic] task, but it is a real man's job as you know."[64] The Circuits never backed down on the guarantee. No matter how much pressure the committee brought to bear, Circuit managers staunchly defended its existence.

The Circuits made two arguments in favor of the contract. The first was that it bound them to the community by assuring local support. One pamphlet argued: "No responsible management that operates in the bounds of responsible Chautauqua standards can long survive without adequate local backing in some substantial form." That local support, created by the guaranteed contract, would then support the formation of "a working unit and either contract . . . for the outright purchase, or pledge . . . themselves to the advance sale of a specified number of season tickets."[65] These advance sales meant that significant numbers within the community were supporting Circuit Chautauqua before they knew what its specific offerings would be. The second argument was that the local committee, comprised as it was of discerning community leadership, could reassure more ordinary folks that Chautauqua would be beneficial to them. Another such pamphlet emphasized: "The things that enable the Chautauqua to score big, as an institution of real education and progress, are not popular with the masses until they are seen and heard. Hence the necessity for the underwriting contract, pledging the advance sale."[66] These arguments were made more frequently as committees continued to question their need to take financial risks, especially in the 1920s as agricultural communities began to experience the early effects of the Great Depression.

Convincing local committees that the contract was in their best interests grew more difficult, and throughout the 1920s committees became increasingly resistant to the contract's requirements. In 1926 booking agent C. B. Wait described the prevailing attitude: "[Local committees believe] that they are playing your game for you, and that there is absolutely nothing in it for them. That is the big objection which I meet on every hand. They say to me, 'Why sign a guarantee for Vawter and then get out here and work our heads off just simply to keep even with where we were when we started?'"[67] Trying to "sell the 'Chautauqua idea' to the community as a duty, a privilege, a consecration of local spirit" was no easy matter. Booking agents, superintendents, and managers "would not talk about profits or financial values to the town but hold fast to uplift, inspiration, and culture."[68] Circuit personnel strategized more and more desperately to keep towns, but those efforts were less and less successful as the 1920s wore on.

Ultimately, what was important to the community was not the stiff terms of the contract or the sales techniques of the managers but the talent who appeared on the Chautauqua platform. The term "talent" covered everyone from William Jennings Bryan to the Military Girls singing group. When the spectators walked up to the characteristic brown tent, they expected to hear great music, edifying lectures, and challenging ideas. Lectures on "Pie, People, and Politics" or "How to Master One's Self" were standard fare.[69] Described by many as "Mother, Home, and Heaven," these lectures were a familiar part of Chautauqua. For those who attended Chautauqua, such lectures were not greeted with cynicism. Whatever the nature of the talent's presentation, spectators valued the Chautauqua experience. Sue Humphrey stressed that "the town [Havensville, Kansas] never was the same after Chautauqua started coming [in about 1910]. The Chautauqua brought a new touch of culture which we immediately applied to our lives: new ways of speech, dress, ways of entertainment. . . . It broadened our lives in many ways."[70] Women saved money from their household budgets and saw Chautauqua as a way to better their children's lives. Humphrey's observations foreground the pleasure and importance of Chautauqua—it entertained, educated, and expanded people's lives.

Renowned public figures were also a vital part of Chautauqua. William Jennings Bryan, who in the days before the Scopes trial was known as the "Great Commoner," drew the greatest crowds. Famous Progressives such as Robert La Follette and reformers such as Ida Tarbell (who wrote the influential exposé of Standard Oil) were a key part of the Chautauqua experience. Interpreters or elocutionists who read plays, poems, or fiction were also ubiquitous. Gradually, fully produced plays performed by actors made their way into the repertoire, and after 1913 theater routinely appeared on the Circuits. This form of performance soon became the most popular aspect of the Chautauqua, despite people's prevailing moral and religious suspicions of theater. "Bringing in the theater has a great influence on the Chautauqua. It was not altogether an unmixed asset. . . . The play gave a tint of commercialism, without a doubt, and yet many thousands of customers had their first opportunity to enjoy the thing."[71] People certainly did come to "enjoy" the theater; by the end of the 1920s there would often be two fully mounted productions presented in as few as three or four days. Music, from popular to classical, from ethnic to patriotic, also had a prominent place, with opera singers, singing quartettes, bell ringers, yodelers, and "novelty" acts making up half the program of any given Chautauqua.

Spectators, as one talent noted, were "in awe" of the talent and saw them as glamorous, comparable to movie stars.[72] While performing on the Circuits may have seemed glamorous, most talent found the Circuits grueling, even boring. Living conditions were spartan at best. Many a performer "could write a library on the fly-infested, mosquito haunted, bathless and comfortless hotels of the United States of America."[73] Touring with the Circuits was challenging to those who did it, as they could "face . . . six to fifteen or more weeks of solid booking, or as much as 120 consecutive daily appearances."[74] Stories about the difficulties of travel and sleep are omnipresent in Chautauqua reminiscences. In her nostalgic 1939 memoir, Marion Scott remembered: "I learned to sleep anywhere. In a crowded, noisy, smelly coach. Hunched up on a wretched iron-armed bench at a station. In later years in the seat of an automobile over unspeakable roads. . . . The custom . . . of indulging in small, unimportant acts that you believed essential to your happiness and well-being. You got rid of those."[75] But audiences appreciated their effort. "The average Chautauqua audience . . . will sit for an hour and a half under a tent where the heat is concentrated essence, and listen, without even fanning, to the most serious discussion of great problems."[76]

Talent who occasionally lost sight of the meaning of Chautauqua for their audiences were reminded in no uncertain terms that Chautauqua was worth the sacrifice and discomfort. One manager recalled:

> Marge [talent] was on her way to the tent . . . one hot, disagreeable windy dusty day. She was joined by a local lady who said she was also going to the Chautauqua. Marge remarked "If it were not my job, I would certainly not be going on a day like this." The reply came back, "If you lived in this part of the country where the Chautauqua is your only chance from one year to the next to see and hear programs like these, you would not miss it for anything."[77]

Marge felt suitably chastened and ashamed. She saw firsthand how Chautauquas were supported with fervent devotion by practitioners and spectators alike. Whether as "our oasis, our lifebelt," "something which broadened our lives," or as an event "you would not miss for anything," people held Chautauqua in great affection. It was uniquely theirs, of their community, of their country, and the Chautauqua experience was bound up in the lush rhythms of the summer landscape, making it seem as natural as the fresh food and relaxed times of the season.

"To be sure the Chautauqua supports a great mass of mediocrity. Many of its plays and concerts are insipid and not a few of its lectures are 'bunk.'"[78]

Despite its carefully controlled programming, its appeal to self- and civic improvement, and the great affection many held for it, Chautauqua was not uncontroversial. Chautauqua's championing of the rural way of life came at a time in the United States when many, especially those in the cities, believed that life in the rural United States was narrow-minded, provincial, bland, and unsophisticated.

Probably the best-known critique of the Circuits on these grounds was expressed by Sinclair Lewis in *Main Street*. Lewis, while working on his book, visited a small town in Iowa and was given a free season pass to the Chautauqua, where he saw Charles Zueblin give a community lecture.[79] Zueblin, a professor of sociology at the University of Chicago, lectured widely in Chautauquas, Lyceums, civic clubs, and schools as a "social and civic evangelist," proclaiming that "democracy is not a form of government, but a faith and a life" and offering "civic revivals reaching whole communities."[80] His academic field was municipal sociology, which "investigates the means of satisfying communal wants through public activity."[81] For Zueblin, Chautauqua was the place where his scholarly work had its greatest effect. He told one Chautauqua manager, "I make the people want to be good citizens."[82] This earnest boosterism, with its bland suggestions for reform, must have been a tempting target for Lewis.

Lewis's disdain for Chautauqua and Zueblin is revealed in the disdain of Carol Kennicott, Lewis's *Main Street* heroine. Kennicott is excited about Chautauqua's arrival, believing it will relieve some of the shallowness, emptiness, and sheer boredom she finds in rural life. She hopes to find "a condensed university course brought to the people." Instead, she experiences "a combination of vaudeville performance, Y.M.C.A. lecture, and the graduation exercises of an elocution class." While she is "impressed by the audience . . . eager to be made to think . . . eager to be allowed to laugh," Chautauqua itself is "nothing but wind and chaff and . . . the laughter of yokels at old jokes, a mirthless and primitive sound like the cries of beasts on a farm." Charles Zueblin, whom Lewis witnessed in Iowa, is imagined as "a plain little man with his hands in his pockets" who points out the obvious defects of the town. Rather than the rousing response the Circuits claimed such lecturers received, the inhabitants of Gopher Prairie "grumbled, 'Maybe that guy's got the right dope, but what's the use of looking on the dark side of things all the time? New ideas are first-rate but not all this criticism. Enough trouble in life without looking for it!'"[83] Circuit Chautauqua had its place in Lewis's stinging critique of small-town life. He saw it not as the Circuit billed itself, the savior of the small town, but as others found it to be, supportive of the smug complacency of small towns.

This self-righteous confidence reflected a growing sense that learning and self-improvement were no longer valued as labor-intensive activities worthwhile in and of themselves. For those excluded from the social and educational elite, as scholar Janice Radway describes, learning was becoming "a transitive, utilitarian activity with concrete social effects."[84] Education and its benefits were being transformed into commodities to be purchased, rather than culture to be inherited or earned. Journalist Gregory Mason scorned Chautauqua in 1929:

> The peasant afflicted with this appetite [for self-improvement] sees Chautauqua as an agency through which he can gratify his longings for almost nothing. He is "sold" the idea that by paying $1.80 for five days of Chautauqua, he can get himself a liberal education, a whole carload of canned culture. It is cheaper than Dr. Eliot's sixty inches of printing and a darned sight easier. It is infinitely easier than trying to think.[85]

"Dr. Eliot's sixty inches of printing" first became available in 1906. Charles W. Eliot, president of Harvard University, was fond of remarking that "a five-foot shelf of books . . . would furnish a liberal education to anyone willing to devote fifteen minutes per day to reading them."[86] Eliot was approached by the publishers P. F. Collier and Son about creating just such a collection of books. This collaboration gave birth to the enormously popular Harvard Classics.

While the series stressed quality and perseverance, it also seized upon the "desire for information and making it consumable."[87] But its critics, usually published in elite literary and cultural magazines like *American Mercury*, *Nation*, and *Atlantic Monthly*, derided the Harvard Classics for the same reasons they critiqued Chautauqua: both were, as Radway notes, "vulgar," "mundane," and "utilitarianism . . . carried too far."[88] These attitudes were reactions against what was characterized as the cheapening of liberal education, transforming value and status into commodities. That "culture . . . could be acquired" rather than earned was a disturbing trend toward the disintegration of genteel standards. The scornful images of "yokels" and "peasants" who fail to "maintain the fences cordoning off culture from commerce, the sacred from the profane, and the low from the high," as Radway puts it, are a long way from the claims to rousing entertainment and challenging intellectual discourse made on behalf of Chautauqua in various articles, advertisements, and letters.[89]

The Circuits were not without avenues of response. Keith Vawter was invited to speak to Philadelphia's Poor Richard (Advertising) Club in December 1921, and he used the occasion to reassure his audience that Chautauqua was not the business depicted in *Main Street* but one of America's hidden assets. Most large newspapers ignored their existence, Vawter reported, but when those publications do look into Chautauquas themselves, rather than rely on secondhand opinion, they find, as one Arkansas editor did, that Chautauqua was "a great nation-wide institution being managed and largely controlled by some very serious-minded gentlemen with the highest of idealistic motives upper-most."[90] Critiques like Lewis's, Vawter argued, deserved to be treated with scorn because Lewis just did not know his subject.

> Some of you may have had so much time on your hands these last few months that you wasted several hours reading a certain much advertised book called "Main Street," and you may recall that Mr. Sinclair Lewis' idea of a Chautauqua is not such that would prompt you to go far out of your way to hear a Chautauqua program, however, Mr. Lewis misses the main point and the big thing in Chautauqua just about as far as he missed sensing the real community life of the average Mid-western town. Any time a blazé [sic], sophisticated snob past forty attempts to write a present day problem story based on recollections of events in his childhood he is liable to make about as bad a mess of it as Sinclair Lewis has made of "Main Street."[91]

Vawter remonstrated his audience that he and the other Circuit managers knew more about small towns than Lewis possibly could. Vawter's refrain was that Lewis wrote through limited personal experience, while the Circuits had experience that was both broad and intimate. This harsh dismissal of Lewis and his novel does not, however, refute the primary claim in Main Street that the Circuits were mediocre and unoriginal and that their commercial organization forced them to cater to the lowest common denominator.

Chautauqua had been charged with those faults before. William James had visited the Chautauqua Institution in 1896 and written his brother, Henry, that he found it "depressing from its mediocrity."[92] This experience prompted him to write in his 1899 essay "What Makes a Life Significant" that despite being "held spell-bound by the charm and ease of everything, by the middle-class paradise, without a sin, without a victim, without a blot, without a tear," he was relieved to return to the "dark and wicked world." Chautauqua was "too tame, this culture too second-rate, this goodness too uninspiring."[93] James turned to the greater but more unstable world to find excellence, excitement, and inspiration. For both Lewis and James, the worst aspect of Chautauqua was how its claims to quality and improvement were contradicted by the lack of intellectual challenge and complexity.

Even supporters who were committed to the idea of the Chautauqua Institution found much to criticize in the commercial Circuit. Frank W. Gunsaulus, an inspirational lecturer on Lyceum platforms and at the New York Chautauqua who helped to establish the Armour Institute of Technology in

Chicago while also serving in the pulpit of Chicago's Central Church, used most of his Chautauqua earnings to support students at the Armour Institute. He firmly believed in the Chautauqua mission and claimed that "ten percent of the students [at the Armour Institute] owed their presence in classes to the 'Chautauqua influence.'"[94] In 1908, observing that the Circuits were supplanting many of the independent assemblies, he accused Vawter of "ruining a splendid movement" and the Circuits with "cheapening Chautauqua, breaking it down, replacing it with something that will have neither dignity nor permanence." Eventually, Gunsaulus embraced the Circuits, but many thought that his original assessment was the accurate one—as Victoria Case and Robert Ormond Case editorialized: Gunsaulus "died without realizing that his first judgment was correct."[95]

The independents were the ones chiefly affected by the rise of the Circuits. They found it difficult to compete with both the Circuits and one another for resources, and too few people in their communities were interested in providing the labor necessary to operate them. The Dunbar Chautauqua Bureau, trying to lure Ethel Hinton and her Hinton Verdi Company to perform at the independents, wrote, "Circuit Chautauquas are a case of lyceumized Vaudeville and are looked upon as sort of a circus stunt."[96] The reference to circuses and vaudeville is a damning comparison, as many communities believed these popular entertainments undermined respectability and morality.[97] Thus the Dunbar Bureau representative could urge Hinton to sign on with his bureau because it would, by definition, offer her a more community-based experience than the Circuits could. "I have deliberately gone into the independent Chautauquas because they are the real Chautauquas. There is an entirely different feeling among talent and people who are connected with them. . . . Of course the managers of the circuit Chautauqua business are in it absolutely for the money, no matter how much they prattle about uplift and all that. They are using that talk to commercialize the real Chautauqua ideal."[98] Luring Hinton to the independents through appeals to authenticity, the Dunbar representative was arguing not against the Chautauqua ideal, as James did, but against the Circuit realization of that ideal. Sense of community, "social feeling," and education were the values held by all forms of Chautauqua, but at stake was which form could best realize them.

Castle's breezy words that began this introduction are straightforward and uncomplicated. But I have found, as Andrew Rieser did, that "the movement defie[s] easy summation."[99] One particular challenge has been that of the audience for the book itself. There is little scholarly historicization and theorization of Chautauqua. Given its ubiquity at a crucial moment in U.S. history, it is a rich site for examining the ways in which performance and culture can function as an ideological apparatus continuing the interpolation of people as subjects and citizens. Concomitantly, it was the location in which the body was further rationalized and disciplined within the growing cultural commitment to professionalism and modernity. Examples abound, moreover, of how that body was racialized, gendered, and nationalized. Chautauqua's ideological functions and disciplinary effects can be traced in these pages, but the theoretical arguments that influence them are not overt. The primary reason for this is that there is another audience for this book, one in addition to academics.

In 2001 an article quoting me on Circuit Chautauqua appeared in *Texas Highways*. An enterprising Florida man tracked me down in the College of Fine Arts dean's office to find out how he could get my book. He wanted a copy for an elderly relative who had had family who worked on the Circuits. When I told him it was not yet finished, his disappointment was palpable.

Another Chautauqua veteran, Harriette Kohler Smith, now in her nineties, attended the Swarthmore Chautauqua as a child, the only kind of performance her father, Wilbur Jere Kohler, a minister in the Evangelical and Reformed Church in Richlandtown, Pennsylvania, would let her frequent. Like many conservative Protestants, he abhorred the theater, but Chautauqua's mix of entertainment and education was a morally safe venue for his daughter to enjoy music, lectures, and drama. But this did not seem a limitation to her; in fact, Chautauqua seemed to be greater than any other form of live entertainment. Her father could not have understood how his exception for Chautauqua provided his daughter with the opportunity for intellectual exploration and fulfillment in the guise of moral, religious, and patriotic uplift. Years later, as a young housewife, that experience was part of what led her to become involved with the Bucks County Playhouse, a highly respected community theater, during World War II. As she described her Chautauqua experiences her body trembled, and before my eyes I could see the young girl who seventy years or so earlier had looked forward to Chautauqua as the most intense and exciting experience of the year. She made it clear that I could not even begin to imagine how liberating Chautauqua was and what it meant to those who attended. Every time she has seen me since she has asked me when I am going to put this book in her hands.

Richard Oram, whom I was able to interview twice before his death in 1999, not only attended Chautauqua but was one of the last generation of young people to run off and join the Circuits. He, too, indicated to me that something precious had been lost when Chautauqua slipped out of the American national memory. These powerful voices kept the question of audience before me throughout this project. Hopefully, people like the man in Florida, Smith, and the Oram family will find much of value in these pages, even as the book contributes to scholarly debates about the historiographical and theoretical implications of the subject.

One could use the Circuits to write a history of the United States during the beginning of the twentieth century. All the relevant concerns of the time—citizenship, race, community, gender, politics, government, quality of life, foreign affairs, family—were debated and examined by Chautauqua. While the following chapters do not attempt such a large and ambitious project, they do attempt to incorporate the diversity of concerns, subjects, and people associated with Circuit Chautauqua. Each chapter emerges from a particular moment or type of performance to illustrate how tangibly Chautauqua addressed its audiences' concerns. The audience/platform dynamic is what made Chautauqua the "most American thing in America" and is what needs to be explored to comprehend Chautauqua in the American landscape.[100]

The first chapter takes the largest view of Chautauqua and its audiences by examining how Chautauqua aligned itself with national interests. Chautauqua reveled in the pronouncement that it was the "most American thing in America," and definitions and discussions of the nation—its meaning, its workings, its appeal—were central to most activities on the Circuits. The discourse about Chautauqua, as well as discourse within it, returned repeatedly to its Americanness. Even its signal quality—uplift—symbolized its patriotism. As one historian wrote in 1911: "This quality of 'uplift' . . . is synonymous with the word 'American.' To be an American means to have an indisputable right to rise above the environment."[101] How the nation that was so symbolized by its citizens' commitment to upward mobility was defined and enacted is explored through a number of examples, most specifically through the programming Chautauqua offered to children and its participation in mobilizing the nation during World War I.

Central to debates over defining America was community. Community is a place, an idea, and a commonality among people. Chautauqua believed that it offered all these aspects of community to those who participated, and performance was the medium through which these ideas were communicated and debated. Implied in the idea of community are connections among people, shared interests, and linked futures. Community is the articulation of a way that people are bound together. It has both positive connotations (support, inclusion, empowerment) and negative ones (control, exclusion, and surveillance). Ultimately, it is a set of dynamic relations among people that need to be tested, renewed, and represented. Why and how the Circuits seized on notions of community as a crucial focus for their performances is the subject of chapter 2. This topic is one that contemporary participants themselves iterated and reiterated, and approaching it through a focus on race and gender reveals how community was formulated as much to exclude as to include.

Chapter 3 locates the Chautauqua discourses around community and democracy in performance by examining the tent both as a literal entity and a metaphorical idea. The tent was the crucial nexus of community, democracy, and performance. The Circuits implied that Chautauqua shared the circumstances of other institutions that defined the community. Unlike the church or the school, however, Chautauquas were not housed in permanent structures, controlled by residents, or produced by local resources. The brown tent was set up each year in an appropriate location, usually in a large field near the county seat or accessible small town. At the end of Chautauqua the tent was struck, and only the barest traces of its vibrant presence remained behind. How the brown tent became a sign of Chautauqua moral and religious respectability and stood in for the community and the nation is examined through a series of theoretical and practical maneuvers that parallel those around performance.

The last two chapters focus on how performance itself was at issue. Chautauqua was not simply a venue for live performance; it was a way of performing that both confirmed and confronted contemporary ideas about performance and its uses. Chapter 4 concentrates on oratory. In the nineteenth-century United States the various types of oratory—lectures, speeches, and elocution—were influential ways in which democracy was tested and refined. Extended discussion and debate allowed audiences to work with orators to forge understandings of the nation and their place in it. While Chautauqua came at the end of what is often called the "golden age of American oratory," it nonetheless became both the repository of that tradition and the site of its failure. Oratory also revealed Chautauqua's paradoxical relationship to theatricality. The Circuits promised that their entertainment would help its audiences navigate the changing world while not bringing any of the alarming aspects of that world to the community. Oratory, whether it was a William Jennings Bryan speech or a delivery of a familiar poem, was a comfortable and recognizable American practice that was encouraging theatricality even as it condemned it.

Chapter 5 continues the examination of performance by investigating how and why theater was introduced to Chautauqua and what changes this brought to the Circuits. Audiences' desire for theatrical experience without the label "theater" presented a seemingly insoluble paradox. Chautauqua's challenge was to answer the community's demand for dramatic representation without provoking rural Protestant America's abhorrence of the corruptive power of theater. This chapter illustrates how theater eventually became a celebrated part of the Circuits as a result of manipulations of the tensions among different definitions of theater that circulated during this period. Chautauqua's presentation of theater was enabled through an ingenious redefinition of theater, which began with elocutionists and readers and continued through the presentation of fully staged plays, a redefinition that distinguished reputable dramatic literature from the material attributes of theatrical illusion—costumes, scenery, and, most particularly, makeup—all of which audiences regarded as signs of corruption and immorality. In doing so, Circuit Chautauqua changed the possibilities for representation within the communities it served.

The conclusion assesses the effects of Circuit Chautauqua and points to its legacies. Circuit Chautauquas were a casualty of the Depression. Since the late 1920s the Circuits had been in decline; the economic disasters of the 1930s finished them off. Radio and film had made inroads into their audiences, as did the greater mobility brought about by the automobile. Rural people were no longer as isolated and could afford to be more discriminating about how they spent their leisure time. Forty years later, Chautauquas were revived. The new version acknowledged its debt to the Circuits, but it was a publicly funded, nonprofit adaptation of the Circuits rather than an imitation of them. These Chautauquas are not the proudly commercial businesses of the early twentieth century. They are community outreach programs born out of the liberalism of the 1960s and 1970s. Towns in Oklahoma, Nebraska, the Dakotas, and California saw tents being set up, scholars performing one-person shows about historical figures, and workshops offered in history and the humanities. The focus is now on the nation's past, with the idea that history unites, rather than divides, people as citizens. Chautauquas still adamantly state, however, that they are not theater. Despite the fact that these historical figures are performed, grant applications and promotional materials go to great lengths to define Chautauqua as education, not representation. They dissociate themselves from theater, implying that theater is trivial and deludes people by presenting illusion rather than substance, fiction rather than fact. Clearly, the complex and paradoxical legacy of Chautauqua's intersection with community and performance continues.

Remembering Chautauqua is no simple task. It requires reconciling both the plentiful materials found in archives and publications easily identified as evidence with its palimpsestic traces in the national landscape and living memory. Circuits Chautauqua's live performances are long over. Traces of performances, while elusive, are available in the intersection of the archive and the everyday. One mother told Marian Castle that her young daughter had been transformed by her experiences in the children's activities. "And now she's crazy about gallivanting around in cheesecloth!" Castle explains how she understood this revelation: "What she was trying to say was that beauty starved little Mary had tasted for the first time the ecstacy of self-expression."[102] Harriette Smith said something very similar when asked to define her love of Chautauqua. "It was a way of expressing myself," she recalled passionately.[103] It may be impossible to remember Chautauqua fully, but looking for it through live performance creates an understanding that accounts for the ecstatic expression of lived experience.

This is the original speaker's platform at the Chautauqua Institution. It was later replaced by an auditorium that seated 5,000. The poles on the center aisle are for torches to illuminate night meetings. Chautauqua Institution.

Each year the Chautauqua Institution sponsored a recognition day for the participants in that year's Chautauqua Literary and Scientific Circle (CLSC). One of the most memorable events of the day was the elaborate parade. Girls, dressed in white, were a standard part of the parade. Chautauqua Institution.

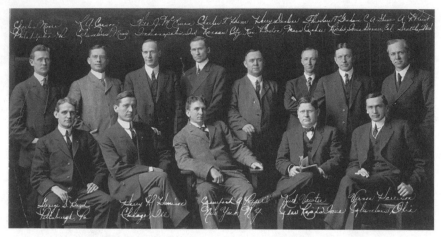

The managers of the different Redpath Circuits gathered infrequently, usually only once a year, to discuss strategy and policy, as well as review financial information. This 1912 photo captures all the major Redpath players including, in the front row second from left, Harry Harrison. Next to him is Crawford Peffer, who would bring theater to the Circuits. On Peffer's other side is Keith Vawter, the architect of the Circuits. Texas, HRC.

This map, from 1912, gives a visual sense of how Circuit Chautauquas were distributed across the country during the early years. By the early 1920s there would not be a state in the Union without a significant Circuit presence. World's Work.

Setting up the tent and selling tickets were
always very public events. Most of the men who
provided the physical labor were college students
working their way through school. Iowa.

This tent outfit in Iowa City is typical. The canvas fences prevented those who had not paid from gaining admission, and the "kitchen" can be seen on the left sticking out from the tent proper. Iowa.

Tent sides were often rolled up to allow whatever breezes there were into the tent. Audiences and talent alike commented on the heat generated by the crowds. Iowa.

This setup in Edgerton, Wisconsin, demonstrates how small the platform was in comparison to the rest of the tent. *Iowa.*

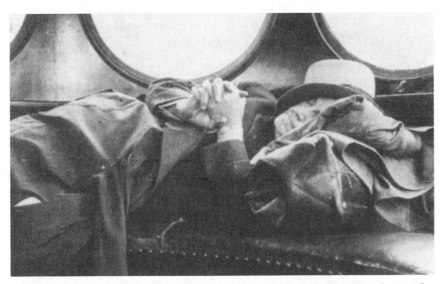

Talent adapted to the conditions of life on the road or quit. William Jennings Bryan, whose zest for life on the Circuits was legendary, knew to sleep whenever he could. *Author.*

CHARLES ZUEBLIN
Publicist, Civic Revivalist, Lecturer on
Democracy in Literature, Education and
Life. ❦ Author, American Municipal
Progress, etc.

Charles Zueblin was one of the more
accomplished Chautauqua lecturers. Iowa.

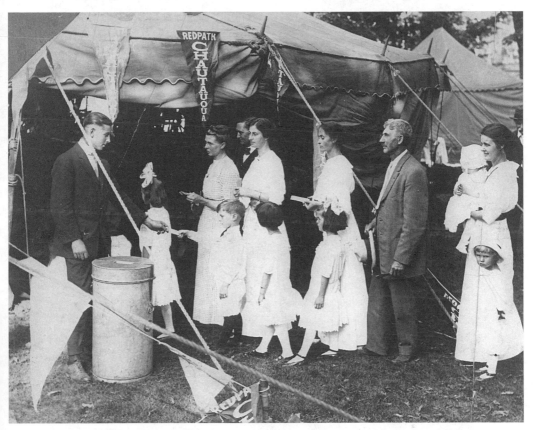

These spectators lining up to enter the tent are all from one family. The third woman from the left, Fannie Redpath Boyle, was still alive and in her nineties in 1975. Iowa.

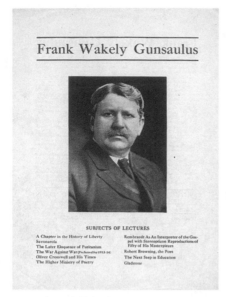

Frank Wakely Gunsaulus

SUBJECTS OF LECTURES

A Chapter in the History of Liberty
Savonarola
The Later Eloquence of Puritanism
The War Against War (Preferred for 1913-14)
Oliver Cromwell and His Times
The Higher Ministry of Poetry

Rembrandt As An Interpreter of the Gospel with Stereopticon Reproductions of Fifty of His Masterpieces
Robert Browning, the Poet
The Next Step in Education
Gladstone

Gunsaulus's publicity brochure was typical of the many lecturers who were the foundation of the Circuits. The speaker almost always is looking directly at the viewer, and the serious expression seems to assure audiences that they will be hearing an important message. Iowa.

Once Ethel Hinton signed with the Dunbar Chautauqua, she also reworked her act to appeal more broadly. Iowa.

Circuit Chautauqua may have been a highly professionalized enterprise, but its equipment was always informal. This ticket booth could obviously be set up and struck very quickly. Iowa.

CHAPTER ONE
America on the Platform

Those attending the 1917 Lincoln Chautauqua in Mooresville, Indiana, for six days in late July must have had the European war very much on their minds. Mooresville is only about ten miles southwest of Indianapolis and at that point had a population of just over 2,000.[1] While the war had been raging in Europe for almost three years, the United States had been involved for just over three months, since April 6. Little of the programming overtly addressed the war, which had begun after arrangements had been finalized, but individual speakers and the superintendent must have referred to it. Alonzo E. Wilson, Lincoln Chautauqua president, promised patrons that the "Lincoln Chautauquas will render real service in their propaganda of patriotism this year and local citizens are asked to catch the spirit of the times and lend their hearty support and cooperation."[2] This folksy message might have come at any moment from the Circuits, but at this particular time its meaning was unmistakable: communities and Chautauqua needed to work together to win the war.

The performances were typical Chautauqua fare that emphasized self-improvement and communal development. The Craven Family Orchestra opened the six days of Chautauqua with both instrumental and vocal music. Their music offered more than just mere entertainment; the program assured audiences, "their presence brings with it the real spirit of true home life which the Chautauqua aims to develop."

Later in the week, Maude Willis, "interpreter of masterpieces," gave a dramatic recital that promised to depict "a more constructive and happier living of life." Each day included two or three lectures with titles like "This New Age," "Health Attained and Maintained," and "Miracles of Electricity." James R. Howerton, for example, on day four spoke on "The New Patriotism," "the subject matter of which is as timely as is the subject itself."[3] In the context of Wilson's characterization, it is clear that attention to domesticity and productivity was part of winning the war.

Children were not expected to be interested in most of the lectures and entertainment. They participated in the "Youth's Chautauqua." Mostly this consisted of supervised play, with an emphasis on athletics. But the children also rehearsed a pageant to be performed for their parents and the community the last night of Chautauqua, Sunday, July 29, as the opening event of that evening. The same pageant was performed over 350 times that year by communities across the United States as one way to affirm and assert their patriotism in the face of the new war.[4]

"America, Yesterday and Today" was written for the Lincoln Chautauquas by Nina B. Lamkin, a professional recreation worker and author of several books on how to use performance to teach children civic and moral responsibility. Lamkin was no stranger to the Circuits, having spent most of the 1910s organizing similar pageants and children's activities for several different Circuits.[5] This pageant intended to make Americans aware of their communal past, and the program urged them to keep that past in front of them. "Our people, and particularly our boys and girls, have very little conception of the significance of the march of the pioneers across this vast continent and its settlement and growth. The community pageant of American history comes to interpret to us true Americanism."[6] What had been implied by the adult activities was overtly stated through the children's activities: Chautauqua guaranteed that it provided the best opportunity for expressing and strengthening each citizen's commitment to her or his country.[7]

Such public performances of Americanism were not unique to Chautauqua; pageants like Lamkin's for the Lincoln Chautauquas had been an important part of the cultural life of the United States, most notably since the end of the nineteenth century. But the performance of America was not limited to the pageant alone. It suffused the entire Chautauqua experience, and the Circuits themselves, as well as influential supporters, were relentless in their embrace of an identity that linked them intimately with the nation. This chapter looks specifically at how that process occurred. Circuit Chautauqua's conflation of itself with the United States was not simply a matter of declaring itself

American. It was a dynamic intersection of several discourses—among them religion, reform politics, and citizenship—in performance both on and off the platform.

> "No one can understand the history of this country and the forces that have been shaping it . . . without some comprehension of the work of that splendid institution that was, and is, Chautauqua."[8]

Richard T. Ely, Christian socialist and labor reformer who wrote in his 1938 memoirs the epigraph that opens this section, was a leading economist and scholar who spent most of his influential career, from 1892 on, at the University of Wisconsin in Madison. He often taught in the New York Chautauqua at the express invitation of cofounder Bishop John Vincent. He was an avid supporter of Chautauqua, especially in its mission of adult education. In the introduction I argued that you could tell the history of the United States in the first third of the twentieth century through the history of Circuit Chautauqua. Ely might well have agreed, and he was not the only one who saw the connection between Chautauqua and the United States as one that was mutually defining.

Many Americans and foreign visitors who came into contact with Chautauqua in the nineteenth and the beginning of the twentieth centuries shared U.S. Senate Chaplain Edward Everett Hale's 1906 opinion: "If you have not spent a week at Chautauqua, you do not know your own country."[9] Almost 120 years after Chautauqua's founding and 55 years after Ely published his memoir, prominent historian and public intellectual David McCullough, speaking at the New York Chautauqua, echoed his predecessors. "Chautauqua is part of the American imagination . . . one of those places that helps us define who we are and what we believe in."[10] For over a hundred years scholars, politicians, journalists, clergy, spectators, talent, and public figures generally have been characterizing Chautauqua as the place where the elusive and abstract qualities that define what it is to be "American" are made concrete and tangible. In order to understand what it means to claim that Chautauqua performed America, it is crucial to understand why there was a need for such a performance, what that performance was, and how it functioned.

It is likely that, when pressed, any Circuit Chautauqua spectator would have agreed that what it meant to be an American seemed open to question. The period of Chautauqua, roughly 1870 to 1930, from the time of the New York institution's founding to the close of the Circuits, saw extreme shifts in the composition of the citizenry, national identity, political practices, and the nation's relation to the larger world. Historian John Whiteclay Chambers II has observed about those who themselves were not recent immigrants in the years surrounding the war that "order seemed to be dissolving into chaos. Collapsing so it seemed, were not only the traditional structures for ordering economic and social life but also the religious and cultural traditions on which national well-being allegedly rested."[11] In every aspect of life, wherever people looked, a majority believed they were witnessing inexorable change, change that they often found threatening, unwelcome, and difficult to explain.

A complex political transformation in the national understanding of democracy came in part from the pressing issue of immigration. Between 1870 and 1910, 21 million people immigrated to the United States.[12] Since the 1870 population was almost 40 million, this represented an enormous increase in new citizens.[13] These newly arrived people differed greatly from the groups that had preceded them. Nell Irvin Painter, in her influential study *Standing at Armageddon*, points out that it was not simply the numbers that had shifted. "Between 1880 and 1920 the provenance of the foreign-born population shifted away from Germany, Ireland, northwestern Europe, and China to central, eastern, and southern Europe."[14] These staggering changes, both in numbers and in ethnicity, unsurprisingly created friction and tension.

One side of the debate believed only certain groups could become American because they possessed the appropriate natural and racial characteristics. Another side believed just as strongly that Americanism could be taught and that almost anyone coming into the United States could assimilate. These two understandings represented, as immigration historian Matthew Frye Jacobson has indicated, strong national "tension[s] [that] existed between the necessity of huge numbers of immigrants as laborers on the one hand, and the menace posed by these same immigrants as ill-equipped citizens on the other."[15] Essentially, the debate was asking fundamental questions: When and how did one become American? Was everyone capable of doing so? From the beginning of the United States in the eighteenth century, Americans stressed "fitness for self-government" as the bedrock of republicanism, and that concept would continue to be the one on which the United States "would favor or exclude certain groups."[16]

Performance served both sides of the debate. In support of assimilation, it could demonstrate the ways in which those who seemed different from Chautauqua audiences were in fact less so because of the devotion to Chautauqua they shared with the audience. In this case, difference was positioned as a misleading first impression and the shared morals and beliefs revealed by performance as more reliable measures of a person's value. For example, foreign-born talent, particularly lecturers, who performed a version of middle-class gentility and bourgeois respectability were an argument for the possibilities of assimilation. But the irrevocability of difference could also be apparent. When performers were exoticized, as was the African children's choir discussed at length in the next chapter, an unbridgeable gulf between spectators and performers was created that made assimilation seem both impossible and undesirable. These views were variously performed on the Chautauqua platform, demonstrating that the Circuits operated within a rich context, one that was ripe for interpretation and intervention.

One reason rural Chautauqua audiences welcomed these performances was that they understood that while the impact of these new immigrant populations was felt most directly in urban centers, questions about them were equally applicable to the situation of the nation's rural citizens. The United States was moving from a largely agriculturally based economy and culture to an industrial, urban one. This meant that assumptions that predated the American Revolution about the character of the nation were being questioned and, in some cases, discarded. "The yeoman farmer, the symbol and hope of America in the Jeffersonian era, became an anachronism in a land of large-scale production. An increasingly urban nation looked on small farmers as a relic of the past, while farmers became radicalized because of their plight and turned to political action to save themselves and their vision of America."[17] This widening gap between those who lived in rural areas and the increasing number of urban residents created great discontent among those whose lives were bound by agriculture. While the political battle was primarily waged through Populism or Progressivism, the cultural struggle was fought in part by Chautauqua performance, where programming reflected a desire to address farming's waning dominance as the quintessentially American way of life.

For those already citizens, their duties and responsibilities were undergoing transformations that were equally a part of that complex context. During a twenty-five-year period, from 1890 to 1915, champions of "direct democracy" inaugurated primaries to select candidates rather than have them handpicked by party machines, popular elections of U.S. senators, and widespread implementation, especially in western states, of referenda and ballot initiatives.[18] This new mode of deciding public policy allowed voters to bypass monied corporate interests and even their elected officials to enact legislation. As a contemporary reformer noted about these radical shifts, "to have told the campaign managers of [18]84 and [18]88 that within a quarter of a century the whole nation would be voting a secret ballot, the candidates nominated in two-thirds of the American states by direct vote of the people . . .—such a tale would have set the [party bosses] of those days cackling in derision."[19] These new political realities also included women's suffrage, guaranteed in 1920 by constitutional amendment. These reforms of the political system were attributable, in large part, to Progressive direct and indirect influence. Whether or not a particular spectator identified herself or himself as a Progressive, she or he would have been well aware that Progressives were at the forefront of articulating both optimism and concern about the nation's future.

Progressivism, often said to have been sustained by Chautauqua, took up the questions nearest Chautauqua audiences' hearts, including the regulatory relationship between government and business, the rights and entitlements of rural versus urban areas, and societal reform.[20] Progressive activists and politicians employed a range of strategies, from legislation to social activism like settlement houses, that helped integrate the poor and immigrants more fully into the nation. As historian Steven J. Diner summarizes, during the Progressive Era (roughly 1890–1920)

> a common discourse dominated American political debate. . . . Struggling to redefine the meaning of American democracy in the age of corporate capitalism, Americans of diverse backgrounds asked how government could protect its citizens . . . and how the polity could use government to regain control of the nation's destiny. . . . Many Americans brought their search for economic security, autonomy, and social status into a spirited conversation about the relationship of citizens to their government and how that government should shape the future of an industrial nation.[21]

The enormous changes in the United States could be stressful and debilitating, and many citizens found them so, but they also provided opportunities and challenges that others (particularly younger generations) found invigorating and promising.

Looking at Chautauqua roughly twenty years after it ended, Harrison John Thornton claimed that "any Chautauqua audience was a microcosm of American Society."[22] If there were those both contemporaneously and later who believed that the nation could be found at Chautauqua, then it was not surprising that Chautauqua was used to understand the nation. Nineteenth-century literary scholar, novelist, and Columbia University professor Hjalamar H. Boyesen wrote that, at Chautauqua, he "had such a vivid sense of contact with what is really and truly American. The national physiognomy was defined to me as never before, and I saw that it was not only instinct with intelligence, earnestness, and indefatigable aspiration, but that it revealed a strong affinity for all that makes for righteousness and the elevation of the race."[23] Similarly, Frank Gunsaulus, minister and college president, wrote expansively of his experiences in the tent: "I never tired of sitting where I could watch the upturned faces and the play of human emotions. The plow-boy would go back to his plow—but not the same—he would remember. The farmer's daughter would go back to her cooking and baking and dishwashing—but she would not forget."[24] Boyesen's and Gunsaulus's descriptions demonstrate that while watching the performances onstage, Chautauqua audiences were offering a performance of their own. Collectively they performed America, their reactions and responses taken by those observing them as proof that the nation was interested in, responsive to, and concerned about their mutual circumstances.

Performance's transformative abilities worked both ways: as Chautauqua itself represented what spectators and participants alike wanted to be American, notions of what "American" meant were constructing Chautauqua. For Circuit manager Charles Horner, writing in 1954, Chautauqua had been "the essence of an Americanism in days gone by."[25] What Chautauqua claimed to present was a true depiction of a United States that was predominantly homogenous, unconflicted, and stable, thus making real through performance a much-longed-for America. Irving Fisher, the preeminent mathematical economist who taught at Yale from 1890 to 1935, noted enthusiastically: "The success or failure of a Democracy depends on public opinion. The Chautauqua has probably done more toward keeping American public opinion informed, alert and unbiased than any other movement."[26] Fisher was just one of many commentators who believed that the United States had never been more fractured or more riven by differences and discord and that a single experience, based on reasoned social intercourse, could address these problems. That what the Circuits were arguing and how they argued were out of step with the United States and that their argument often stemmed from a blinkered nostalgia were not acknowledged within the circle of Chautauqua's advocates.

The absence of a national media, until the arrival of radio in the 1920s, positioned Chautauqua as one of the few ubiquitous experiences that linked people across the United States. Touring performances and performers helped forge these links. Theater historian Thomas Postlewait has noted about touring performance more generally: "Entertainers went everywhere. Even before the country was united by films and radio, touring performers were able to establish a national culture of shared experiences."[27] While the Circuits went to great pains to disguise their variety show nature because of religious and community objections to what was considered the morally questionable theater, they had more in common with variety theater than any other form, even the New York Chautauqua itself.

The New York Chautauqua, leading American studies scholar Alan Trachtenberg observed, "in its original moment viewed itself as an agent of national life."[28] Trachtenberg's description could be easily extended to the Circuits as well. Chautauqua saw itself as an "agent" in that it understood itself to be acting on behalf of the American citizenry to bring about an improved democracy while simultaneously constructing the very improved democracy it advocated. In its greatest flights of fancy, Circuit Chautauqua imagined itself providing a return to the original Greek idea of democracy—a place where citizens presented themselves to conduct the business of governing without intermediaries. There were many influential people ready to make that sort of argument on Chautauqua's behalf.

Glenn Frank, editor most notably of *Century Magazine*, was a frequent speaker on the Circuits and a major supporter of Chautauqua. He argued that Chautauqua was one way "sustained discussion of public problems" could occur, thus preventing "national policy" from being decided by "political leadership of shifting personnel and uncertain qualities of mind and purpose."[29] Even George Vincent, son of the Chautauqua cofounder, argued that the Circuits used their national presence to foster direct participatory democracy. "With occasional crudities and violations of good taste, the commercial chautauqua circuit is rendering a service to democracy by fostering an interest in things of the mind, by quickening the social spirit, and by helping to create the public opinion which in response to leadership slowly gropes its way to collective action."[30] The ideas Frank and Vincent imply about citizenship have persisted throughout the history of the United States: someone who is diligent on behalf of the nation. Judith N. Shklar, noted government scholar, asserted in her celebrated Tanner Lectures on Human Values that citizens "are public meeting-goers and joiners of voluntary organizations who discuss and deliberate with others about the policies that will affect them all, and who serve their country . . . by having a considered notion of the public good that they genuinely take to heart."[31] Circuit Chautauqua was a site where one would encounter uncontested performances of good citizenship and where good citizens themselves would be found.

This uncomplicated patriotic view of how Chautauqua functioned masked the specificity of the vision at work. The Circuits, and indeed all the incarnations of Chautauqua, were adept at presenting a spectacle that appeared to be neutrally inclusive. Religion scholar Clifton Olmstead dryly observed in 1961: "No institution in American history so effectively blended religion and culture and presented them in such a palatable form."[32] As Olmstead implies, Chautauqua did not simply "blend" religion and culture through performance, it blended them to present a seemingly monolithic and unchallenged image of the nation. The United States of the nineteenth and early twentieth centuries was dominated by white Protestants of British descent. This period was marked by the belief that they had the power to "translat[e] their moral vision into the law of the land." This "public" Protestantism, highly evangelical in nature, dominated all public spheres—from politics to education, from literature to popular culture.[33] Despite Circuit Chautauqua's official claim to a non-denominational platform, a claim buttressed by the appearances of rabbis and Catholic priests, the Chautauqua platform was one of the most prominent promoters of what many thought of, as what Robert T. Handy has called it, "the national religion, a religion of civilization," presented simply as universal moral values and the American way of life.[34]

Chautauqua served as a reassuring example that religion and public culture could be productively engaged with one another. The Chautauqua argument was, as Chautauqua historian Andrew Rieser points out, that "Americans . . . could import many of their religious beliefs into realms often viewed as secular, such as municipal governance and popular entertainment."[35] Underlying this is a covert assumption that to be an authentic citizen is to be Christian and that religion is properly infused throughout the culture as a whole, not simply contained within church walls.

When Ely referred to the "forces shaping" America in this section's epigraph, he may well have been thinking of discourses as complex as citizenship, religion, and performance. Whatever he may have been implying, it is clear that Circuit Chautauqua's contemporary supporters argued for an acritical and celebratory linking of Chautauqua and America. For them, Chautauqua was the highest expression of American democracy. Ely, Glenn, Frank, and the rest probably would have been puzzled by the characterization of all Circuit presentations as performance. For them, such a view would have been an insulting reduction of those presentations to the merely false and trivial. Instead, as the programming for children and during World War I demonstrates, Chautauqua's performance of America was in earnest and could not have been a more sincere and affecting, if troubling, transformative experience.

"The Good Citizen's Creed: As a good citizen I believe it is my duty to my country to LOVE it; to obey its laws, to respect its flag, and to defend it against all enemies."[36]

On July 29, the final day of the 1917 Lincoln Chautauqua in Mooresville, the last event of the afternoon was a lecture by Helen B. Paulsen. Billed as "Play Magician, Child Welfare Worker, Authority on the Boy and Girl Problem, Juvenile Community Builder, the Children's Troubadour, A Hundred Mothers in One," Paulsen was no novice to contemporary questions about how to raise and educate children effectively and appropriately.[37] She had trained at Columbia University, taught kindergarten, and taught at "normal" schools (teachers' colleges) in West Virginia and Oklahoma. In addition, she had also worked with children through the Chautauqua Circuits and as field extension director of the American Institute of Child Life.[38] Her lecture that Sunday, "If We Only Knew," probably was similar to other ones she had given before and would give well into the 1920s. "This lecture . . . shows plainly and conclusively how by proper handling children can be developed and molded in their natures and characters."[39] Paulsen was by no means unique. Chautauquas urged parents and communities to take their responsibilities to their children very seriously as part of a larger agenda of making audiences conscious of their identities as citizens. Local children were part of specific performance strategies aimed at entwining the Circuits' identification with the nation.

In 1890 journalist Frederick Perry Noble had enthused, "Chautauqua is Americanizing America. It is a potency in the growth of the consciousness of nationality, a large factor in producing a homogeneous American life."[40] His excitement about Chautauqua as a process for creating citizens placed the institution squarely in the camp of those who believed citizens could be made. The Circuits were working within this established belief when they encouraged children to recite publicly the "Good Citizen's Creed," which begins this section. Performance, such as the repeated recitation of the "Creed," resists fixed beliefs of identity and behavior because it easily enacts the processes of change, learning, and transformation. The Circuits were able to assure audiences that Chautauqua was preparing children for what Noble called the "homogeneous American life." Even if only for the fleeting moment of performance, Chautauqua gave its audiences a promising glimpse of the future. Those audiences could see their children enact, however briefly, the model citizens that they had the potential to be.

All the Circuits offered supervised activities for children, which allowed their parents, particularly their mothers, to attend the daily programming. The supervisor, usually called the Junior Girl or Lady, was often already professionally associated with child care. She might have been a settlement worker, teacher on vacation, or college student. Typically her pay was around $16 a week, especially in the years before World War I.[41] Children's activities varied but almost always included a performance on the tent platform. These enterprises might be *A Mother Goose Party*, Children's Town, or mock weddings, which Richard Oram remembers doing in 1919. "Of course the parents came and were terribly proud," Oram noted about the final children's event.[42]

Most of the programming promised parents that their children would be improved through play, just as the adults were being improved through lectures and other activities. Progressive reformers had been focusing on the productive use of leisure for both adults and children for many years before the Circuits existed. In 1910 Jane Addams argued that to "fail to provide for the recreation of youth is not only to fail to provide all of them of their natural form of expression, but it is certain to subject some of them to the overwhelming temptation of illicit and soul destroying pleasures."[43] Addams was typical of reformers who worried that without constructive alternatives for leisure-time activities, people would fall into moral and social degeneration. This was a danger because of the larger threat it posed to families and communities. These concerns about the risks inherent in leisure were one expression of a larger Progressive anxiety over citizenship. As one scholar has recently noted: "Worried that many Americans were not yet equal to the task of self-government, Progressive reformers promoted civic and democratic education in schools and settlement houses."[44] The education they "promoted" was largely performance based. Participants could learn appropriate behavior and ideas by engaging in aesthetic forms of interaction, ones that encouraged the imitation of what Noble called "consciousness of nationality" as a way of adopting it.

It seemed obvious that play, when properly framed and supervised, guided the child's development as a member of the community and nation. One Chautauqua contemporary and prominent theorist of structured play, George Ellsworth Johnson, believed that such activities developed loyalty, citizenship, and teamwork over a taste for cheap pleasures. "The play impulses of children then, we may affirm, have one all-important office of giving rise to habits and permanent interests. . . . There is a time when the habit of activity, that is the *habit of work* and the enjoyment of work may be formed. . . . The opportunity of play is the opportunity of work."[45] There were calls to build playgrounds, include children in dance and dramatic activities (particularly folk dancing and pageants), and sponsor civic celebrations that encouraged entire communities to participate actively. No one questioned that the ways in which they were instructed to use their bodies as children would come naturally to participants as adults.

Nina Lamkin, author of the pageant that concluded the Lincoln Chautauqua in 1917, wrote in a reference guide for such endeavors:

It [community involvement] gives a civic backing to activities in which all
   may participate. It is this universal participation in various kinds of
   recreation and club activities that helps to make a satisfied
   community. . . . Interest and responsibility of the right sort . . . bring
   joy, recreation, leadership. These things bring a desire for more.
Play is the serious business of childhood.
It is the safety valve of youth.
It is the re-creation of middle-life.
It is the re-juvenation of older years. . . . It is the way to keep our vigor
   for work and our joy in life.[46]

All the suggestions for making "a satisfied community" took advantage of the
public and collaborative experiences of performance. It was not simply that
performance-based activities could be participated in and witnessed by great
numbers of people but that they encouraged people to reenvision themselves
in light of the work they did together.

Chautauquas responded to this call for productive play through performance. Lecturers, the staple Chautauqua performance, abounded. Women like
Helen Paulsen crisscrossed the nation offering their testimonies in performance to the pressing need to involve children in public enterprises. The
Radcliffe Chautauqua, for example, offered a lecture on "modern organized
play" as part of the regular programming.[47] Minna Mae Lewis, early in the second decade of the twentieth century, made the connections for parents between
children's lives and their achievements as adults in "The Children of Today and
the Public of Tomorrow."[48] In her lecture "The Child in Our Midst," Mary
Lawrence Kamnitz asked audiences, "Have you stopped to think? That the Boys
and Girls of YOUR city are YOUR city's contribution to the America of TOMOR-
ROW? That if our boys and girls are going to successfully solve the problems
ahead of them we must prepare them mentally, morally and physically to meet
them?"[49] Women dominated this type of lecture, drawing on the Progressive
belief that women's roles as mothers and housewives particularly suited them
to speaking authoritatively on matters pertaining to children. They were taken
seriously as they performed a public version of these private roles, part of the
popular notion of reform as "civic housekeeping."

Pageants were another extremely popular way to inculcate patriotic productivity in the young. David Glassberg has noted that "to [Progressive educators and playground workers], historical pageantry," a common approach to
municipal and national expressions of a shared historical past and patriotism,
"was an elaborate ritual of democratic participation . . . a way to . . . lead all

local residents in the ritual construction of a new communal identity and sense of citizenship."[50] Pageants modeled the Progressive potential of performance because they demonstrated the ways in which performance was not only an affective exchange between audience and performers but within the audience and among the performers. *A Mother Goose Party*, a pageant written expressly for the Circuits, made the argument that play was an important element in the process of becoming citizens in its opening song:

> We juniors claim that every one
> Must learn to romp and play.
> It's as of much importance
> As working is—they say.
> For when a boy knows how to play
> To give and take—you know
> He'll work a great deal better
> And he'll conquer every foe.[51]

Throughout, the verses celebrate the potential within each child to be a model citizen and imply that any transformation performed onstage will be effected offstage.

Performing the pageant was equated with the cardinal virtues of citizenship: hard work, cooperation, and bravery. These first two are ones the pageant rehearsal would have already promoted before the audience was in place. Rather than simply tell children that they must work together diligently, creating performances allowed them to experience these conditions firsthand and osmose this message naturally. As Shannon Jackson has theorized about Hull House performance, "The uses of theater in the reformist cultivation of aesthetic and moral sensibility lay in the embodied, environmental, and enacted nature of the medium itself, one that uniquely facilitated the transformation in sensibility and behavior."[52] While the word "theater" would have raised questions and concerns among some Circuit audiences (an anxiety explored in chapters 4 and 5), audiences and Circuit personnel would have agreed that the ways in which children's bodies and minds were manipulated through the staging process anticipated the ways in which they should function as adults.

A Mother Goose Party closed with a self-justifying and reassuring song that echoed the points it had made throughout:

> Now is the time for us to be good Americans
> Now is the time for us to be strong and true

Our country's sons are we, and we must ever be
The citizens she needs so much today!
   Ready to work and never shirk we all must try
To keep that Peace our boys have earned so dear,
So here's to glorious days—better in a thousand ways.
Now is the time for us to bring them here![53]

Just as the regular Chautauqua programming attempted to create for adults the milieu in which they could become perfect citizens, the junior Chautauqua tried to mold children in the culture's image. The important argument, however, was one that must have been obvious to all spectators, regardless of age. Citizen is not a passive condition one can merely absorb but an identity to be actively pursued and earned.

Even children who attended Circuits that were not able to or did not offer such elaborate activities found ways to use performance in the service of future responsibilities. Richard Oram remembered participating in a "little wedding." Mentone, Indiana, was a very small town in 1919; Oram remembered the population as about a hundred, and the junior girl was thrown on her own resources. Her idea for a wedding was fortuitous in part because, as Oram remarked, "You had a great many people, not only do you have your bride and groom, but you have attendants and a choir, that made everyone in the show."[54] But it was also significant because marriage has been (and is) an essential element of citizenship. In her landmark study of the history of marriage as a nationalist enterprise, feminist historian Nancy Cott emphasized that marriage has immediate consequences for the future of the citizenry. "The laws of marriage must play a large part in forming 'the people.' They sculpt the body politic. In a hybrid nation such as the United States, formed of immigrant groups, marriage becomes all the more important politically. Where citizenship comes along with being born on the nation's soil as it does here, marriage policy underlies national belonging and the cohesion of the whole."[55] Even in the seemingly artless performance of a ubiquitous adult activity, children were being schooled to anticipate their future responsibilities through pleasurable repetition.

Edith Williams Way, an alumna of Swarthmore College who worked on the Swarthmore Chautauqua in 1914, kept a notebook recording the children's activities she led and the conclusions she wished them to derive from the various stories and games. One such activity was the "Citizenship Information Hour," in which lessons about how one becomes a citizen were related through a parable she told the children.

Once upon a time there was a town that had a new lighting system—was very proud of its main street—but all the side streets and little yards were filled with scraps—man saw this—tried to get town to straighten up— grown-up friends did not do as much—asked children to help—companies, captains—how did they do it—1st looked into their own backyards—vegetable gardens as pretty as flower gardens—2nd had slogan of "pick it up"—3rd had a slogan of "swat the fly"—keep yourself clean and tidy—put away things.[56]

The idea of citizenship Way sketches here is similar to that of A Mother Goose Party. Citizens were those who were active on their community's behalf and tireless in improving it. Specific notions of hygiene were even part of citizenship: taking care of one's body and attending to one's physical surroundings were interconnected. The individual body and the body politic were experienced as continuous in the performances Circuit Chautauquas produced with local children.

Children were also taught to respect order and hierarchy. Citizens were clearly those who submitted to organization. Way understood her teaching as a new definition of citizenship and noted parenthetically that the "old idea of being a citizen was to salute the flag and sing 'America.'"[57] Progressives had a more dynamic, if vague, model in mind. They "defined citizenship as patriotic virtue, moral integrity, and broad participation in public life."[58] The model proposed to children was one that mimicked the philosophy of Chautauqua itself—proactive improvement aimed at both the self and the community— and positioned itself as a contemporary understanding of what it meant to be an American. Chautauqua emphasized that "whether in private or public, the good citizen does something to support democratic habits and constitutional order."[59] Chautauqua thus shaped children by championing itself as the agent of an order to be internalized. Way admonished her charges: "You should begin to notice these things and talk about them."[60] She encouraged them to embrace the Chautauqua definition of citizenship as their own.

Parents were urged to understand the value of Chautauqua activities for their children in similar terms. While the Junior Girls structured play to shape young citizens, the Circuits were not reticent to point out the importance of these endeavors. Redpath's 1923 season advertising brochure encouraged parents not to underestimate the importance of their children's attendance. "Every child is taught to salute the flag. This is well. All boys and girls ought to be furnished with a season ticket to chautauqua [sic] that they may learn what this flag means and wherein it differs from other national emblems, and what it means to them that is different from flags of other nations. Teach the boy to salute the flag and also teach him why the flag should be revered and loved."[61] Like Way, Redpath espoused the Progressive notion that citizens had to go beyond simply saluting and singing to signal their citizenship. Those actions had to be undergirded with the knowledge that could make them a deeply held belief rather than superficial gestures.

The most obvious way that children were taught to love the flag or, in other words, be citizens, was through junior town. Throughout Chautauqua week, junior town allowed children to mime the activities of local government. While their parents were attending lectures and other performances, children performed the civic activities of their parents' daily lives. The 1929 Redpath Chautauquas urged parents to bring their children because they would "learn to take the responsibility of citizenship. Out of this we should produce citizens for tomorrow who will not shirk the tasks of honest, loyal, home town government."[62] The link between Chautauqua and the molding of citizens could not have been more explicit. The Circuits held out the promise that the next generation could be trained to carry on the best of what the current generation had wrought. They also reinforced the most general notion of citizenship, that it, as social scientist Evelyn Nakano Glenn describes, "refers to full membership in the community in which one lives. Membership in return implies certain rights in and reciprocal duties toward the community."[63] The activities of junior town (elections, holding office, carrying out one's duties) trained children not only in the tasks of government but also in the idea of participatory democracy, where one earns the right to be self-governing. Those who witnessed junior town found the inculcation of these values moving, as Arthur Row testifies.

> Under her [the Junior Girl's] tutelage they learn at least the rudiments of citizenship. A mayor is appointed and all the lesser officials, at the end of the week they read their reports from the platform and electrify their relatives with their poise and savoir faire (acquired in a week or less, if you please). . . . To see an embryo "Mayor" aged maybe ten, solemnly mount the platform and give a "report" on his week's "rule" is to see America in the making as well as something that is more often impressive than funny.[64]

Row, an actor on the Circuits, was neither a performer nor a member of the local audience but a specialized audience member with participant knowledge. He understood firsthand the artificiality of what he was seeing, which may account for his mocking tone, but he cannot help but be moved by the performance of "America in the making." This effect represents what Shannon

Jackson has termed an "infectious example," that is, the ways in which performance intervenes in self-formation without apparent effort.[65] These children may not have realized it during the Chautauqua week, but they were being encouraged to imbibe knowledge and experience in seeming spontaneity. They were not overtly being taught to be responsible citizens but were encouraged to find continuing pleasure in its behaviors. Such pleasurable performances now, reformers were sure, would later translate into desirable embodiments and affects. This mimetic performance of democracy was a reassuring repetition that seemed to promise a utopian future.

"We are glad . . . to fight thus for the ultimate peace of the world and . . . for the rights of nations great and small and the privileges of men everywhere to choose their way of life and obedience. The world must be made safe for democracy."[66]

Woodrow Wilson, calling for a declaration of war on April 2, 1917, was not speaking of Chautauqua. Yet by the time the United States entered the war, the Chautauqua movement had been striving for more than forty years to make the United States "safe for democracy." The Circuits' work during World War I, like their work with children, was an unqualified articulation of the Circuits' identification of themselves, as one Chautauqua participant put it, as "the machinery necessary for the successful operations of democracy."[67] That Chautauqua had a special relationship to America and, more pragmatically, that it reached a large number of people every summer were not lost on the federal government. When it became apparent that many communities across the country were canceling their 1917 Chautauqua contracts in the belief that such activities were disrespectful in a time of war, the president of the International Lyceum and Chautauqua Association (ILCA) lobbied hard in Washington to get an official statement from the government that supported the Circuits. "It was thought that nothing short of a statement from President Wilson would save the business."[68] It was probably not solely out of respect and admiration that Wilson wrote to commend Chautauquas on their work and encourage them to continue. As Wilson said elsewhere: "It is not an army we must train for war. . . . It is a nation."[69] What better way to train the nation than to utilize the democratic institutions already in operation?

It has been on my mind for some time to thank your organization for the very real help it has given to America in the struggle that is concerned with every fundamental element of national life. Your speakers, going from community to community, meeting people in the friendly spirit engendered by years of intimate and understanding contact, have been effective messengers for the delivery and interpretation of democracy's meaning and imperative needs. The work that the Chautauqua is doing has not lost importance because of the war, but rather has gained new opportunities for service.

Let me express the hope that you will let no discouragement weaken your activities, and that the people will not fail in the support of a patriotic institution that may be said to be an integral part of the national defense.[70]

Every Chautauqua and Lyceum bureau in the United States received a copy of the letter and was offered unlimited reproductions. Initially, 70,000 were requested, and ultimately 85,000 were distributed.[71] It was reprinted in almost all 1917 season programs, as well as in numerous other publications.

Wilson's letter implied that there was more to the war effort than simply winning on the battlefield. What was truly at stake was the survival of the United States. The effort to preserve the nation was unimaginable without a partnership with Chautauquas. Wilson's argument echoed the typical justifications linking Chautauqua with democracy: it shaped political thought, it facilitated otherwise difficult connections among people, and it shaped citizens. After reading this letter, local guarantors and spectators must have understood very clearly that refusing to participate in Chautauqua could threaten the nation's ability to win the war.

Mobilizing the home front during World War I put the country in a state of near-hysteria. Any critique of the war was considered unpatriotic at best and traitorous sedition at worst. The government did little to check the vigilante justice that was often meted out against those who even merely appeared to be against the war.[72] This enforced patriotism seemed right to many Americans who, through both public and educational discourse, had been imbued with what Stewart Halsey Ross in his book on World War I propaganda describes as a "narrow chauvinism" that prized "American achievements as noblest among all countries."[73] Conformity became conflated with Americanism.

One of the most outspoken supporters of the war was former president Theodore Roosevelt. Roosevelt was untiring in his promotion of the war and in his demand for "100% Americanism."[74] Populations still marked as immigrant, such as those who called themselves "German-American" or "Italian-American," were pejoratively referred to as "hyphens" or "hyphenated Americans." These citizens were seen as conditional Americans because they had not embraced Americanization. Public figures warned Americans that "hyphens" might form a fifth column within the United States and therefore should not be trusted. For celebrities and performers, such charges were particularly dangerous, as they were at risk for becoming scapegoats for fears about the outcome of the war.

In training the nation for war, Wilson and his government had, as Ross reminds his readers, "to convince a lukewarm population that the nation was engaged in a life-and-death struggle against the forces of darkness."[75] This was no easy task, because strong isolationism had kept the United States out of the war when it began in 1914. A massive propaganda campaign was launched in, as Chambers portrays it, a "nation-wide publicity apparatus that included newspaper reporters, authors, academics, actors, orators, screenwriters, songwriters and artists. . . . Using modern advertising and public relations techniques [they] sold the war to America."[76] National mobilization was nothing new to the Circuits. For more than ten years they had been constructing just such an effort.

Circuit Chautauquas played a crucial role in "selling" the war to the United States. Even before Wilson's 1917 letter, Circuit managers had joined the huge federal efforts to transform the country for war. By the end of 1917 Harry Harrison, manager of the Redpath-Harrison Circuit, had been appointed by the War Department to head the War Finance Committee of the War Entertainment Council.[77] The twenty-member committee was a who's who of Circuit Chautauqua, including Arthur Coit of the Coit-Alber Circuit; Montaville Flowers, head of the ILCA (who had solicited the letter from Wilson), W. V. Harrison and Charles Horner of the Redpath Circuits, and Paul M. Pearson of the Swarthmore Circuit. Only one theater manager of note, Marc Klaw, was tapped. Klaw, with his partner, Abraham L. Erlanger, ran the powerful Theatrical Syndicate for about twenty years beginning in 1896. The syndicate was a booking monopoly that provided theater with the greatest degree of centralization and standardization it has ever known and controlled most American commercial theaters between 1900 and 1916. The committee's composition suggested that the U.S. government looked to Chautauqua, not to the theater community, when it needed a national patriotic effort to offer morally acceptable entertainment.

The committee members focused on the Smileage Campaign to get the public to buy coupon books that would allow the military to attend various types of entertainment. This early forerunner to the United Service Organization (USO) emerged from the belief, as the Smileage News put it, that "giving [military personnel] some of those forms of amusement and relaxation to which they had become accustomed in civil life is of tremendous value in wholesomely filling the hours in camp which are not occupied by military training."[78] Chautauqua was ready to provide "wholesome" entertainment, thus supplanting the kinds of amusements soldiers had turned to in previous conflicts. As Raymond B. Fosdick, head of the Commission on Training Camp Activities, noted, in earlier wars "there was absolutely nothing for them to do . . . nothing but saloons and a well-organized red light district. In this war we are driving those vicious agencies out of business and setting up clean entertainment in their place."[79] The actual Smileage tickets themselves marked the moral mission of the campaign by quoting Secretary of War Newton D. Baker on every coupon: "Plenty of hard work and clean fun make for vigor and manhood, the prime requisites for a soldier."[80] Each ticket emphasized the connection between moral behavior and the ability to defend democracy.

In training camps with no access to cities, Chautauqua tents were erected and became Liberty Tents. In cities, preexisting theaters and auditoriums became Liberty Theaters and Liberty Auditoriums. Chautauqua and Lyceum used their usual talent, and F. W. Keith of the Albee Vaudeville Circuits also provided some entertainment.[81] Soldiers were admitted to the Liberty performance spaces with their Smileage Books.

Using the Circuit booking and advertising structures, the Chautauqua managers on the committee launched a national campaign urging citizens to purchase books for military personnel. Local committees, charged with the task of selling books, were told to use "telling war cries such as 'If you can't put the "I" in fight, put the "pay" in patriotic.'"[82] The goal was to sell $1 million worth of books. By April 9, 1918, they had sold $692,942, demonstrating that the goal was within reach.[83] If there were people ignorant of Chautauqua, the Smileage Campaign was a way to address that. "The words Lyceum and Chautauqua appear frequently in the Smileage articles and people cannot help becoming aware of the service being rendered by these institutions in the way of bettering the morale of the nation," *Lyceum Magazine* assured readers.[84] Chautauqua's service to the nation when citizens were intensely aware of their role as defenders of democracy further identified Chautauqua as a primary institution of democracy.

The government turned to Chautauquas to organize the entertainment efforts, and citizens supported these efforts. Chautauqua managers relied on Circuit selling techniques and were reaching most of the same audiences. The call to support the war by providing entertainment comparable to that on the Circuits resonated with Chautauqua patrons because that created a link between the Chautauqua audiences and soldiers. Soldiers and Chautauqua audiences were both witnessing many of the same performances, and this reas-

sured families that their sons were seeing the same morally acceptable entertainment as they did at home.

The Circuits fulfilled their mandate to be "an integral part of the national
defense" in many other ways besides the Smileage Campaign. The platform
continued to be a site of democracy that molded citizens. One obvious strategy was to turn the platform over to various government agencies and personnel. "With a daily programme with a patriotic tinge Chautauqua is helping to
make real Americans no matter what their pedigree."[85] The platform was used
to sell Liberty Bonds, inform people about the activities of the Red Cross, and
generally provide the latest war news. By the second summer of the war, many
of the lecturers offered firsthand accounts of the fighting. On the 1918
Redpath-Vawter Circuit, for example, audiences heard Private Ernest Lovell
discuss "Thrilling Experiences in German Prison Camps," and journalist-
turned-lecturer Fred Dale Wood considered the question of "Financing the
War."[86] The Circuits also brought the war itself onto the platform. In his study
of the Circuits, John Edward Tapia observes: "Although brief film clips of the
war could be seen in populated areas, in rural areas where the movie house and
radio virtually did not exist, the Chautauqua program was the main avenue of
'seeing' and learning about the European war."[87] The Circuit platform could
almost literally bring the war home to rural citizens, but it was careful to con-
textualize this new information in familiar Chautauqua dialogues.

One of the most significant pieces in that repertoire was the play The Melting-
Pot by Israel Zangwill. In it, poor young Russian Jewish immigrant and com-
poser David Quixano's greatest wish is to compose a symphony that expresses
his experiences of and love for America. "America is God's crucible," he tells
another character, "where all the races of Europe are melting and reforming!"
The races will not be separate for long, as "these are the fires of God you've
come to, . . . into the crucible with you all! God is making the American. . . .
The real American has not yet arrived. He is only in the crucible, I tell you—he
will be the fusion of all races, perhaps the coming superman. Ah, what a glorious Finale for my symphony."[88] David also plays violin at the settlement
house, where he meets and falls in love with one of the workers, Vera, who is
a Russian Christian. They plan to marry, until David finds out that her father
led the pogrom that exterminated his family. David turns from her in hatred,
just as she turns from her father, rejecting the terrible actions that her father
continues to defend.

The final act occurs after David's America symphony has been successfully
played for the first time. The other characters, inspired by the triumphal performance, connive to reunite the lovers, who reconcile after David declares that

Vera cannot be held responsible for her father's crimes. The play ends as David describes his vision of America—the only place where their love is possible. "Ah, Vera, what is the glory of Rome and Jerusalem where all nations and races come to worship and look back, compared with the glory of America, where all nations and races come to labor and look forward! (*He raises his hands in benediction over the shining city*). Peace, peace to all ye unborn millions, fated to fill the giant continent—the God of our *children* give you peace" (185). The final image onstage is the Statue of Liberty, with an offstage chorus singing "My Country 'Tis of Thee."

The play premiered in Washington, D.C., in 1908. President Theodore Roosevelt attended the premiere, and his enthusiastic appraisal was subsequently quoted everywhere: "A Great Play; a Great Play."[89] When it was produced in New York in 1909, it quickly became one of the most popular plays that season, indeed, of its generation. Theater scholar Harley Erdman comments in his book *Staging the Jew*: "If the concept of the melting pot, discredited as it may be, remains an influential metaphor for American acculturation, then one can posit Zangwill's play as one of the most influential events in the history of Broadway."[90] The same claims could be made for the play on the Chautauqua Circuits. *The Melting-Pot* first toured in 1915 when Arthur Kachel, an "enacter of plays," did a one-man version.[91] The play was first fully produced on the Circuits in 1916 and then annually for many years after that. During World War I, the play was a particular favorite because of the way in which it answered questions about assimilation and becoming American.

The importance of assimilation is emphasized in the development of subplots, which also focus on the complexities of immigration, and minor characters. The most significant such character is Kathleen, the Quixanos' Irish maid. Kathleen is the typical stage "Brigid," representative of the 700,000 single Irish women who immigrated to the United States during the time of Chautauqua, most of whom found employment doing domestic work.[92] The stage Irish figure was a familiar stereotype in nineteenth-century theater. While the Irish themselves were not welcome in many places, "audiences for legitimate theater . . . couldn't get enough of authentic Irish accents, which invariably prompted great bellows of laughter."[93] But Kathleen represents more than the simpleminded Irish maid; she is also another example of the possibilities and benefits of assimilation.

At the start of the play, Kathleen exhibits an ignorant anti-Semitism. She cannot understand why Frau Quixano is angry at her for putting meat on the butter dish and responds sharply, "bad luck to me if iver I take sarvice again with haythen Jews" (3–4). Kathleen's speech is rendered in the stage Irish dialect audiences had been laughing at for years, so she largely serves as humorous counterpoint to David and Vera's seemingly tragic love story. At the end of the play, Kathleen comically anticipates David and Vera's reunion. Assimilation moves her from her earlier anti-Semitism (based, it is suggested, on a lack of familiarity with Judaism) to an acceptance of her Jewish employers by hybridizing their traditions and behaviors with her own Catholicism. She scolds David for suggesting that his grandmother ride in the settlement house elevator on a Saturday ("Troth, I'll try to explain to her that droppin' down isn't ridin'" [168]) and that they eat the settlement house food ("Give her refreshments where they mix the mate with the butther plates! Oh, Mr. David" [169]), but the moment intended to be the most humorous is also the moment where Kathleen's assimilation is most apparent. Frau Quixano has exited and Kathleen follows, calling to her "(In Irish sounding Yiddish.) Wu geht Ihr, bedad? Houly Moses, komm' zurick? Begorra we Jews never know our way" (170). Most discussions of the play understandably focus on David and Vera, but Zangwill's melting-pot message of assimilation is sounded throughout the play in a variety of ways. Through Kathleen and common, everyday practices, he demonstrates that assimilation happens at a simple level as well as a grander one.

The play participated in contemporary discourses that conflated race with culture. If "American" was a race, could immigrants become American? Blood, a common metaphor for race, is invoked throughout the play. When David leaves Vera he cries, "You cannot come to me. There is a river of blood between us" (155). Earlier, he described the Old World as being marked by "blood hatreds" (33). Zangwill offered a visceral version of the racialist discourse popular at the time. Inviting Roosevelt to the premiere, Zangwill explained that the play's message "dramatizes your own idea of America as a crucible in which the races are fusing into the future America."[94] Zangwill believed that a new race would emerge after the old ones were "melt[ed] and fuse[d]" in the "roaring and bubbling" of the "great purging flame" (184–185). Harley Erdman explicates: "Americanization-through-deculturation may always have been implicit in the very metaphor of the melting pot, the alchemical roots of which would suggest the conversion of worthless material into something valuable. When appropriated across a generation, however, the melting pot became a process through which immigrants would lose their differences as they conformed to a higher standards of 'American-ness.'"[95] This was not mongrelization or miscegenation but the creation of something new. The old races (or cultures) would disappear, and a new and better race would emerge. This message countered the fears Americans voiced about the massive influx of immigrants (especially those from southern and eastern Europe). Zangwill suggests that there is nothing to fear, that the conformity of America will transform the heterogeneity of the immigrants.

It must have been precisely this message that made The Melting-Pot so attractive to the Circuits and their audiences when first presented on the Circuits in 1915. The play was "a new vision of America" in which disparate peoples were forged into a "common brotherhood and civilization," publicity assured audiences.[96] During the war, the play was advertised as proof that "hyphenated Americans" would be loyal to the United States. Redpath-Horner's program trumpeted: "'The Melting Pot' has never been more eminently fitting than it is in this momentous year of 1917. Never before has there been so much discussion as to the effectiveness of this country acting as the great melting pot for the people of all nations. Present events promise to reveal in striking manner whether such fusion of nationalities has been successful."[97] As one Circuit lecturer noted about Chautauqua audiences, "Here and there are little groups of foreign-born. One or two of my audiences consisted practically of Germans and Swedes. But they are good Americans. They are through with the hyphen. They are sending their boys over to beat the Kaiser and they do not want them home until the job is done."[98] While Chautauqua used the play to ask whether "the fusion of nationalities had been successful," the audiences were evidence that the answer would be resoundingly positive. Asking such questions allowed the Circuits to position themselves as providing the answer to questions of loyalty, assimilation, and Americanism.

Not surprisingly, after World War I the Circuits used the play to reinforce further their emphatically positive answer. "It is intensely patriotic and is especially appropriate at this particular time. The products of the melting pot have been tried in the refining of the great war and have stood the test."[99] The play, as the 1919 brochure goes on to argue, demonstrates why German American or Italian American soldiers stayed loyal to the United States and fought better than the Germans or Italians. "Why? Because these men were products of the great American Melting Pot. They had come under the influence of American ideals and American institutions."[100] Staging this play between 1915 and 1919 documents Chautauqua's commitment to defining "American." It also illustrates the way the Circuits positioned themselves as the primary platform from which to resolve that debate. The Circuits wished to become identified as the best expression of "100% Americanism."

Sometimes this desire translated into tangible service. Ernestine Schumann-Heink, the German contralto of the New York Metropolitan Opera who had long since made her home in the United States and was a staple on the Circuits, turned to Chautauquas when her loyalty to the United States was questioned. She wrote to Harry Harrison of her work selling Liberty Bonds: "Here is a proof for my loyal enthusiastic working for the Government. . . . Thanks for all you do for me, dear friend. Three cheers for USA forever and ever."[101] It is not surprising that someone as prominent as German-born Schumann-Heink would come under suspicion given the American suspicion of hyphenated Americans. Harry Harrison later wrote a friend that Schumann-Heink "said she would do anything for me for the good work I did for her" because he contacted Washington to "kill the report of her being a German spy."[102] That the Circuits had the power to speak behind the scenes to someone's loyalty demonstrates the national influence they had. It also demonstrates a disavowal of any distance the Circuits might have claimed to have from the government. Andrew Rieser documents this significant shift in the early Chautauqua mission. "The propaganda function of the circuits revealed that it had abandoned Chautauqua's historical role as an independent proponent *for* the modern state, and had instead become an agent *of* the state."[103] Chautauqua's claims to Americanism and democracy must have been taken seriously, not simply by those who bought season tickets to the Circuits but also by those in power. When Wilson called for Chautauquas to be "an integral part of the national defense," the Circuits accepted this charge and extended it far beyond the platform.

In 1917 the president of the Lincoln Chautauqua assured those in Mooresville (and elsewhere): "Let us make then Lincoln Chautauqua in your town a real factor for the promotion of patriotism and the propagation of higher American ideals, molding the sentiment of the public along lines that will make the people of the community better citizens and if need be—better soldiers."[104] Chautauqua did not want just to help Americans hear about the war, it also wanted to define what the war meant for them. The Chautauqua themes of progressive improvement, constructing the citizenry, and democracy had greater weight in the period immediately around the war.

The 1917 program cover for Redpath-Horner illustrated the relationship that Chautauqua promoted between the United States and the Circuits (see page 70). With a benevolent smile, Uncle Sam looks over his shoulder at the spectator holding the program.[105] Uncle Sam grasps two guy wires attached to the two main poles of the tent, each flying an American flag. He supports the tent by cradling it in his arms and embracing it, he encourages spectators by inviting them into the tent, and he nurtures Chautauqua by strengthening the tent itself. Uncle Sam, the master puppeteer, animates the entire Chautauqua through his manipulations of the tent. That Chautauqua tent is filled with a standing-room-only crowd. The message is clear—Chautauqua is nestled in the bosom of democracy.

"AMERICA YESTERDAY AND TODAY"

(Copyrighted 1917)

A PAGEANT, by NINA B. LAMKIN

We take pleasure in announcing that on one night of the Chautauqua a costumed pageant will be presented by the boys and girls of the community, under the supervision of our trained directors. This will be a very happy event for the young people, a culmination of their week of pleasure and profit. We urge your fullest cooperation in this feature of the Youths' Chautauqua program.

Pageantry is an expression of community interests, whether an outgrowth of play-work among the boys and girls or among the grown-ups; it is symbolic of the live issues which stand for the best in history, in patriotism and in real community building. Our people, and particularly our boys and girls, have very little conception of the significance of the march of the pioneers across this vast continent and of its settlement and growth. This community pageant of American history comes to interpret to us true Americanism. It is your pageant, given by the young people of your community, and was written for the exclusive use of Lincoln Chautauquas. It deserves your enthusiastic support.

Lincoln Chautauquas promised Mooresville, Indiana, that the pageant would stand for the "best in history, in patriotism, and in real community building." Since the pageant was newly written that year, there were no pictures of it for the program, but pageants were so ubiquitous that these illustrations indicated that this pageant would not differ from the typical format. Iowa.

There were few people who did not dress their best for Chautauqua. When Circuit supporters rhapsodized about Chautauqua audiences as true representations of America, they were encountering audiences like these. Iowa.

Athletics were a popular junior activity. These children in Enid, Oklahoma, played volleyball while their parents attended lectures. Iowa.

Children's programming was one way Chautauqua advertised itself in the town. There were usually parades, like this one in Mount Sterling, Kentucky (showing children on horseback), and events anticipating the Circuit's arrival. In Darlington, Wisconsin, Lincoln Chautauquas used children as part of their advance sales strategy, as shown by the children on stage. Iowa.

The women who organized the children's events could
be in charge of large numbers of children. Iowa.

Mother Goose *performances were so prevalent that Circuits had materials just to advertise them. Iowa.*

Many Circuits supplied children with costumes for pageants and other games. Impersonations of American Indians were ubiquitous. In Darlington, Wisconsin, boys competed with one another from different "tribes." Iowa.

Girls were called upon more often than boys to perform ethnic nostalgia. These Darlington, Wisconsin, girls are supposed to represent England, France, Holland, and Sweden, although it is not clear who is which country. Harriette Kohler Smith remembers that the costumes smelled, and she would not wear hers until her mother cleaned it. Iowa.

A common junior Chautauqua activity was a flag raising. This public activity was just one of the things that assured adults that children's Circuit experiences were inculcating the appropriate values. Iowa.

One of the few surviving photographs of Richard Oram's childhood is this one of his participation in a "little wedding" when he was five in 1919. Oram and his "bride," Margaret Mentzer, remained friends. She lived in Mentone, Indiana, her entire life. Courtesy of the Oram family.

Children's performances of adult activities were reinforced through costuming. Iowa.

Children's parades, like this one in Somerset, Ohio, were quickly co-opted to communicate the appropriate war messages. Iowa.

A 1918 "Win the War" parade in Brookville, Indiana, featured the Red Cross. Iowa.

This brochure emphasized the assimilationist message of the play, although literalizing the melting-pot metaphor also underscores its latent violence. Iowa.

Arthur Kachel's one-person performance may have worked to support The Melting-Pot's emphasis on similarities, as he embodied all the characters himself. Iowa.

Ernestine Schumann-Heink's schedule never permitted her to take an entire season's contract, but she impressed Harry Harrison with her generosity to children and the elderly. Her public gestures to them may have helped influence him to act on her behalf with the federal government. Iowa.

Redpath-Horner was one of the few Circuits to
acknowledge the war overtly on a program cover. Iowa.

CHAPTER TWO

Community on the Platform

When Ben R. Vardaman, an Iowa businessman and editor of *Merchants Trade Journal*, stepped off the train platform in Valley City, North Dakota, "one July, eleven bands met [him]."[1] The small town rang with the glorious sounds of music, cheers, and anticipation. Crowds gathered at the station eagerly awaiting the guest of honor. Vardaman had pioneered the idea of a special "Business and Community Betterment Day" as a staple on the Chautauqua Circuits. Advertising himself as "The Community Builder and Business Missionary," he built his lecturing career on such topics as "Human Science in Community Building" and "How to Make This Community Better."[2] Audiences and Circuit managers alike saw his work as a natural outgrowth of the theme of uplift and improvement so central to the Chautauqua mission. The crowds, however, were not really there to welcome and honor Vardaman. They were there to celebrate themselves and "boost" for their town, as the contemporary vernacular would have it. Vardaman was there simply to validate those efforts. Valley City, the county seat of Barnes County, sits on the banks of the Sheyenne River in the southeastern corner of the state. Sixty miles west of Fargo, its population in 1910 was 4,606 and had climbed to 4,686 by 1920.[3] Those North Dakota citizens probably did not think their small town was in the mainstream of America, but for a few hours, at least, Vardaman was going to make them feel that they were one of the nation's most valuable assets.

Self-improvement and community improvement were identical concepts to Vardaman and other lecturers who did similar work. Sinclair Lewis's choice of Charles Zueblin as the focus of his parody was no coincidence; there was no type of lecture more identified with Chautauqua than the community lecture. People looked forward to it because it functioned, as *Outlook* enthused in 1922, "to wake . . . up . . . sleepy towns. Long after the Chautauqua tent has been taken down the newly awakened community spirit remains. All up and down Main Street there is an added warmth in the greetings exchanged between the passers-by."[4] Community lecturers performed community back to its inhabitants to affirm their way of life. Circuit Chautauqua affected feelings but rarely effected substantive change.

Vardaman took his charge seriously and prided himself on the growing number of requests for lectures that he received from communities throughout the country. "I believe that it is right that the people should be given a broader teaching along these lines than they have had in the past."[5] This notion, that community could be taught, was basic to Chautauqua. In the spirit of uplift, the Circuits believed they could define Chautauqua as the driving force behind community.

While there was pessimism about small communities' chances for survival in the face of growing urbanization, immigration, and cultural shifts, Vardaman and others like him were optimistic that the United States was a realization of the necessity of community. He wrote W. Frank McClure, a fellow businessman and lecturer, in 1914:

> It seems to me—and I believe that I am in the position to feel the trend of these things, being in touch more or less intimately with communities in every section—that the people of this country are coming to realize that the community centered around our towns and centers, is infinitely more than a business center, and believing this to be true, I feel that the masses of the people should be given an insight into the fundamental principles of these things in a clear, practical, and straightforward manner. And my experience has been that people of all kinds and classes appreciate these things, when given to them in this way.[6]

In a typically Chautauquan move, Vardaman framed the impetus behind his talks as democratic service to his fellow citizens. People are hungry for his information, he argued, they just need to be able to put it to work. Although he stressed utility and practicality, Vardaman knew that while community can be reduced to "fundamental principles," it cannot be reduced to the physical boundaries of the town or county. It is the less tangible but more valuable connections among people, and Circuits and audiences together seemed to believe that community lectures would help communities survive and thrive. What this meant to Vardaman and his fellow Chautauquans was fundamental to Circuit Chautauqua's place in national life—the place it wanted to occupy, the place that others understood it to occupy, and the place performance enabled it to occupy.

Community was performed in many ways on the Circuit platform. The most overt treatment of community was from lecturers like Vardaman who exhorted citizens to attend to their obvious community responsibilities. Less obvious were the other ways in which civil society was performed. More complex formulations of community, like those of citizenship, focused not only on inclusion but exclusion and its ramifications. Vardaman was not the only "missionary" appearing on the platform. The solid relationship between Chautauqua and evangelical Protestantism was not always visible but undergirded every performance. Persuasion and conversion were strategies adapted from religious practices and used directly and indirectly to articulate the standards for community inclusion. The two constituencies that make the vexed relationships of inclusion, exclusion, and grounds for both most visible were women and people of color. The performance of gender and race was often the surrogate for more penetrating discussions of community than lecturers like Vardaman provided. In Chautauqua, community, race, and gender were all contextualized within Christianity. An exploration of these links provides the "infinitely more" for which Vardaman hoped.

"Chautauqua has served to reveal the American community to itself at its best."[7]

In small-town America, American identity and democracy often found definition in discussion and debate over shared community values. In large part, the ideal of community as shaped and promoted by local leaders provided the basis for an understanding of the entire nation. Circuit Chautauquas certainly embraced the notion that the local and national were inextricably linked. Moreover, the Circuits used *Lyceum Magazine* and the platform to urge communities to develop "the new localism" that would serve as the foundation for American preeminence. "The idea is this: The way to build anything from a house to a civilization is to start at the bottom and build up. National laws cannot make prosperous, contented local communities. But happy, industrious, beautiful, democratic, righteous communities all over this country will make a strong, powerful and just nation."[8] Rather than looking for the national to be defined at the national level, it was to be defined by ordinary people in their everyday lives. Community could not be legislated, but once it existed it would define the direction of the nation. Communities, therefore, had to be the focus of the Chautauqua effort.

Circuit Chautauqua's concept of community sprang from a particular set of political, cultural, and social circumstances. As the United States moved away from its nineteenth-century agrarian roots toward the industrial power of the late nineteenth and early twentieth centuries, the ensuing geographical shifts brought with them questions about how people should conceptualize their connections to one another. Urban centers increased in importance, while rural ones, the ones traditionally understood as "communities," became less influential. For the many people who lived in rural areas or critiqued the cities, these shifts were at best disturbing, at worst a harbinger of accelerated national decline. These worries often found their expression in discussions and debates about "community" and the belief that these new developments threatened its very existence. As one Chautauqua pamphlet titled "I Am What I Am" boasted about the Circuit: "I fuse aggregations of individuals into communities."[9] Ronald Wiebe has noted that in the nineteenth century, the United States was a country of "island communities." By the end of the century these communities were supplanted by new social organizations based on "the regulative, hierarchal needs of urban industrial life" alien to those who lived outside these urban centers.[10]

Rural communities were the site for much of this national uncertainty. Their experience that, as scholar David B. Danbom describes it, "to live in the countryside by 1900 was to have the sense that the nation was passing you by, leaving you behind, ignoring you at best, derogating you at worst," was based in part on tremendous population shifts that fueled the growing urban domination.[11] From 1880 to 1930 rural population increased 150 percent, but during the same period the urban population expanded 500 percent. Another sign of this radical change in the distribution of the population is that in 1880 only 26 percent of the population lived in towns with more than 5,000 residents, but by 1936 56 percent of the population were urban dwellers.[12] At the end of the nineteenth century, Wiebe argues, even though

a majority of Americans would still reside in relatively small, personal centers for several decades more, the society that had been premised upon the community's effective sovereignty . . . no longer functioned. The precipitant of the crisis was a widespread loss of confidence in the powers of community. . . . Countless citizens . . . across the land sensed that something fundamental was happening to their lives, something they had not willed and did not want and they responded by striking out at whatever enemies their view of the world allowed them to see.[13]

Those who had fought to establish their communities during the nineteenth-century expansion across the continent were angered by their loss of "effective sovereignty" and the growing demands of national industrialization. For them, scholar Thomas Bender points out, the "common denominator of local life was . . . the experience of community."[14] Those struggles were too recent and too personal to be threatened by young people abandoning the farm for big cities or farmers choosing mail-order catalogs over the local general store.

"Confidence in powers of the community" was not lost without a fight, as Wiebe, Danbom, and Bender indicate. Many in rural communities, as well as several observers, believed, as John Whiteclay Chambers II describes it, "that the metropolises, with their congestion, hectic pace, lack of adequate air and space, and crime, violence and pollution, would destroy not only their residents but American civilization as well" and that they were fighting not simply for their community or way of life but for the survival of the nation.[15] Chautauqua offered itself as a place to stage the battle for rural communities as the source of American values, morals, and beliefs. According to Paul Pearson, Swarthmore Circuit manager and lecturer, Chautauqua was "the medium through which the community may express itself at its best."[16] This sentiment was reiterated in every piece of Chautauqua literature and by most of the contemporary articles on the movement. As one Circuit system, expediently named the Central Community Chautauqua system, announced in its 1916 program: "Our Creed: We believe in our Community. . . . We believe that out of hopes and labors now will grow a community, democratic, prosperous and strong."[17] The emphasis on community was seen as the inevitable outgrowth of the investment in uplift. No community could help but be improved by its association with the Circuits because Chautauqua, as one newspaper flourished, "was charged with the vital essence that leads to higher life."[18] Community survival was a paramount concern, and the Circuits were embraced as a very effective solution.

Circuit Chautauqua claimed that community was more than the "three characteristics [that] are usually agreed upon as a minimum, namely locale, common ties, and social interaction," as community theorist Jessie Bernard explains.[19] These aspects, while indisputably important to any understanding of community, only begin to evoke the complexities of community. Bender argues:

Americans seem to have something else in mind when they wistfully recall or assume a past made up of small-town communities. This social memory has a geographic referent, the town, but it is clear from the many layers of emotional meaning attached to the word *community* that the concept means more than a place or local activity. There is an expectation of a special quality of human relationship in a community, and it is this experiential dimension that is crucial to its definition. Community, then, can be defined better as an experience than as a place.[20]

While the "place-ness" of community was crucial to Chautauqua, the Circuits were appealing to more than locale. Community invoked history and identity. Those invocations had powerful effects, not the least of which was further binding the experience of Chautauqua to the experience of being an American.

The Circuits understood that "the word *community* has quite positive connotations that are associated with visions of the good life."[21] What Chautauqua envisioned as the "good life" was small town, Protestant, agricultural, and patriotic; in short, mainstream midwestern America. Chautauqua was creating this "good life" even as it was performing it on the platform. Arguments were variously and heterogeneously made that authentic American community, community that was unified and homogeneous, could be found in the small towns and rural life so fervently celebrated by Circuit Chautauqua. The Circuit's vision of a nation, a community, and a life was a vision of something that did not exist in actual lived experience, as Wiebe and others have pointed out, but it was a nation, a community, and a life that many wanted to exist, willed to exist, or even imagined and performed into existence.

In his widely cited delineation of "nation," Benedict Anderson states it is "an imagined political community—and imagined both as inherently limited and sovereign."[22] Imagination is crucial to the existence of a nation for several reasons. Since no one individual who claims citizenship in a nation can ever know all others who make the same claim, "meet them, or even hear of them," and thereby verify their tangible existence, the nation exists largely in the realm of assumption and trust. What distinguishes one community, or nation, from another is not, for Anderson, a question of the quality of the representations or their natural basis but rather "the style in which they are imagined." Style stands in for substance, allowing a nation's constituents to recognize it as such or, as Anderson puts it, "in the mind of each lives the image of their communion."[23] The "image of their communion" that the Circuits hoped lived in the minds of many rural Americans was one that in part emerged on the Chautauqua platform.

Chautauqua helped Americans imagine "the image of their communion," partly by emphasizing the ways in which Chautauqua was ubiquitous. Charles Horner stressed precisely this feature as one of the strengths and founding assumptions of Chautauqua. "Chautauqua people are not likely to forget that their own community is part of America, and that the whole nation is a great family of neighborhoods."[24] Chautauqua gave substance to Horner's metonymic equation by creating a subcommunity ("Chautauqua people") and relating that subcommunity to the larger community (the United States) in order to link the two. As spectators looked around the Chautauqua tent, they were encouraged to fuse what they saw with the whole of the United States. "Chautauqua people" are the citizenry, and the citizenry at its best is made up of Chautauqua people.

One effect of the Circuit's understanding of all small towns as alike is that audiences could imagine others, just like them, sitting in the same tent, seeing the same talent, and enjoying the same experiences and know that shared experiences connected them profoundly. The effect of imagining the United States as contiguous communities suggested what Anderson terms a "deep horizontal comradeship" and stressed the positive and empowering nature of those bonds—or "the good life," in Bender's terms. This also obscured the "inequality and exploitation" of relationships among citizens in practice.[25] Audiences were invited to disregard their differences and embrace the homogenized vision of the United States performed on the platform.

What Chautauqua performed, the idyllic life of small-town America, was one manifestation of the ideal of community. Community lecturer Alex Miller, appearing on the Redpath-Vawter Circuit in 1922, promised to help attain that ideal. He was "the champion of the small town. . . . He has lived all his life in a small town. His business has often taken him to the city, where he has felt its loneliness and crass cheapness."[26] His experience was reassuring evidence that choosing the small town was choosing community, democracy, and comradeship over dissolute anonymity. "He knows from experience the neighborliness of 'Main Street.' He knows the beautiful, the helpful, the genuine good, typified by its unpaved streets and shaded walks. He knows by intimate touch of neighborliness, the rich, the poor, the needy, the happy and the sad. He has ever been the exponent of the best there is in all such."[27] The America that Miller's lecture imagined was one of communities connecting everyone from across many boundaries. He promised uplift and a unified stand against forces that would destroy community. Like Ben Vardaman, Miller "boosted" for the survival of community in its current form and implied that it provided the best life for the greatest number of people. For some, however, this message was not quite so compelling.

"Enclosed you will find [the] street car schedule in regard to Camden. The Camden people cannot find a place in their town to take colored people, so would suggest that you drive over to Rockfield and catch a car out."[28]

Community was often invoked through continuity. Alex Miller, who knew Main Street "from experience," was particularly adept at this sort of invocation. He was worth heeding because he knew the community, as each spectator did, through firsthand knowledge. Fred Eastman, who spoke on the Central Community Chautauqua in 1915, was another such expert. He offered his services as a "community doctor." As a result of his appearance in one town, "good roads were built, libraries and a clubhouse followed, and the town became a leader in its locality."[29] This sense of community stresses materiality—its boundaries and definitions are geographical but malleable. T. Dinsmore Upton, a Circuit veteran by the time he appeared on Redpath-Vawter in 1926, defined community less physically than Miller. "The thought of service before self. The desire to perform those duties of civil life that will mean the greatest good for the greatest number. The aspiration to win victories for the benefit of those who watch us as we play our game. To so construct the family, civic, and national life that tomorrow may find each better than today."[30] Community could be understood physically through location, as Miller did, or metaphorically through common experience, as Upton would have it. For both, however, commonalities were paramount.

Community could also be created by discontinuity. Spectators sometimes had to compare themselves to those who were unlike them and whose experiences seemed alien. "Six dark-skinned, black-eyed people got off the train. . . . The magician's troupe . . . [included] a girl about twelve years old who, if she lived here in this small town, would probably be in the eighth grade, but she didn't look like any little girl anywhere and couldn't even speak English."[31] These six people, by their mere presence at the train station, suddenly made boundaries tangible. Community as "common ties and social interaction" could be acutely discerned in their absence as well as in their presence. Race, as the magician's troupe illustrates, was often the marker of the tension around the boundaries of the community.

Race is, as American studies scholar Matthew Frye Jacobson argues, a "theory of who is who, of who belongs and who does not, of who deserves what and who is capable of what."[32] One form of this in the United States was assigning and defining degrees of whiteness. Citizenship itself had always been a perquisite of whiteness. In 1790 Congress passed the first bill concerning eligibility for citizenship, which declared that citizens could be made from all immigrants who were "free white persons."[33] Factors like religion were also crucial, but race emerged and reemerged during the Chautauqua period as a defining factor. Racial violence was prevalent during this time—an explosion of lynchings in the South and the riots of 1919 across the Midwest, for example. Racism, whether directed toward native-born African Americans or newly arrived immigrants, evinced a struggle over inclusion and exclusion. As one eugenicist noted about the second and third decades of the twentieth century, immigration was not about importing exploitable labor sources but looking at an immigrant as "a parent of a future-born American citizen."[34] Communities are more than national citizenship, and Chautauqua performed the contradictory criteria of belonging for communities' entertainment and edification.

Circuit Chautauqua performed race in two ways. One was through the traditional way race had always been performed in the United States—minstrelsy or speakers tirading against social and political equity for people of color. The second and newer way emerged from Protestant missionary work. The results of missionary work—both at home and abroad—complicated ideas about community because missionary work both made the argument for social equality and emphasized the obstacles to achieving it. In the eyes of Chautauqua, white Christian civilization was surely the pinnacle of human achievement, and membership in its community was very desirable. Hanging in the air was the question: would the community still be superior and enviable if those previously excluded were admitted?

Certainly the predominately white Protestant Circuit Chautauqua did not intend to fight the battle for racial justice. Progressives, in fact, tended to support segregation, believing that some differences could not be overcome. Separate spheres, many European Americans thought, would reduce violence and conflict. The promotion of moderate and conservative African American voices on that issue and the alteration of programming to avoid offending southern sensibilities, including dropping potentially offensive speakers and observing segregation, were not actions likely to foster change.[35] Circuit Chautauqua's response to the Ku Klux Klan's 1924 Chautauqua was cautious, for example. The Ku Klux Klan was a powerful force in the United States and had enjoyed a resurgence of interest and respectability after a lull at the end of the nineteenth century. The revision of attitudes toward Reconstruction as corrupt, disorderly, and "tragic"; the 1905 publication of Thomas Dixon's widely popular novel *The Clansman*; and the 1915 release of *The Birth of a Nation*, D. W. Griffith's film adaptation of Dixon's novel, Shawn Lay's 1992 study of the Klan points out, "completed the process of rationalizing and romanticizing the activities of the original Klan."[36] By the 1920s millions of Americans had joined the Klan, including, in a special White House ceremony, President Warren Harding.[37] It seemed entirely possible at that moment that the Klan, Lay indicates, "might establish itself as a[n] enduring influence in American society."[38]

Chautauqua thought otherwise. When faced with the "Klantauqua," with a reported attendance of 1,000 to 5,000 and run by evangelist Rev. LeRoy Mitchell, Circuit leaders played down the implications.[39] Noting that the "Klantauqua divides communities, and therefore cannot be permanent," Circuit Chautauqua argued that holding open gatherings might bring an end to the Klan as an organization because "a good many klansmen [sic] will lose interest when it becomes public, ungowned, and intelligent." This moderate response tried to divorce Circuit Chautauqua from divisive racial discourse, claiming it "doesn't want to be an antagonist of the K.K.K., for it isn't, nor an antagonist of the anti's, for it isn't. The Chautauqua is out for the best interests of all."[40] "All" is an inclusive word, but "all" here appears to be less than inclusive since it could hardly be in the best interests of Catholics, Jews, or African Americans (the groups predominantly persecuted by the Klan) to support a Klantauqua. Chautauqua's attitudes toward the Klan are disappointing, but many white Protestants believed in white supremacy to varying degrees. There must have been significant overlap in many places between Klan and Chautauqua supporters.

Audiences did not present a united front on issues of race, and it is not possible to construct a monolithic Chautauqua position on race. When white supremacist senator Benjamin Tillman of South Carolina (who served four terms beginning in 1894) gave a lecture, he demanded that the African American spectators sitting in the front move to the back of the tent. "'Down in South Carolina,' he shouted, 'we don't allow "niggers" to sit on the front benches. You go to the back seat and then I'll speak.'"[41] Despite some protests from others in the audience, the African American spectators moved. "The crowd was about fifty-fifty in their disgust and admiration," *Success* magazine reported.[42] Senator James K. Vardaman of Mississippi (who served 1913–1919) held similar views. His platform was a combination of Progressive positions (he was for railroad regulation, antitrust laws, and the abolition of child labor) and white supremacy (he supported lynching, favored limited education for African Americans, and was against racial equality of any kind).[43] Vardaman campaigned in a white suit "driving a white lumber wagon drawn by white oxen," keeping the state in "constant turmoil."[44] The Circuits booked

Vardaman to speak on the "race problem" because he had given it "a lifetime of research, experience, and thought."[45] Vardaman's reputation obviously preceded him because the 1915 Redpath-Vawter program went to lengths to reassure audiences about the lecture. "Senator Vardaman is not a fire eater, as some imagine. He is forceful, but not abusive; full of conviction but not bigoted or blindly partisan; southern yet of national sympathies; strong yet kindly. He ranks high as an orator and fully sustains the traditions of the South in eloquence. He deserves the largest possible hearing."[46] The Circuits' seemingly moderate position on race was belied by their attitude toward the Ku Klux Klan and their supportive inclusion of speakers like Tillman and Vardaman.

Individual managers were less temperate in expressing their personal positions. In 1929 First Lady Lou Henry Hoover invited the wife of newly elected African American congressman Oscar De Priest of Chicago to the White House as part of a series of teas to welcome the wives of new congressmen. The event was handled discreetly, but news soon broke and there was a "storm of protest from Southern Democrats" and others over the party.[47] Among those debating the incident were L. B. Crotty, an Ellison-White manager, and C. E. Backman, of the Redpath Bureau. Appalled that "they are sending to the halls of Congress some of the Southern illiterate 'niggers,'" Crotty commented with disgust on a *Chicago Tribune* clipping Backman had sent about the De Priest tea. President Hoover and "the northern people" "do not understand the Negro," he added in a postscript, "they are making their own problems."[48] Backman responded at length in paragraphs interspersed with Circuit business. He called Crotty "a rabid southerner" and argued that the North could address racial discord better because "intelligent Northerners believe that problems of this kind can be solved through education." This approach contrasted with that of the "low-brows of the South [who] have handled the Negro problem in a way that has made it difficult for the whole country."[49]

Crotty's position was that of many white supremacists, who believed unwaveringly that the "real Southern 'nigger' is much more happy than the 'nigger' that has come north and been placed on an equal footing with the white man."[50] The painful and delicate question of racial equality was one that plagued the United States. Many who believed as Backman did when he wrote, "I am for that race, or any other race, to get ahead," could not ultimately embrace the ramifications of that message of equality and equity. It was not a contradiction, unfortunately, for Backman to add, "I am afraid, however, incidents such as happened at the White House, makes them a little more cocky and a little harder to get along with."[51] The exchange of letters between Crotty and Backman is one example of a debate over community membership. Their correspondence evidences the contradictory and conflicting positions of European Americans. White superiority was normalized—witness the laconic tone of the letter to the Ethiopian Serenaders that opened this section. For the managers, the reality that the Serenaders cannot stay in the town where they perform is merely another logistical detail, ultimately inconveniencing only the performers themselves. If, as W. E. B. DuBois famously asserted, "the problem of the Twentieth Century is the problem of the color line," then it was so in part because many early-twentieth-century European Americans could not acknowledge the privileges and responsibilities that line afforded them.[52]

Much of the Circuit's overt acknowledgment of race in performance was familiar from other venues. White and Myers billed the Black and White Minstrels (all European American performers, a fact made clear to patrons in the program) as "a la *Bert Williams*!! Yea Bo!" and this meant that audiences could expect the usual minstrel fare that had long been a part of American performance.[53] White women, too, participated in these performances. Mrs. John McRaven, who "entirely lost herself in her impersonation, succeeding faultlessly with the negro dialect," toured her one-woman show, *Mammy*, in 1915.[54] The story followed a slave who faithfully served generations of a plantation family until her death. Her last request was that she be buried "close by whar Mars Gus gwine by put when de wa' am done. I want to be allus close by you, Missy." This racist fantasy of the antebellum South was promoted by its publicity as "a true picture of a Southern home, a society that has passed away, and condition that will come no more."[55] Most European Americans believed these minstrel images to be accurate portrayals of the community structure or at least wanted them to be so.

There was another uniquely Chautauquan way race was performed. The platform offered various versions of the fruits of foreign and domestic missionary labor. These performances encouraged Americans to understand race and its meanings for the community in alternative ways. Circuit Chautauqua connected audiences to the new discourses of Progressive-reform Protestant liberalism rather than the old traditions of slavery and minstrelsy. Faith in the ability of humans to improve themselves was bedrock to Chautauqua. "To men and women with . . . convictions Chautauqua is a crusade and their part in it a mission. They see it as an instrument of service, bringing happiness, beauty, and melody into drab lives, stimulating thought in hungry minds, and implanting hope, courage, and aspiration in weary souls," argued Circuit lecturer Harry Hibschman in an article in the *North American Review*.[56] Most American Protestantism, by the end of the nineteenth century, had its roots in the "evangelical commitment to social reform [as] a corollary of the inherited enthusiasm for revival."[57] The evangelical Protestantism undergirding Chautauqua had spread through domestic mission work. The vigorous evangelicalism that converted a rapidly growing America, as religion scholar Andrew F. Walls reasoned, had stressed "the delivery of the elements of the Christian gospel. The delivery was couched in terms which sought individual commitment yet recognized the family unit and created and strengthened local *communitas*, which both channeled emotion and permitted the development of a popular culture, which suggested a continuity with old traditions while being manifestly free of old institutions."[58] This nineteenth-century fusion of local and national, individual and community, and innovation and tradition sowed the seeds that germinated the Chautauqua and its emphasis on community and democracy.

It was strongly believed that it was incumbent upon Protestants to bring their message to others in hopes of converting them, and conversion was synonymous with improvement. Protestants, however, desired continuing evidence that this fight for souls was succeeding, that the world was a better place because of Chautauqua, and that the community was strengthened through these efforts. The Chautauqua platform was the ideal public site to present live testimony to the efficacy of missionary work's success. Chautauqua is "part of the great missionary movement that began with Christianity and moves onward with Christian civilization," exclaimed U.S. commissioner of education Dr. William T. Harris.[59] Chautauqua created through performance one kind of connection between white Protestants, who largely comprised the communities that supported Chautauqua, and people of color, whose mere presence raised questions about and caused anxiety and tension over community citizenship.

Jubilee singers were an enduring and popular Circuit attraction, sometimes performing day after day for the same audiences. Over fifteen different jubilee groups toured the Circuits over the years, making them a Chautauqua staple. Jubilee singing emerged directly from missionary work. After the Civil War, the American Missionary Society (AMS) redefined its mission from the abolition of slavery to the education of the newly freed slaves. Fisk University was one of the newly founded, but inadequately financed, educational institutions sponsored by the AMS. Desperate for funds, treasurer and music teacher George White took a small choir on the road in 1871 to sing popular and religious music. The choir barely met its expenses until it added the private songs previously only sung among themselves, "slave hymns," "plantation songs," or "sorrow songs," later known as spirituals, to their repertoire. They had not thought the songs appropriate to perform, as jubilee singer historian Andrew Ward describes, and, "it was sometimes difficult for northern missionaries to persuade freedmen to sing for them. 'The slave songs were never used then by us in public,' wrote Ella Sheppard [former slave and a founding member of the group]. 'They were associated with slavery and the dark past, and represented the things to be forgotten. Then, too, they were sacred to our parents, who used them in their religious worship.'"[60] Once audiences heard these songs, however, the Fisk Jubilee Singers became one of the most popular singing groups of their time. The group was named from a Bible passage, "proclaim liberty throughout the land to all its inhabitants; it shall be a jubilee for you" (Lev. 25:10), and George White "target[ed a] mainly white Christian audience." The singers were seen as "convincing proof of what higher education could do for the freedmen."[61]

Education of former slaves was a missionary effort to "bring . . . every emancipated slave to Jesus" and "turn them into Protestants of the Northern stripe."[62] The Jubilee Singers's first audiences were drawn from AMS membership, but these former slaves (and children of former slaves) soon turned the tables on their audiences and began missionary work of their own. "People came to despise, to ridicule, to wonder, but remained to bury their foolish prejudices," G. D. Pike wrote in 1873.[63] Tales were told of their music's power, convincing audiences of the "dignity, intelligence, and educability of black Americans" and making a forceful argument for their inclusion in the community.[64] One northern town threatened to cancel the Swarthmore Chautauqua if the Tuskeegee Singers performed. The local Klan chapter was adamant that the group not appear, and Paul Pearson was equally adamant that they would.

> I, too, had to stand my ground—we prefer to lose a town to compromising with a principle like this—and the Tuskeegee Singers made their appearance. As usual when a protested attraction shows up, the tent was full to capacity. . . . There is something in that simple yet lofty music of those grand old spirituals before which narrowness cannot live. And when those colored boys and girls had finished and the soothing waters of their great human melodies had flowed over the souls of those people it was a very much chastened audience . . . which left our tent. We heard no more about canceling the Chautauqua there.[65]

Anecdotes like this one abound in stories of jubilee groups. Many believed the singers would achieve what social and political activism had not: full membership in the community.

Many played down the message of social equality, however, pleading instead for harmony without inclusion. M. Eliza Walker Crump, a former Fisk singer who founded her own group, argued in *Lyceum Magazine* that "surely these programs to which the two races listen, with no fear of social equality, are bringing a saner and more righteous understanding."[66] Often the groups were presented by white managers as nostalgia, as Redpath-Vawter did in 1918. "How these old melodies do push back the years and bring to us all of those tender memories that live in the heart of age; they people the earth with those who have gone away into a far and unknown land, and arouse voices that have been still through the long, long years."[67] However the groups were presented—as civil rights pioneers who proved that "there was something of lasting value in African American culture" or as a longing for slavery's golden past through the "simple ecstatic utterances of wholly untutored minds"—it was undeniable that they offered images of African Americans other than those usually presented on the American stage.[68] Whether or not European Americans wanted to admit it, jubilee groups made a powerful argument for the success of missionary work. Chautauqua audiences could see visible proof that missions spread the culture and society that white Protestants believed were superior.

Another type of domestic missionary work was the sort being done by Booker T. Washington and his disciples. Washington spoke frequently on the Circuits and even organized his own Chautauqua at Tuskegee in 1893 [69] Laurence C. Jones, founder of the Piney Woods Country Life School near Jackson, Mississippi, focused on training students for agricultural work and trades.[70] He went on the Circuits, according to Beth Day's 1955 biography, to carry the "story of their school throughout the North" and earn money "for food and school supplies."[71] Jones lectured, and his wife sold pine-needle baskets and rugs she and the students had made. Another part of the presentation was a jubilee group, the Cotton Blossom Singers. Circuits assured audiences that Jones did not "preach social equality, neither does he discuss the rights and privileges of the negro. He realizes that his people are primitive folk and that, like all primitive people, they are better off amid primitive surroundings."[72] Characterizing Jones's students as "primitive" both justified the need for missionary work and reassured Chautauquans that community boundaries were not really permeable. African Americans were seen both as Backman would want, "trying to better themselves," but also as Crotty would want, in their proper place.

Foreign missionary work had its place on the Circuit as well. Reform efforts were not simply about improving national conditions, they were also about promoting American Protestant superiority. The United States was the "chief source of missionaries in the early part of the twentieth" century; more Americans traveled with the purpose of conversion and education than did people from any other western nation.[73] This work implied that others desired the community values that Americans were gathering in Chautauqua tents annually to celebrate and reaffirm. Foreign lecturers abounded—every continent and most countries were represented in some way on the platform and brought information about the wider world. Ng Poon Chew, the "Chinese Mark Twain," "unfold[ed] the true story of China and Her Problems"; Dr. Gregory Zilborg spoke on "Russia in Revolution"; lecturer Bagdasar Baghdgian was "A 100% American from Armenia"; Edward Johnson came as a "recognized authority on South American"; Yutaki Minakuchi advocated "the interests of friendship between the United States and Japan"; and Dr. Sudhundra Bose "address[ed] the canvas covered college of the people" on "The Awakened Orient."[74] These speakers reported on exoticized foreign conditions by offering titillating hints and evidence of foreign inferiority.

Other foreign talent served a different purpose: to demonstrate the success of foreign missions and the desirability of Christian values. Dr. Wherahiko Rawei, an enduring and popular presence on the Circuits, was a Maori orphan adopted by an English officer and his wife and later educated at Rugby and Cambridge. He began performing with his wife, Hiné Taimoa Rawei, in 1903 (later adding his children), presenting songs ("love songs, war chants"), "strange rites and ceremonies" (tattooing young girls, for example), and "fine stereoptican views" of "many beautiful scenes of their native land."[75] Billed as "Portraying the Rise of a Primitive People from Savagery to Culture" and, alternatively, "The New Zealanders in Song, Story, and Picture from Cannibalism to Culture," his family was "queer but picturesque" and a "wonderful and inspiring example of the value of Christian effort."[76] The Raweis were a study in contradiction. Audiences were drawn in by the exotic aspect of their performances. The Raweis focused on the "native," not the Christian, as did their reception by audiences and critics alike. "The audience is held under a spell of fascination by the weird ballads . . . and incantation."[77] Equally important, however, was their Christianity. "There is no stronger argument for the spread of the missions than this company."[78] The Raweis struck a delicate balance— exotic enough to be on the platform and Christian enough to characterize their origins as primitive.

Missions "often create Christians who are either completely culturally deracinated from both their original and European societies . . . , or who have creatively meshed Christianity with their indigenous culture where Christianity is often a veneer," Eric Langer argues in *Historicizing Christian Encounters with the Other.*[79] Whether Wherahiko Rawei, Hiné Taimoa Rawei, or their children were either cannot be said with any certainty. Wherahiko Rawei did seem to have a sense of his contradictory position, however. He asked in 1923 to be billed as a "Highly Cultured and Gifted Polynesian Native Gentleman" because this "would be very much more appealing to *Redpath* clients than any statements that I am a kind of Reformed Savage, etc. Such talk is not only absurd but I believe would keep any but carnival patrons and similar sensational folk from booking me."[80] This resistance expressed a discomfort with being exoticized. "You will no doubt use the pictures of myself in native dress for they arrest attention and awaken curiosity, but please give the pictures of myself in European dress 'as a cultured gentleman' greater prominence."[81] There are no surviving flyers or brochures that prominently feature Rawei in European dress. He was eulogized in 1928, however, as "everything that the word gentleman implies."[82] He performed for Chautauqua audiences the tensions between gentleman and primitive, the mission and the tribe, and the community and its other.

The Circuits relied heavily on those tensions to avoid arguing explicitly either for racial inclusion or racist exclusion. Consider, for example, the experience of spectators attending the 1915 Redpath-Vawter Chautauqua. James K. Vardaman delivered his message of white supremacy. Arthur Kachel "interpreted" *The Melting-Pot* and offered "a new vision of America." Ng Poon Chew reported on his native China, and the Cambridge Players performed excerpts from *Macbeth* and *An Evening at Sylvandale*. "One of the surprises of this Chautauqua season" was the presentation of J. H. Balmer and his Kaffir Boys Choir. They appeared in "gorgeous costumes of their native tribes" and presented music "ranging from Hottentot chants to classic English music." Spectators were assured that the singers were "a fine bunch of young fellows. Each one tries to outdo the rest, and all simply beam with delight at the thought that they are able to entertain civilized peoples, and are excused from dodging poisonous reptiles and wild beasts in their old home."[83]

It is hard to imagine a program that laid out any more clearly the economy of race and civilization. Indeed, if spectators were in any way unsure of the hierarchy, they could simply refer to Redpath's taxonomy (see page 105). "From Shakespeare to the Hottentotts [*sic*]" illustrates the superiority of European American culture over all others without ambiguity or irony. Depictions of happy, benign African Natives enjoying the fruits of civilization had been part of the missionary project since the late nineteenth century, and Balmer had played a significant role in the performance of that project.

In 1891 and again in 1894 Balmer and two associates organized tours of Zulu choirs of Europe and the United States. Musicologist Veit Erlmann observes: "The venture failed dismally. . . . By 1893 . . . losses of more than £1000 had been incurred, and with most of the musicians having fallen ill or been abandoned by their white agents in London, the whole enterprise ended in a fiasco." The North American tour "suffered the same fate as its predecessor."[84] Despite these setbacks, or perhaps because of them, Balmer reemerged a few years later and went on to organize several tours of boy choirs, their earliest Chautauqua appearance occurring in 1901. These performances allowed audiences to experience, as Balmer put it bluntly, "what can be achieved through the rough human material of the Dark Continent."[85]

Unlike Rawei, who had some input into his image, the choirs were never anything but representatives from "Savage Africa." The children's "picturesque garb," as their publicity put it, further emphasized their differences from audiences.[86] This practice departed from Balmer's adult choirs where, in order to represent success visually, the "missionaries . . . had made clothing one of the most morally charged mediums of their message. By restyling the outer shell of the 'heathen,' they reasoned, the inner self of the newly converted would be reformed and salvaged."[87] While Rawei had struggled to present himself as a gentleman, it seems that those performing on the Chautauqua Circuits as "Kaffir Boys" were not allowed to be anything more than "Hottentots," *Everybody's Magazine* opined, "collected painstakingly from the wooziest wilds of Africa."[88]

The complexities of race—its politics, its representations, its performances—were familiar to Chautauqua audiences. The fact that those audiences were largely, if perhaps solely, European American meant that those complexities tended to favor views that reinforced, rather than challenged, white superiority. Audiences must have reflected on how their communities were constituted. Was being Christian sufficient? If "Hottentots," "Savages," or "Heathens" embraced the values and appearances of white Protestants, would that provide them with an entry to white institutions and societies? This is not to ignore the potential agency of the performers themselves. They were paid comparably to other performers and probably seized opportunities to influence audiences through their work. Surely Rawei believed he was presenting a positive model of success through conversion, proving that community virtues and qualities could be learned. Some in the many companies of jubilee singers must have believed that their singing made a powerful argument against racism and that, as an 1880 account put it, those "who would not sit in the same church pew with a Negro, under the magic of their song were able to get a new light on questions of social equality."[89] More than one message about the constitution and continuation of community was communicated through these performances.

"As Vawter would have said, girls were good merchandise then, as now."[90]

Racial differences and encounters foregrounded definitions of community by juxtaposing (and sometimes confusing) inclusion and exclusion.

Gender issues brought into confrontation two different arenas of community: the public and private spheres and women's place in them. From 1865 to 1920, as women's historian S. J. Kleinberg documents, "rising levels of female education and a growing awareness of social problems encouraged women's involvement in a broad spectrum of non-domestic activities, even if these were sometime rationalized in terms of their maternal roles."[91] In 1870 single women employed outside the home made up 14.8 percent of the total work force; by 1920 it was 24.2 percent.[92] The period of Chautauqua coexisted with amazing changes for women. The growing tide of reform in the late nineteenth century saw women campaigning for suffrage, temperance, access to education, labor laws, sanitation and health improvements, and pure food laws, among other things. As women took their places in the public sphere, they did so conditionally, each woman invoking (whether she wanted to or not) the private sphere of domesticity. Feminist historian Glenda Riley cautions: "Although women's 'sphere' had definitely expanded by 1914, it was still a bounded space. Thus it continued to be segregated and limited in many ways."[93] Women's professional and personal identities in the community were a matter of some concern to all who participated in Circuit Chautauqua.

Whether they were arguing that women could make special contributions to public life because of their maternal and domestic experience or fighting to enjoy equal standing with men, women reformers during the Chautauqua movement were a formidable presence on the national scene, as Sara Evans explores in Born for Liberty: A History of Women in America. "Between 1900 and World War I the old Victorian code which prescribed strict segregation of the sexes in separate spheres crumbled. The women's movement reached the apex of its political power achieving new laws . . . , protective legislation . . . , [and] prison and court reforms."[94] Many of the women who worked for these gains appeared at some time or another on the Chautauqua platform. Among these were well-known suffragists like Susan B. Anthony and Anna Dickinson or lesser-known women like Mrs. Demarchus Brown, who lectured on the 1915 Central Community Chautauqua. "Her Long Road" dealt with "women's struggle for social, industrial, and political justice."[95] Fola La Follette, Robert La Follette's daughter and sometime actress, spoke on the 1914 Midland Chautauqua Circuit on "The Democracy of Women's Suffrage."[96] Women reformers on a variety of issues became familiar faces on the platform. Maud Ballington Booth, the "little mother of the prisons," spoke movingly on prison reform from 1904 onward.[97] Carrie Nation brought her controversial approach to temperance into the tent. Less sensational on the issue of temperance was Frances Willard. Jane Addams, when she could find the time, toured the

Circuits, and Florence Kelley, also of Hull House and later president of the National Consumer's League, used the platform to get her message across. Anna Howard Shaw, one of the first ordained woman ministers, was also a familiar face. In 1909 Leonora Lake, who believed in "equal pay for equal work" and who had drafted the bill that became the factory inspection law of Pennsylvania, spoke on "The Cornerstone of Our National Superstructure, Our Home" for Redpath-Vawter audiences.[98]

One popular speaker who had both impeccable reformer and Chautauqua credentials was Ruth Bryan Owen. Following in the footsteps of her father, William Jennings Bryan, Owen was often a headliner on the Circuit. In 1923 the Redpath-Vawter twentieth-anniversary season featured her lecture "From Cairo to Jerusalem with General Allenby" on the cover of its season program. The program ensured that everyone knew her lineage: "patrons . . . who have heard W. J. Bryan will have a great interest in meeting also his talented daughter."[99] She went on to represent the fourth congressional district of Florida for two terms (1928–1932), and President Franklin D. Roosevelt named her envoy to Denmark and Iceland in 1933. Owen was celebrated, as Eleanor Roosevelt said, for "blazing a trail in diplomacy just as women in covered wagon days had blazed a trail in geography."[100]

There is no record that any African American woman, or indeed any woman of color, was featured as a serious lecturer. African American women seemed to have been limited to jubilee companies and related activities and other women of color to exoticized displays. In 1928 Princess Blue Feather, who appeared with "her Indians," was "a star with her rope spinning and her clever comment on current affairs."[101] "Esquimau lecturer" Olof Krarer held forth in 1906 on "the strange customs of her homeland [and] her education by missionaries," another reminder of missionary success.[102] The absence of women like Ida B. Wells-Barnett or Mary Church Terrell, for example, meant that reform was being represented to the primarily white audiences as a primarily white activity. When African Americans organized Chautauquas, their approach was different. In 1910 a committee of prominent African Americans in Owensboro, Kentucky, rented the local Chautauqua grounds for a week, and Wells-Barnett was one of the speakers. Chautauquas like the one in Owensboro "served as arenas for discussing community problems and searching for political solutions."[103] Such goals differ greatly from those of predominantly white Chautauquas.

The community that some of the reformers argued for was one that was little different from what already existed. Suffragist and reformer Belle Kearney was very active in the Woman's Christian Temperance Union (WCTU) and became "after women achieved the vote . . . , the first woman senator in the Mississippi legislature."[104] From 1910 to 1912 she spoke on various Circuits on a range of topics: "Russia As I Saw It," "Lectures on the Great Reform: Who Is Responsible?" and "Woman Suffrage in the United States." Her featured lecture was "Old Days in Dixie Land," an "enthralling word painting of the times of cavaliers and of chivalry" in which the "Civil War and Reconstruction are touched upon as somber shadows in the sunlight of American history" and "the negro dialect is given to perfection."[105] Kearney fought for women's rights but solely for the rights of white women. In 1896 she lectured that enfranchising African Americans would halt the movement toward Prohibition. Glenda Gilmore notes about Kearney's success: "Quickly white women's local temperance strategies shifted to complement the Democratic party's white supremacist platform."[106] Similarly, in 1903 Kearney argued unequivocally that the "enfranchisement of women would insure immediate and durable white supremacy, honestly attained."[107] She also railed against miscegenation as a prelude to "barbarism." Were Booker T. Washington to return to Africa, she argued, his "half white blood" would alone save him from savagery.[108] This repellant image of community illustrates the complexity of women's presence on the platform and the constitution of community.

There was no aspect of the Chautauqua in which women were not involved.

> Chautauqua gave young women opportunities they had never enjoyed before. Not only was the platform open for dramatic readers, singers, and artists of all kinds, but female lecturers were permitted—even encouraged—to troupe the country in greater numbers than the country had seen before or has since. And Chautauqua did not discriminate between men and women on the business side of the circuit. Any woman who could book the contracts could have a job instantly, with the same pay, expense allowance, and bonus offered the men. Women were managers, superintendents, ticket takers, and diplomats. Sponsors asking to see a representative from the bureau learned not to be surprised when a woman turned up.[109]

Chautauqua's message may often have been qualified on race and gender, but it provided women with a huge number of professional and community opportunities. The cultural arena was often represented as a women's sphere, and Chautauqua was an important part of that sphere.

Women usually created the support for booking and sustaining Chautauqua. Commentators noted repeatedly women's resolute resolve to attend Chautauqua at any cost, as Marian Castle remembered in 1932. "I shall never forget the first of these farm women. The committee man and I repeated to her the good old ballyhoo. . . . As we talked I saw a spark flicker in her dull eyes. She brushed back her wilted hair, shifted the baby to her other hip, and listened. Presently a sort of holy determination shone in her face. When we left, money that ought to have gone for shoes, or flannel outing, or window screens, went for three season tickets."[110] Despite these tales of earnest impoverished women, it was middle-class club women who were often the greatest force behind Chautauqua.

A typical club woman was Anna J. Hardwicke Pennybacker. A resident of Austin, Texas, she was active in local clubs and the University of Texas. She held several offices, including president (elected in 1912) in the General Federation of Women's Clubs.[111] She helped to found the Boulder Chautauqua in 1898, an Independent Assembly and cooperative effort between Texas and Colorado. In addition, Pennybacker was also an active participant in the Chautauqua Institute in New York, where she was president of the Chautauqua Woman's Club and on the board of trustees. It was said of her that "to hear of Mrs. Pennybacker was to hear of Chautauqua."[112] Pennybacker strongly believed not only that Chautauqua was a moral force for good in the United States but that it also was a good venue through which women could advance their causes. When nominated to the board of trustees, she "declared that she really made up her mind to accept when she heard that a man had reported Chautauqua to be running down hill terribly—women were being elected as trustees!"[113]

Few club women were out to challenge the Victorian moral code that dominated the United States. While issues like the vote, temperance, and children's welfare were popular areas of reform, sexual and moral liberation were not. Circuit Chautauquas extended the community surveillance of women by subjecting their female talent and employees to rigorous standards of moral behavior, further emphasizing the view of women as sexualized and dangerous. In her autobiographical *Morally We Roll Along*, Gay MacLaren explored life on the Circuits for women through the example of Opal May Spencer. There is no record of such a performer. She may have been real, a composite of several women, completely fictional, or a version of MacLaren's own experiences.

It was seeing Spencer perform as a child that inspired seven-year-old MacLaren to dream of a Chautauqua career. As adults, they were roommates on the Circuits. As MacLaren related them, Spencer's experiences illustrate how Chautauqua could be an oppressive experience for women. Spencer's mother had given up her own company upon marriage and "'preluded' [opened] for Daniel [Spencer's father], much as she might have washed and scrubbed for him had they lived within the four walls of a home."[114] Her mother's domestic existence of unquestioned subservience was simply transferred to the platform. Spencer's birth brought her into an existence similar to her mother's—committed to life on the Circuit by an authority she had few resources to challenge.

It was years before Spencer doubted the life into which she was born. "Throughout her childhood it never occurred to Opal May to question her father's convictions—shared by thousands of other Americans—that Chautauqua was the vestibule to utopia. She believed with him that Chautauqua was the greatest movement on earth, next to the church and the school; that it would . . . eventually mold the thought of the entire world to its ideals."[115] But while studying music in Chicago, she discovered the world was more complex than her father's Chautauqua philosophy acknowledged. Spencer "became confused, however, in trying to merge her Chautauqua ideals and her own observations into a logical philosophy." A "very rich man" offered to send Spencer to study voice in Europe. His wife was "an invalid who he would not divorce," and "Opal May, who had been taught she would go straight to hell if she ever 'defiled her body,' rejected his overtures, of course. But the incident confused her. She said she used to think about it on nights when her body was covered with filthy quilts in bug-ridden hotels, and when she dragged her body around on dirty trains for a week at a time without a bath. She puzzled long about the man in Chicago."[116] What she learned about morality and gender on the Circuits failed to sustain her when faced with such seemingly clear choices. The double standard dictated Spencer's actions but did not serve to still or satisfy her confused questioning.

While Opal May Spencer may or may not have existed, it is clear that MacLaren believed her biographical sketch depicted ubiquitous experiences. MacLaren uses Spencer's story to gesture toward the larger experience of Chautauqua for women. This pointed toward a recurring obsession around the presence of women on the Circuits: regulating their sexuality. MacLaren summarizes: "As a matter of fact the whole Chautauqua movement was merciless to young ladies who 'defiled their bodies.' When one of the Junior Workers was suspected of being a little indiscreet, her bureau sent a superintendent to 'try her out' to find out if she was a 'good girl.' She fell for his lovemaking and was discharged from her job. He made his report and went on with THE WORK."[117] While there is no archival evidence to support MacLaren's contention, it is clear that the managers and supervisors worried about women's conduct and perceptions of it.

In a reference for Fern Donahue, Charles Horner grudgingly admitted that the former superintendent was intelligent, dynamic, and focused; "also she has considerable talent as a musician."[118] He cannot, however, recommend her. "The reason we could not continue her in our employ was that she gave the wrong impression as to her relationship with men. I do not think there is anything wrong with her morally, but her unfortunate mannerisms seem to be incurable, and we felt that we could not afford to have any of our folks misjudged on this score."[119] This may be a far cry from "trying her out," but Donahue's perceived behavior, not, as Horner noted, her actions, implied something illicitly sexual. Implication enough for the conservative managers, despite her clear ability, she was "not continue[d]."

Female sexuality, particularly that of unmarried women, posed a significant threat to the Chautauqua moral order. Chautauqua women had privileges enjoyed by few women: both geographic mobility and economic independence. Often without any chaperonage, hundreds of women were paid to traverse all parts of the country, stay in hotels, and work in close quarters with men—conditions that must have seemed fraught with the potential for moral disaster. This situation titillated the public imagination. Dime novels since the mid-nineteenth century had depicted working women "who were less notable for their skills than for their unsupervised sexuality."[120] Single women were particularly suspect. Chautauqua had many single women in its employ, and, as Shannon Jackson explores about settlement house work, the "specter of the unattached female often evoked images of uncontrolled sexuality."[121] This immorality would have been particularly ruinous for Chautauqua. It was essential, then, that Chautauqua avoid even the hint of illicit sexuality. Of course, Chautauqua assumed that immorality was a female failing.

The Circuits were particularly vulnerable to pressure from communities to enforce high standards of behavior and appearance for women, and there is no indication that the Circuits were reluctant to do so. In 1922 a letter was sent to all talent because "several communities have written in criticizing the dress of several different lady members of the Redpath family, that there is an undue exposure of the person."[122] While it ostensibly addresses both men and women, women are singled out. "All the lady artists shall have beautiful and becoming gowns but the style must not cause unfavorable comment by the conservative men and women who make up the large part of the audience, and who in nearly every case, are responsible for every course."[123] Chautauquas saw a relationship between women's moral standing and the Circuits' continuing financial success. Manager Charles Horner documented about his Redpath colleague: "[Keith] Vawter would have been the first to reprimand or remove a youngster who stepped out of line. . . . A girl in slacks, or with bare legs or a plunging neckline or even too much make-up might have created an undesirable situation. Perhaps all that was hypocrisy in moral concept, although the Chautauqua didn't think so at the time, and, anyhow, it was good business policy."[124] Many women supported this policy. Evelyn Bargelt, of the Bargelt Concert Company, who "combined cartooning with reading and music," cautioned young women to "remember, dear girl, that when one is careless she not only hurts herself but the whole lyceum. If she allows liberties to be taken with her, the lyceum suffers in general, and the persons who follow in particular."[125]

Redpath and their communities were probably fighting a losing battle. Performance was one of many social practices that were challenging strict moral codes. Jean Handley Adams remembered, with some discomfort, her mother preparing to perform. "Mother unself-consciously stripped to her slip . . . and began putting on her make-up. Male performers and crew men wandered by. Gosh! How embarrassing! Seeing Mother rosy with so much make-up and so immodest was a shock."[126] It is not difficult to see that such a situation might cause worry for those who were responsible for ensuring Chautauqua's moral standards. If performance could actualize a nation (as chapter 1 argued) or a community, it carried the potential to effect transformation in the bodies on the platform. The extent to which women, whether they performed in Chautauqua or not, were responsible for both their own moral probity and that of the community was something no individual woman was allowed to forget.

Men were also cautioned about moral behavior. Male conduct, however, was the least important part of the problem, in the Circuit's opinion. The most challenging part was the conduct of the women the men would encounter. In 1918 crew men were admonished that it was "bad form to thrust your attentions upon any young woman whose acquaintance you have made through your connection with Redpath." They were also reminded not to accept invitations from women who "know you only as 'one of the Chautauqua men.'" "The young woman who extends an invitation under these circumstances is, to say the least, indiscreet. She probably is careless as well, and failure on your part to observe these injunctions will be jeopardizing the good name and reputation of the Redpath—as well as your own."[127] Crew and talent behavior influenced Redpath's ability to return. As the memo shouted: "THE NAME REDPATH INTRODUCES YOU TO A COMMUNITY, NEVER TO ITS INDIVIDUALS."[128]

Spencer's moral confusion, MacLaren's decision to foreground it, and injunctions about women's behavior speak eloquently to the myriad ways in which women must have experienced the material and ideological conditions of Chautauqua as contradictory. While Spencer's narrative may be suspect, the ideas and experiences it explores are not. They are repeated and expanded upon in other women's Chautauqua texts. Consider again, for example, the experiences of violinist Enola Calvin Handley, the subject of an affectionate but questioning memoir by her daughter, Jean Handley Adams. "Mother traveled in Chautauqua every summer from the time I was ten years old [1921] until I was twenty. It was disconcerting to have a career mama who was not at home when I wanted her to be, and who had a completely different concept of living from that of my friends' mothers. So it took years for me to appreciate the specialness of my mother."[129] The primary dilemma for both women is Handley's driving need to escape the domestic sphere. Adams records, perhaps unintentionally, her mother's highly gendered experience of Chautauqua, providing not simply a record of a Chautauqua performer but also of the costs and effects of being a woman Chautauquan. If "what Mother did was daring and scandalized her friends and neighbors," then one cannot lose sight of what it meant to "scandalize" one's friends and neighbors in small-town America in 1921.[130]

Handley struggled with her decision to tour and argued with her husband over the matter.[131] One form of resistance was probably her domestic ineptitude. "Jerry [Adams's brother] remembers being embarrassed when all five of us appeared [at church suppers], more than once, with one bowl of Jello [sic] as our contribution. Oh well, more ladies could cook than could make beautiful music."[132] Chautauqua women often had to prove themselves domestically, as if to demonstrate their legitimacy as women and their ability to conform to community standards. MacLaren's own publicity materials affirmed that "[husband Ralph Parlette] will tell you she can cook as fine a dinner, if the necessity arises, as can the exotic chefs of the Loop hotels."[133] This testimony reassured readers that despite the public nature of her performance, she was still capable of women's traditional tasks. Women who did choose both a public and private, or primarily a public, life caused anxiety both for their families—Adams was "conscious of Mother's two worlds—show business and home" and concomitantly worried that "she liked the other world better than ours"—and their communities.[134]

The question of whether a woman can be effective both domestically and publicly was (and continues to be) the subject of much vexed debate. Maud Ballington Booth was emphatic. "I have been in public life since I was seventeen, but I believe it has made me a better mother, wife, and homemaker than would the narrower life that limits to household duties only." One opera singer, citing Ernestine Schumann-Heink as an example, said glibly, "Motherhood and a career, why not?"[135] But as Handley's experiences demonstrate, it was not quite so simple. Women had to negotiate complex and changing discourses of domesticity, public and private spheres, morality, and public sentiment. Circuit Chautauqua afforded women great opportunities to test the limits of these discourses. Whether arguing for social reform, acting, singing, or playing an instrument, women on the Chautauqua platform offered new examples of women's membership in the community. No longer solely mothers, daughters, or wives, they were now reformers, politicians, and businesspeople.

Defining community exactly is a difficult, if not impossible, task. It is, as feminist scholar Iris Marion Young theorizes, "an understandable dream, expressing a desire for selves that are transparent to one another, relationships of mutual identification, social closeness and comfort."[136] In the face of tremendous and ongoing change, Circuit Chautauqua promised that dream. But waking differences continued to assert themselves. They were present in Enola Calvin Handley's determination to perform; the jubilee singers' gentle call for understanding; Belle Kearney's, James Vardaman's, and Benjamin Tillman's promotion of white supremacy; Wherahiko Rawei's insistence on himself as a Christian gentleman; Laurence C. Jones's resolve to educate his people; and Charles Horner's refusal to recommend Fern Donahue. Depending on how closely audiences were watching, they might have seen traces of these struggles that belied claims to transparency and identification.

ALEX. MILLER

Alex Miller, community lecturer. Iowa.

James K. Vardaman. Iowa.

Their publicity promised that people who "love to listen to the darky" would find this group "in the realm of white quartets." Despite reassuring audiences that they are "refined and educated," Redpath was not above depicting the men through typical racist iconography. Iowa.

MAMMY

MRS. JOHN McRAVEN
Premier Presentation of the Drama
"MAMMY"

" 'Good' is not the word for Mrs. McRaven in 'Mammy.' She is wonderful."

"Her dialect is perfect."

"A sob-show and a laugh-fest in one, is Mrs. McRaven's interpretation of 'Mammy.' "

"In the tragedy scenes Mrs. McRaven grips the heart until it aches. In the comedy scenes her dialect and negro impersonation is irresistible."

"Out of its sobs and smiles comes one of the most appealing pleas for peace ever made."

Mrs. McRaven was careful to put an actual picture of herself on the outside of her publicity brochure and save one of herself in character for the inside. Those who booked her would not have to wonder about her race. Iowa.

The Fisk Jubilee Singers were careful to point out their status as the original jubilee group and even more careful that their singers always met the highest standards of bourgeois respectability. Iowa.

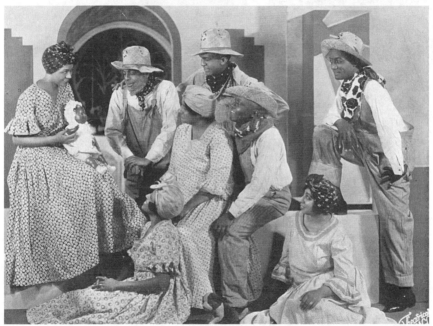

The Eureka Jubilee Singers would have appeared late in the Circuit's history, but their materials emphasize the ways in which race was a performance for white audiences. This group could perform whichever version of jubilee singing an audience demanded—the elegant and refined or the simple peasant, as the contrasting images from two different brochures demonstrate. There is no record of what the group itself thought of these materials or the ways in which their material was presented. Iowa.

For the benefit of Harry Harrison and Chautauqua, Laurence Jones was careful to emphasize that he was born in Iowa. Jones's secretary assured Harrison that "they travel in their own house cars equipped for cooking, eating, and sleeping." They thus avoided the fate of the Ethiopian Serenaders. Iowa.

The contradictions that Wherahiko Rawei embodied were often presented without acknowledgment. It is hard to imagine an image of someone looking less "educated and cultured" than Rawei does here. In spite of, or perhaps because of this, he was an enduring attraction. Iowa.

The entire Rawei family was eventually part of the act, and much was made of the fact that his family performed with him. Iowa.

On his letter-head, Rawei carefully reproduced pictures of himself and his wife in Western dress, perhaps in order to remind those doing business with him that he was thoroughly experienced in Western culture. Iowa.

The surviving publicity materials for Rawei
demonstrate how he was positioned as exotic
during his performance career. There were no
pictures that depicted him pursuing his work as
a medical doctor, for example. Iowa.

Redpath-Vawter intentionally positioned Shakespeare and the "Hottentotts" as polar opposites, and the "diagonal design" did not simply "set forth the idea," as the program declares, but instead reified a value system. Iowa.

The woman who accompanied the Kaffir Boys Choir was Elsie Clark, born in South Africa. While her primary job was musical support, she also gave, on occasion, "intimate talks on her own life in Africa." Iowa.

Ruth Bryan Owen. Iowa.

Belle Kearney's publicity literature stressed her reformer credentials, her speaking ability and experience, and the wide range of topics she addressed. No overt mention was made of the unrelenting work she did to further white supremacy. Iowa.

The North End Women's Club was primarily responsible for Chautauqua's presence in an unnamed town in 1911. Iowa.

Involvement in Circuit Chautauqua was one of the few ways women could participate in public events without raising any questions about their conduct. Concomitantly, supporting Chautauqua was often seen as women's work. Iowa.

Anna J. Hardwicke Pennybacker is pictured here with the Chautauqua Women's Club at the Chautauqua Institution in New York. She is holding the gavel near the platform. Texas, AHC.

An advertisement for Gay MacLaren was placed in a local store window alongside one for her husband, popular inspirational lecturer Ralph Parlette. Iowa.

Evelyn Bargelt's publicity underscored the claims she made to respectability. The brochure signals that sentimentality will figure prominently in her presentation. Iowa.

European-trained violinist Enola Calvin Handley (far right) led her own group, the Philharmonic Ensemble, which was able to "adapt the works of the world's masters to present day tastes." Iowa.

CHAPTER THREE

The Platform in the Tent

Chautauqua's visit was heralded with the transformation of the town by pennants, window displays, and placards. Large signs hung across streets exclaiming that "Chautauqua is coming!" The breeze would set these notices fluttering, and the whole town quivered with the excitement of it all. Chautauqua boosters and guarantors (often the town's leading citizens) wore buttons boasting "I'll be there." The trains themselves were bedecked with banners and signs, alerting everyone that the long-awaited event had arrived. Buildings emptied as crowds swarmed to the station to see Chautauqua come into town. Excited residents decorated their cars, wagons, and themselves so they could march with the Circuit folk in a parade celebrating the opening of Chautauqua. Signs went up pointing the way to the tent, reminding all: "Go to Chautauqua Big Doings!"

Rural America embraced Chautauqua so fervently because the enthusiasm was returned. Spectators could be sure that programming would reflect this agreeable relationship. If they saw the Neil Litchfield Trio around 1908, among the group's "musical specialities" and "humorous and dramatic recitals" was the rural comedy "playlet" *Down at Brook Farm*. "It is clean and refined in character, and, without a doubt, is the funniest comedy on the . . . platform today."[1] Starting in the second decade of the twentieth century, Harold Wright Bell's best-selling 1907 novel about life in Ozarks, *The Shepherd of the*

Hills, was a perennial favorite.[2] Readers/elocutionists Myra Casterline Smith, Bess Edith Barton, and M. Beryl Buckley were just a few who brought the story to the platform. Buckley, for example, lived in the house not far from Branson, Missouri, where Wright had written the book and rehearsed her performance there. "The beauty of the surroundings found lodgement in her heart as the lines fixed themselves in her mind. What a studio! What a glorious inspiration!"[3] In the 1920s Jean Barron Hurst joined the list of readers presenting this work. It was also dramatized into a full-length play, and the Standard Chautauqua System featured it in its 1922 program.[4] Audiences never tired of the portrayal of "the lives of these hardy mountaineers who are as clean cut and unaffected by the veneer of civilization as the rock bound hills in which they live."[5]

These were scarcely the only performances to promote the superiority of rural or small-town life. The Detour by Owen Davis was the closing attraction on the Redpath Premier Circuit in 1929. The play followed the struggle within a family between the mother who wants to use family savings to send her daughter to art school in the city and the father who wants to save the family farm. The Next-best Man by Leon M. Pearson dramatized the triumph of the small-town beau over the glamorous and urbane film star to win the heart of the local sweetheart. Turn to the Right by Winchell Smith and John E. Hazzard premiered on Broadway in 1916 and quickly became a Chautauqua staple. As one novel about Chautauqua characterized the play: "It had everything Chautauqua stood for. . . . It paid tribute to the nobility of the farm, home and mother love, and in the end the honest country bumpkin triumphed over the city slicker."[6] Donald Bain offered "A Trip to the Farm" and through whistling and other imitations "puts his audience on a train, whisks them out into the country, takes them through the woods, turns off into a lane through an open field past a pond, then up to the farm house. . . . Then, finally, they are lead [sic] into a farmhouse and are entertained by the unique 'double-whistling' and imitations of musical instruments."[7] Such pieces, whether performed in a reading or as a full-fledged production, served to reassure audiences that their lives were the ones that America most wanted to emulate.

Lectures, too, sounded that theme for audiences. Community lecturers tended to preach community building for the rural town. The primary idea motivating this type of lecture was that the small town was not just worth saving, but improving it would be a boon to the nation. Among his repertoire of lectures in the 1920s, Frank Preston Jones included "Five Miles from Main Street." "This is a discussion of American agriculture and its relation to the life of the nation. A powerful argument for a constructive agricultural policy and a challenge to every town and city . . . to develop rural leadership and preserve our basic industry. An address that is prophetic of a new day in agriculture."[8] Educational sociologist Llewellen MacGarr's potential lectures were variations on the rural theme. "The Amusement Problem of the Country Town" and "The Rural Community—Its Upbuilding" were just two possibilities.[9] Audiences may have looked forward to hearing Otis T. Wingo (Dem., Arkansas), "the 'Rural Credit Congressman.'" "He has successfully lead [sic] the fight for financial legislation in the interest of the farmers of this nation."[10] No matter who the lecturer was or what kind of material was included, the repetitive declaration that America's strength was in its rural communities and that its future lay with the family farm reinforced the audience's already firmly held beliefs.

At the end of Chautauqua, audiences were exhorted to sign up for the coming year in advance, and many did. At the height of Chautauqua, the platform superintendent rarely left a town without securing the next year's contract. As the last spectators lingered, the tent was quickly struck by the crew. Everything from the tent to banners to the ticket booth was loaded onto special railroad cars and shipped to the next location. Physically, only traces, like trampled grass or the odd forgotten poster, testified to what had taken place. In memory, however, Chautauqua lingered on, and people talked it over endlessly among themselves. Chautauqua's visit might be temporary, but many Chautauqua practitioners and commentators argued that Chautauqua's effect and rural America were synonymous and permanent. Chautauqua's very existence seemed to prove that the superiority and strength of rural communities made them the most American part of America.

The argument that rural America was America, however, was not made easily. As the United States grew increasingly powerful through urban industrial might, much of the national attention, both appreciative and derogatory, was turned toward the cities and all that they had to offer. The struggle between the country and the city over claims to American identity was fierce. Chautauqua's solution was to eliminate the city from the equation altogether and present rural communities as a resonant metaphor for America through the agency of Chautauqua.

Whether America was most properly urban or rural was played out through the powerful process of metaphor. Metaphor licenses materiality because metaphor is so often the process through which people understand something new or unfamiliar. The often reductive movement of metaphor, used by talent, managers, and observers, played a controlling part in conceptualizing and utilizing the community landscape, as well as Chautauqua's place in it. It proceeded "by invoking one meaning system to explain or clarify another. The first meaning system is apparently concrete, well understood, unproblematic, and evokes the familiar. . . . The [second meaning system] is elusive, opaque, seemingly unfathomable without meaning donated from the [first]."[11] For the Circuit audiences, the first meaning system was the home landscape with which all Chautauqua spectators were familiar—their own town, village, or county. Circuit materials were a part of the first meaning system, as was the public discourse encouraging rural citizens to think of themselves and their community as America at its best. Given the economic and cultural developments of the period, however, it is clear that such pronouncements were intended as much to convince as they were to describe.

The second meaning system, that which is "elusive, opaque," was the United States itself. Positioning the community landscape with its requisite Chautauqua as comparable to the entire nation was both reassuring and empowering. It reassured because it suggested that audience frustrations and anger would be fleeting and that rural needs, concerns, and practices were not being superseded in the United States. In his study of the Midwest, James Shortridge notes: "Entities such as states and nations . . . are too large for people to 'know' in detail, and so loyalty for them must be created through such devices as flags, anthems, and the formal study of their history."[12] The metaphoric construction empowered audiences because it suggested that they should be able, using the contributions of Chautauqua, to improve and strengthen rural life and that the entire nation would benefit and progress. In short, Circuit Chautauqua was a "device" through which spectators could "know" the United States. Those who were inculcated with greater knowledge and enculturation through Chautauqua conceived of their own experiences within their community landscapes as typically modeled throughout the United States. By comprehending their own tangible space, they comprehended the intangible space of the nation.

As Robert Wiebe has noted, however, this effort was doomed, and many sensed it. The United States was moving away from such "sovereign communities," and Americans, particularly rural ones, "tried desperately to understand the larger world in terms of their small, familiar environment. They tried, in other words, to impose the known on the unknown, to master an impersonal world through the customs of a personal society."[13] "Impos[ing] the known on the unknown" is a process through which the unknown is made approachable and familiar and subsequently stripped of its power to threaten. Ultimately, these efforts would fail, but the struggles to counter the trend away from "sovereign communities" as materialized in Chautauqua demonstrate the power of the idea of community and the magnitude of the changes that occurred. This chapter examines not so much what the Circuits performed to make the case for the small town but how they used the Chautauqua itself to make that case. Split into the two parts of metaphor, the examination looks first at the most tangible and lasting parts of the Chautauqua experience: the tent itself and the souvenir program. The second half of the chapter takes up the relationship between the country and the city, as well as the institutions that Chautauqua used to make its metaphoric movements, the church and the school.

"The system sent a most enticing program, bearing on its cover a deliciously cool-looking tent, a shimmering lake, and a fluttery girl, with a striped parasol strolling off to read her book of verses underneath the bough."[14]

If the Circuits encouraged the metaphor that made the United States and its struggles over community "concrete" and "familiar" through Chautauqua, then the tent was what made Chautauqua familiar, local, and tangible. Everyone who wrote about Chautauqua used the tent to evoke its experiences. Memoirs were titled *Culture under Canvas* or *Strike the Tents*, and articles had similar labels: "Tents of the Conservative," "Tent Universities," "Under the Big Tent," and "Canvas and Culture: When Chautauqua Comes to Town." All of these marked the tent itself as the synecdoche for Chautauqua. Promoting the tent was a risky decision for Circuit managers. While they stressed Chautauqua as essential to the community, in reality it was not locally produced, and the management allowed the community little influence. The guarantors, however, had to sign the "ironclad" contract promising to provide the minimum return no matter what ticket sales brought in. In order to convince local communities that Chautauqua was a stable and permanent constituent, and simultaneously to resist efforts to categorize Chautauqua as yet another traveling tent show, the Circuits embraced the tent as Chautauqua's identity. This embrace helped reduce the risk that the tent would be seen as evidence of itineracy and a mark of Chautauqua's outsider status.

One strategy was simply to make Chautauqua tents look different than any others that might come to town. Speaking of the new tents they had purchased to expand the Redpath reach, Harry Harrison put it succinctly: "That was no circus or medicine show looming up there in the middle of the field. The brown tent after 1912 meant Chautauqua and nothing but."[15] While the new color was not part of an intentional strategy, it became the most visible weapon in Chautauqua's arsenal of respectability. William L. Slout notes in *Theatre in a Tent*:

The white tents of strolling entertainers aroused suspicion in the more puritan minds. Since the church and its auxiliaries . . . were the centers of interest in the social structure of small towns, scorn of theatrical entertainments was perpetuated through the village churchman. Therefore by using brown canvas instead of white, Chautauqua promoters removed any chance of their being identified with "show business;" brown canvas symbolized cultural inspiration—improvement of mind, body, and spirit.[16]

On the inside, Circuit Chautauqua tents continued their battle to distinguish themselves from "show business." "The interior of the Chautauqua tents more closely resembled a lecture hall than a opera house. Wooden folding benches formed into rows supplied the seating. A small stage or platform at one end of the tent was furnished with a 'sylvan backdrop,' electric footlights, two chairs, and a table holding a pitcher of ice water and a glass."[17] Ultimately, the tents evolved into the nostalgic symbol of Chautauqua. Alma Ellerbee and Paul Ellerbee wrote in an article in World's Work: "Looking back over them, we would rather lose almost anything out of our past than those big brown tents and the things that went with them. For there was more of America under their patched and re-patched canvas than we have seen before or since."[18] It is a measure of some success on the Circuit's part that Chautauqua was able to make a sign of its itinerancy and its similarity to despised entertainments a symbol of beloved community status.

Chautauqua's chief competitor for annual dependability and excitement was the circus, and it was against the circus that it often had to define itself. When the circus came to town, at least in the beginning of the twentieth century, everything stopped. "On 'Circus Day' shops closed their doors, schools canceled classes, and factories shut down."[19] Like Chautauqua, the circus was an event that appealed to broad swaths of the community. Circuses had been operating in the United States since the 1790s and, again like Circuit Chautauqua, became an influential national presence through the availability of rail travel. They were variety entertainments that offered the spectacle of trained animals (both wild and domestic) performing impressive feats, people with incredible physical prowess, and exotic spectacles of all kinds. By 1910 circuses had begun to decline, an economic victim of their own investment in increasingly lavish production values.[20]

If Chautauqua tried to make its tent reminiscent of a lecture hall rather than a theater, the inside of a circus tent could not be mistaken for anything else. The multiring presentation had its fullest realization in the early twentieth century, and a spectator could be overwhelmed by trying to sort out as many as five or six rings, although three were by far more typical.[21] Circuses often claimed, as one did in 1894, to "instruct the minds of all classes."[22] Their instruction was much more spectacular than any Chautauqua had to offer. The Spanish-American War was one of the most popular sources of circus education and uplift. In 1899 Barnum and Bailey presented a reenactment of the Battle of Santiago with "a Miniature Ocean of Real Water with Real War Ships, Guns, and Explosives."[23] Chautauqua could not compete on that scale. Of course, it did not want to. Such elaborate showmanship smacked of just the kind of excess and trickery Chautauqua was trying to critique. Similarly, the morals of the circus were famously suspect. Women's bodies were very much on display, scantily clad and athletically active. Circuses, like vaudeville, went to great lengths to assure nervous middle-class audiences that all their performers had the highest morals, but most spectators, as American studies scholar Janet Davis documents, "interpreted circus women's scant dress as a sign of sexual availability."[24] Circus audiences, too, were troubling to communities, as the circus could be an opportunity for rowdy behavior, particularly after the show when fights often broke out.

That circuses and other entertainments endangered rather than strengthened moral character and behavior was a long-standing assumption among Chautauqua audiences. Ida Tarbell, the famous investigative journalist, discovered that such assumptions about the affective power of live performance were common among loyal audiences when she lectured on the Coit-Alber Circuit in 1917. "In several of the towns the women work hard to make the show a success . . . that they might have an antidote to the traveling carnival, . . . which in place after place I was told had done serious harm. They claimed it had encouraged boys in evil ways and unsettled their girls; and in some cases there were tragic tales of young girls enticed away from town, or of boys bitten by the desire to go with the show."[25] For smaller communities, ones likely to have Chautauquas and unlikely to attract the larger circuses of the highest quality, being able to tell the difference at a glance between circus and Chautauqua was an important and reassuring aspect of the Circuits' identity and an inoculation against "evil ways."

The tent never appeared so permanent as it did on the cover of the annual souvenir program. It was the rare program that did not feature the tent. The tent was almost always planted there, surrounded by lush foliage and inviting anyone looking to come inside. Always crisp, never patched or worn, the tent was imposing and reassuring in its dominance of the landscape. Program covers were obviously intended to call up the feelings of connection, continuity, and community that the Circuits promoted in so many different ways. If

Chautauqua was permanent through its effect, its audience, or its dependable return, it was absolutely tangible through the souvenir programs that every ticket holder received. John Edward Tapia noted in 1997: "The brochures were rich with discourse and pictures which invited their readers into vast symbolic fantasy worlds—worlds of intense drama more real than life."[26] Clearly intended to be saved and looked over year after year, the programs presented the Circuit Chautauqua world in ornate visual detail.

Manager Charles Horner encountered one spectator in Chelsea, Oklahoma, who valued the programs for just this reason. Upon learning he managed the entire Circuit, "a Cherokee Indian woman [asked] if [Horner] was going to be present at the night session" because "she wanted to bring him something she thought he would prize." Curious, he "awaited with much interest further developments." That evening the Cherokee woman "presented to him a complete set of his circuit chautauqua program booklets covering a period of ten consecutive years. These she had accumulated during the years and preserved with great care. She told Mr. Horner, with a great deal of pride, that she had missed only one session in the whole period of ten years." For Hugh Orchard, who related this anecdote in his 1923 history of Chautauqua, the incident demonstrates the "far reaching educational contribution" of Chautauqua.[27] It also demonstrates the power of the program itself. The treasured programs were the material evidence of the ephemeral experience of performance.

Programs were usually about ten pages long. A smaller Circuit might produce one that was only the schedule on a single sheet, with a few accompanying photographs. A larger, elite Circuit would offer a longer one, and the program typically included a greeting from the manager, pictures and descriptions of each act, rules and policies, and the schedule. The same program was used for each Circuit's season, the only variation being the name of the location printed on the cover, a schedule that reflected that town's dates (and some Circuits even dispensed with this, indicating only first day, second day, and so on), and, occasionally in the early years, the names of the local guarantors.

Circuit Chautauqua programs did not exist outside general entertainment practices of the early twentieth century. Playbills, single sheets that listed basic production information and inherited from British theater practices, had been a part of American theater since the eighteenth century. By 1900 these had developed into programs, usually defined as "one or more folded sheets, printed on both sides."[28] Programs were also most often purchased or provided at the theater for its patrons. One striking feature of most programs both prior to and in the twentieth century was that they contained copious amounts of advertising. In fact, the balance of the space was given over to businesses seeking customers, sometimes making it difficult to find information about the actual performance. Circuit Chautauqua programs bear little resemblance to these efforts because they never carried advertising.[29] Circus programs, for example, did contain prominent advertisements, especially for nationally available products like Waterman pens.[30] One reason for this difference may have been that Chautauqua saw its audience as a nation of citizens with specific duties. Circuses seemed to have been appealing to a nation of consumers, urging them to purchase the goods promoted in the program. Circuit programs are most like those created for long-running theatrical shows that functioned as a record of the event itself. The American Memory Project describes these efforts: "Managers promoted their shows with souvenir programs of all sorts that were printed on silk, satin, parchment, or other fancy materials. Often, these more lavish programs commemorated landmark performances."[31] While Circuit programs were printed on prosaic paper, they were doing something theatrical programs rarely did. They were promoting the venue itself, Chautauqua, not just what was being presented on the platform.

The program subtly served as a paper Chautauqua—the exterior of the tent (never the interior) graced the cover, opening the program was like entering the tent, and inside one encountered Chautauqua in all its dynamic glory. The interior photographs of the attractions were crucial. The talent were almost always represented by headshots, and in early years the accompanying explanatory text took up as much space. In later years, particularly the 1920s, visuals—photographs, illustrations, and graphics—gained greater prominence than the written text. Also, as the management built up a stock of images, the programs would be stuffed with photographs of previous years' Chautauquas—audiences, talent, crew, and supervisors all enjoying themselves immensely. It is not hard to believe that in the long winters when people were largely cut off from the world, the programs were a source of happy memories and a promise that summer, and Chautauqua, would eventually return.

The cover was the most arresting feature of the program, perhaps appropriately since that was the first thing a spectator probably saw. In the earliest years the covers tended to be very utilitarian, simply written text with basic information. Some independent assemblies had only their name and a letter to participants, like the 1901 Midland Chautauqua Assembly.[32] Vawter's 1909 program was more boldly designed, with different-sized letters and contrasting colors in bands; it even had a thin picture of a tent as a border at the top. But neither of these styles became the Chautauqua signature. They did little to evoke the complicated discourses that Chautauqua was trying to communicate to audiences. The style that finally did emerge centered on the tent—usually depicted surrounded by trees, not blocked by them but framed, putting the tent into relief. In Redpath-Horner's 1914 program, for example, the tent was in the upper quarter of the cover set off on both sides by trees. The tent hovered over the community, represented by an undifferentiated mass of people and a young, attractive couple in the foreground leaving the Chautauqua with looks of great happiness and enjoyment on their faces. Although this does little to connect Chautauqua with community institutions, it does promise an experience worthy of the spectator's investment.

For the 1915 Redpath-Vawter program, a tree acted as the program's spine, folded on the longer vertical edge of the paper.[33] The tent wrapped around both sides of the cover, a strong visual presence. Couples headed toward the tent, mimicking what actual audiences were doing as they clutched this program in their hands for the first time. The viewer can only see their backs, a device that pulls her or him into the picture and signals that the spectator was part of a larger whole. As one performer cheerfully remarked to an interviewer in 1922: "At this season of the year you're likely to meet up with a bunch of Chautauqua people on any train anywhere."[34] This sense, that America was blanketed with Chautauqua and its business, was evoked by the crowds drawing the spectator in. Spectators converge on the tent in their cars and buggies. The tent is nestled in the trees and a church spire looms in the background. The movement is away from the viewer holding the program and toward the tent, creating a sense of movement toward Chautauqua. Let's go to Chautauqua, it seems to urge.

The 1916 Canton, Missouri, Redpath Chautauqua program had a small picture that occupies the upper third of the cover and is largely filled by the tent. Its peak with a waving pennant sticks out of the frame, as does a large, graceful tree. Couples stroll toward the tent, the closest couple moving into the frame of the picture from the cover. It was the same inclusionary device as used in the 1915 program, urging people to open the cover and attend.

The Evening Star Chautauqua of 1917 and 1918 placed the tent on its cover in a valley and showed a large crowd of people emerging out of the hills to descend on Chautauqua. Trees bend protectively over the tent, but it is set off in the distance. This evokes a pastoral setting, implying that there is no community other than the people and the tent, as if the town did not even need to exist for Chautauqua to act as its essence. As Shortridge notes about attitudes brought to bear on the Midwest: "Pastoralism, the concept of the ideal middle kingdom suspended between uncivilized wilderness and urban-industrial evils, was applied to the original American colonies by many European writers and soon became an important part of the new country's self-image."[35] That rural life was not a wilderness but a civilized, bucolic idyll conspicuously lacking any of the vices of urban settings was an idea enshrined in Chautauqua consciousness. If one needed a single Chautauqua image to evoke this "ideal middle kingdom," the Evening Star program could serve.

A tree was the most prominent feature of Redpath-Vawter's 1918 program. It stands in the foreground, and in the distant background a town is nestled in verdant hills. Houses cuddle snugly against one another, and in front of the town is a tent, differently constructed but looking as enduring and appropriate as the houses and church. But it is the tree that first captures the viewer's attention, not an entire forest but a single tree. Although there are suggestions of other trees, it is not the dense setting of the forest. Frieda Knobloch theorized in 1996: "Forests are places where everything else came from, places against which all the animosity of 'civilization' turned in a simultaneous nostalgia and contempt for its imagined sylvan origin."[36] The 1918 Standard Chautauqua program presents the tent with American flags proudly waving and predictably flanked by trees. Like the 1918 Redpath-Vawter program, it suggests nostalgia for the conquered and depleted forest, of which only a few trees remain, enough to remind gently of the lost frontier but not so many as to prohibit development. As if to emphasize the practical use of the land by Chautauquans, a car hovers just on the edge of the picture.

Rarely is the ideological argument as overtly made as on the cover of the 1918 Redpath-Horner program by Fred Craft. In the center is the tent—pennants crisply flapping in the breeze, a road winding invitingly to its entrance, and trees and other foliage flanking the tent and rooting it into the ground. Alone, this would be a standard and unremarkable cover. This program, however, encloses the image in a picture frame hung from a hook made out of the American seal. The picture continues beyond the edge of the frame. On one side is a typical early-twentieth-century school building and on the other an impressive church, evoking a Gothic cathedral. The entire image—the framed picture and the two buildings—is contained within a more modest frame. The shaping human hand that intervenes into nature to organize it into landscape is revealed as the hand of the artist who both creates and legitimizes Chautauqua's place in that landscape through his composition.

Swarthmore chose to silhouette the community/tent relationship in 1924. With a church on the summit of a hill, the tent is the broad foundation on which the hill rests. Between the church and the tent is the town, capped by the church but supported by Chautauqua. This cover, by Harrie Wood, erases the details that make a community specific and offers the Chautauqua landscape iconographically—church at the top, Chautauqua not at the bottom but as a base for all that the community does. Its very starkness makes the message all the more urgent. Religion crowns the community that Chautauqua undergirds.

In 1929, one of the last seasons before the demise of Chautauqua, Redpath Chautauqua, now the operations of Harrison, Vawter, and Horner combined under the management of W. S. Rupe, portrayed the tent in the ubiquitous grove of trees flanked by community buildings, including a church. This scene is different, however, because the tent is also flanked by a huge parking lot full of cars and a large crowd of people making their way to the tent. As the much earlier Evening Star 1920 program exclaimed in a long list of motives for attending Chautauqua, perhaps as a harbinger: "REASONS WHY I am going to take my car and drive over to Chautauqua this summer because I can imagine nothing finer for a cool, summer evening, than to drive over to Chautauqua."[37] With the advent of the car, the country began to seem less pastoral and more suburban, a visual indication of the waning of the Chautauqua and its landscape. Eventually, the drive will be more important than the destination.

"The great cities rest upon our broad and fertile prairies. Burn down your cities and leave our farms, and your cities will spring up again as if by magic; but destroy our farms and the grass will grow in the streets of every city in the country."[38]

For many rural inhabitants, the United States seemed increasingly unknowable. The rise of the cities populated by large numbers of recent immigrants, the radical shifts in cultural life, and the emergence of industrially based businesses were alien to the experiences of Chautauqua audiences. The Circuits championed those audiences and their concerns by creating ways in which they could see themselves as true Americans, as the realization of the founding vision for the nation. They were the bulwark against the lowering of moral standards and the weakening of the national fabric, as the epigraph from a William Jennings Bryan speech that opens this section implies. Iterating and reiterating these beliefs metaphorically was a familiar theme for Chautauqua, and examples of this can be seen in three cartoons in the Circuits' professional journals (see pages 151–152). "A Chance for Cultivation" (1913), "Our Town" (1914), and "The Sower" (1919) are remarkable depictions of the metaphoric strategies Chautauqua employed to connect the communities it served with the larger nation. The cartoons promised that the true and authentic America was Chautauqua's America: rural, agricultural, and traditional.

The 1913 cartoon consists of two panels. The first—a "before"—depicts a chaotic, dark, and dying landscape where the trees are gnarled and bare, the brush matted and dense, and the setting sun weak and pale. In the center, a young man, "The Pioneer," rolls up his sleeves, a hatchet close by, and prepares for action. The second panel—an "after"—shows the Pioneer, now an older man, standing in the same spot with his arm around a young man gesturing toward what he has wrought. Gone are the dead trees and tangled brush, replaced by roses and orderly orchards, streetlights, and buildings. These buildings are labeled with their role, the last in the row a crisp tent marked "Chautauqua." One caption reads: "Let the son continue the fathers [sic] work[.] The greatest inheritance is ambition."[39] But even more significant than an emphasis on physical labor and a gesture toward the belief that inherited wealth was debilitating was the interest in cultivation. Under the cartoon itself, a separate statement reads: "CULTIVATION has changed the jungle into the garden. Cultivation has changed the bramblebrush into the Beauty Rosebush. Cultivation has changed the election by bullets into the election by ballots on the other side of the Rio Grande. STOP CULTIVATION and we revert to the jungles, brambles, bullets and bullfights."[40] Whether or not Chautauquans were aware of it, the words "culture" (what Chautauqua presented itself as) and "cultivation" derived from the same French root word for "to take care of," "to till." Chautauqua made one argument for its permanency and essential American nature by analogizing itself to the activity that created the community and that many believed thinly separated them from a collapse of civilization. Knobloch emphasizes:

> Cultivation, or the arts and sciences of improving nature, is an act of transformation that takes "wild" territory—virgin land—and breaks it as one would break an animal or subjugate a slave, processes, incidentally, accompanying many agricultures supported by states and empires. It is a process of domestication by which a plowman enforces his domination over cropland in such a way as to render the land permanently "improved. . . ." Land not under the plow was not improved and therefore appeared to be unoccupied.[41]

Self-improvement was the goal for Chautauqua, and the very act of improving was American. Had not the pioneers "improved" the land, rescued it from "brambles" by putting it to work? The work of Chautauqua was the work of America.

The 1914 cartoon is also divided into two panels, this time to represent two stark choices facing Chautauqua audiences. A field with straight furrows grows lush crops, each orderly row labeled to identify the fruit for harvest—"Schools" or "Chautauqua," for example. The alternative, also labeled "Our

Town," shows the same field, but the second barn is collapsing, the field is choked with weeds, and randomly scattered signs read "low amusements," "vice," and "loafing." These are only a few of the threats that lurk in the uncultivated and neglected field over which vultures hover threateningly.[42]

The presence of weeds is notable because weeds are often interpreted as disregard for the community and its standards. Again, Knobloch proposes: "A weed is wild and rank rather than domesticated and controlled—that is, it does not flourish through the domesticating agent of a person but through its own agency, hence the disdain heaped on farmers or homeowners who allow weeds to grow on their property. A weedy field, garden, or lawn is a sign of neglect on the part of the owner in domesticating his property."[43] Leaving things to chance, an unwillingness to strive for improvement, was anti-Chautauquan, perhaps even anti-American. Eight years later a program made this same argument, pointing out that you reap what you sow. "Weeds will come into the farmers' fields voluntarily and without any sort of encouragement, soon overrun the place. But corn will come only as a result of careful preparation of soil, seasonable planting, and thorough cultivation. The corn crop insists on being guaranteed by substantial interest and intelligent cooperation. Boost for the corn and it boosts for you. Leave it to compete with the weeds, and the weeds will invariably win."[44] Chautauqua, clearly, was the more desirable corn.

The 1919 cartoon makes a similar point as the earlier two. In a single panel a lanky man labeled "Chautauqua," barely contained within the frame, strews seeds across a field from a sack marked "Information, Inspiration, Clean Entertainment, Community Improvement, Timely Messages."[45] The cartoon's figure obviously is intended to invoke the quintessential American hero Johnny Appleseed, who, through his distribution of apple seeds, helped transform the wild frontier into the cultivated countryside. The Sower's seeds must be the same ones that the Pioneer used to create his garden and that the superior "Our Town" planted to yield churches, schools, and homes. A 1923 program made a comparable argument about the crop yet to come, the crop that Chautauqua was sowing. "I can supply the service. I can make it worth your while. But you yourselves, your young men and maidens, your boys and girls must furnish the seed bed for planting. And the bountiful harvests upspringing from their quickened lives belong to your community, not to me. And I will venture that the aggregate practical values of this service is a thousand-fold greater than my balance sheet will show."[46] The argument is a pragmatic one: invest in the seeds and the crop they yield will be far greater than the value of the seeds.

"A Chance for Cultivation," "Our Town," and "The Sower" depict Chautauqua as first and foremost a predictable feature of the familiar and typical landscape of any small, rural town. Landscape operates as space transformed into "a unit of human occupation," which indicates the labor and existence of the community.[47] These communities, under threat from the external forces of urbanization and industrialization as well as from a more internal one of an agrarian population decrease, seized on Chautauqua and its metaphoric argument as tangible evidence that they could stem the tide of change. The relationship of the platform to community, Chautauqua to landscape, was a complex one that revealed much about how people made sense of the relationships of community, nation, and themselves. In his 1996 *Kinship with the Land*, E. Bradford Burns remarks: "Physical and psychological adjustments to immediate environment distill an appropriate local culture. It, in turn, defines people partly in terms of place, partly in terms of adjustment to and use of that place, and partly in terms of how they relate to each other in that place."[48] Chautauqua provided both a literal and metaphoric space for those processes to be celebrated and contextualized. The American space was the countryside and the authentic American citizen a rural, small-town dweller.

It was an absolute article of faith, as John Tapia notes, that "agricultural life was . . . the natural life from which all good flows," and "competing life styles had to be unnatural and therefore inevitably enervating and corrupt."[49] But America held out a rural life unlike any other—the frontier. As University of Wisconsin assistant professor Frederick Jackson Turner observed in his famous address to fellow members of the American Historical Association at the World's Columbian Exposition in 1893: "In short, at the frontier the environment is at first too strong for the man. He must accept the conditions which it furnishes, or perish, and so he fits himself into Indian clearings and follows the Indian trails. Little by little he transforms the wilderness, but the outcome is not the old Europe. . . . The fact is, that here is a new product that is American."[50] The frontier's disappearance was less important to Chautauqua audiences than the knowledge that a rural life had been carved out of unused wilderness. For them, "native range as pasture was considered an improvement over leaving the native land unused (that is, unplowed)," and this belief was part of their pride in their contributions to the development of America.[51] "Prosperity was attributed not only to the richness of the land but also to the industry of the people. Bountiful rural life fostered independence and self-reliance. . . . With no one beholden to any other person, true democracy could flourish."[52] Chautauqua reminded all in the tent of their pioneer credentials and how those credentials proved that they were the nation's foundation.

These pioneer credentials were not easily achieved, however. In fact, there was considerable contradiction in the rural self-congratulations that Chautauqua encouraged. In his influential work *The Age of Reform*, Richard Hofstadter emphasizes: "For the farmer it was bewildering and irritating . . . to think of the great contrast between the verbal deference paid him by almost everyone and the real status, the real economic position in which he found himself."[53] The ideas behind the passage and implementation of the Homestead Act in 1862 are an excellent example of just this sort of "contrast." The act itself, distinct from how it actually worked, was used to point up American exceptionalism. As scholar Lawrence Bacon Lee notes, "It was copied from no other nation's system. It was originally and distinctly American, and remains a monument to its originators."[54] While the act predates the Circuits by many years, it was the instrument that allowed many of these communities to come into existence, and it was a living legislation for the West, as it was amended in 1909 and 1916, well after the founding of the Circuits.

The original act, "heralded as the greatest democratic measure of all time," among other things, provided 160 acres of public land at a nominal fee to a citizen head of household if he or she would live on it for five years.[55] The linchpin of the act, however, was that the farmer must "improve" the land in order to claim it. The Homestead Act "institutionalized" the 160-acre homestead. Knobloch summarizes: "Together with the plow technology necessary for a farmer using European methods to cultivate even a quarter of it, the size of the homestead indicates at least two things: the determination on the part of the federal government to recode a 'wild' landscape as quickly as possible by creating vast domesticated fields and the commercial nature of western farming."[56] Not only was farming firmly understood as a productive and improving use of the land, but the agrarian myth of the moral superiority of the farmer and rural life was enshrined by the act as the basis for developing the continent. Farming was a moral imperative because of its benefits to the nation. An 1851 speech exhorted: "The life of the farmer is peculiarly favorable to virtue. . . . No other occupation is so well calculated to inspire trust in his creator and charity toward creatures."[57] Some critics charged that the act would draw undesirable immigrants, but others responded that the act would help immigrants assimilate more quickly and teach them to be better citizens. The arguments made in favor of the act all stressed the importance of farming to a nation's moral and social well-being. One commentator emphasized that "a nation will be powerful, prosperous and happy, in proportion to the number of independent cultivators of the soil found within its domain" and the need for land to be improved by settlement and cultivation.[58] No one questioned the assumption that European American settlement and use of the land were improvements.

The act itself was less than a success because land speculators, corporations, cattle barons, and absentee owners grabbed much of the land, and drought and claims too small to yield sufficient crops often starved farmers out. The rhetoric around its passage and the ongoing struggles to keep the act current well into the twentieth century testify to its continuing resonance for most rural, western citizens. For those who did manage to hold on to their claims and for farmers who established their farms in other ways, claiming or owning the land was not the end of the battle but the opening salvo in what was often a painful struggle.

Throughout the nineteenth century, especially after the Civil War, tight currency and high tariffs hurt farmers, particularly those in the West and Midwest because of the debt they had accrued to improve their farms. Falling prices for crops across the nineteenth century had not been accompanied by similar decreases in costs, thus farmers found themselves working harder and harder for less and less. That there was a crisis was clear, but it was not clear to whom to turn. There was no central figure to protest or picket as there was in industrial labor. "The farmer's enemy was not an employer but a *system*—a system of credit, supply, transportation and marketing," observes scholar Elizabeth Sanders.[59] This demanded a different sort of organizing than was being tried in the cities. The first attempt at a solution was the Grange movement. Begun in 1867 as a cooperative to buy and sell goods for farmers, it was officially apolitical, but those in the leadership often sought and won public office. The more activist Farmers' Alliance started in 1877 and stressed education and collective action. The Farmers' Alliance expanded rapidly in the 1880s. As Sanders describes: "The lecturers spread the Alliance 'gospel' of political education, social criticism, and economic collective action to remote rural settlements. In the words of Robert C. McMath Jr., '[the lecturer] was to the Alliance what the circuit rider had been to early Methodism.'"[60] This led in the 1890s to an actual political party, the Populists, which represented rural discontent. Populist leaders sought government ownership of the railroads, federal loans for farmers, an eight-hour workday, direct election of senators, and a federal income tax.[61] Another of the Populists' grievances was the failure of the Homestead Act, despite several amendments.

Democrat William Jennings Bryan's failure to secure the presidency in 1896 (losing to Republican William McKinley) marked the end of Populism and farmers' ascendancy in American politics. The Progressives, succeeding the Populists and offering a less radical reformist politics, ultimately enacted many of the reforms sought by the Populists. Chautauqua did not invent the rhetoric around the moral importance of rural areas, but it certainly employed it. The Circuits echoed some aspects of the farmers' own organizations, for example, their investment in education and self-improvement as a duty to family and community. This familiarity must have lent greater credence to Circuit Chautauqua's metaphoric connection between its rural audiences and the nation.

Progressives' politics and ideas were intertwined with Chautauqua, and many of the Circuits' favorite speakers were Progressive senators and governors, including Robert La Follette (Wisconsin), James Vardaman (Mississippi), Benjamin Tillman (South Carolina), Albert Cummins (Iowa), and Champ Clark (Missouri). These men, in historian Deborah Fink's words, "fully believed and expounded at length the Jeffersonian creed that the farmers were better and nobler than urban dwellers and the well-being of the country as a whole rested on its rural population."[62] Resisting the city and its urban customs was more than a rejection of a way of life with which they disagreed. Fink continues: "The belief that farm people were happier, healthier, and more virtuous than city people was firmly entrenched in American culture." Those who held that belief "saw the evil cities as a unified entity extracting the lifeblood of the countryside. To rally the vigor of the countryside was to strengthen natural immunities and save society from the disease of the city."[63] Chautauqua reminded people that "strengthen[ing] natural immunities" was precisely what it was good at, especially when it came to vaccinating the young, according to an undated but contemporary article on Chautauqua. "It is the younger generation that is drawn away from the village and farm by the lure of the city. The chief defect in rural community life is the lack of means for wholesome recreation and entertainment. . . . The Chautauqua provides just that combination of education, entertainment, recreation, and inspiration that is indispensable to the building up of the rural community."[64] This argument wove throughout Chautauqua publications—keeping them down on the farm would be easy once they saw Chautauqua.

In the program for his 1909 Chautauqua, Keith Vawter warned that the "greatest industrial problem in this country today comes from the congestion of population in the great cities, and corresponding scarcity of labor on the farms."[65] Vawter articulated both threats to rural communities—the departure of people to the cities and the dangers of the cities themselves. When farm youth did arrive in the city they, "generally speaking, land in the lowest stratum of the city's working class, and far too often, the city's criminal class."[66] The destruction of the community landscape posed huge risks—not only was that landscape menaced by abandonment but also by moral and social decay.

The strong presence of Chautauqua, however, could work as a preventative. Vawter continued: "Here is the greatest of the many missions of the modern Chautauqua. It makes life in the country cities more enjoyable, if it furnishes a glimpse of the great outside world . . . , if it makes life in the country brighter and happier, and tends to keep a fraction of those young men and women at home . . . , then Chautauqua is worth all of the support and assistance you can possibly render it."[67] In his program address, Vawter worked to sidestep the difficult contradiction the issue presented. City life was, for many, more interesting and exciting than life in the country. Urban opportunities for employment, entertainment, and socializing were more diverse and numerous than rural ones. Images of city sophistication and glamor abounded, and there was no doubt that the labor of city living was considerably less than that of country life. Chautauqua found itself promoting a sharp contradiction—it claimed to bring the benefits of city life (access to ideas, people, and developments) without the concomitant dangers (immorality, crime, congestion). Employing a strategy they would later adopt for theater, as chapter 5 will demonstrate, the Circuits used their own unassailable moral position to assure audiences that seemingly morally suspect material was not dangerous when encountered within the canvas walls of Chautauqua. One way that the Circuits ensured those walls' dependability was to make Chautauqua's community role clear. Observer Harold Kessinger asserted in 1914 that "these rural communities are the bulwark of our power."[68] Chautauqua was essential to those fortifications.

Chautauqua fortified its place in the community in other ways, too. The Circuits missed no opportunity to compare themselves favorably with the "bulwarks" of the community's power. In "A Chance for Cultivation," the cultivated rows of necessary institutions start with home and church and culminate in the Chautauqua tent, flags proudly flying, seemingly as fixed in space as the buildings that preceded it. Obviously, Chautauqua is analogous to the other institutions. Certainly in "Our Town," that analogy is unqualified. The straight furrows are of equal size and value, making a visual argument for the equality among them. As one observer noted: "By the traveling or circuit plan the Chautauqua is actually taken to the people, the khaki colored tents being located close to the heart of each community's activities and within reach of thousands who could not otherwise avail themselves of Chautauqua advantages, without the purchase of a single acre of ground or the erection of a building, a town may become a real Chautauqua center and unite its influence with that of other Chautauqua centers in far reaching effects."[69] This 1915 article made two contentions that encouraged connections between Chautauqua and civic and religious institutions. The first was that the Circuits were an essential part of the community.

To forgo Chautauqua, the author implied, was to court decline. The second was that the Circuits were similar to institutions familiar for their quotidian presence, and therefore they were not similar to other misleadingly analogous but discredited tent entertainments. In other words, the Circuits argued they were education, religion, and community and that they were not theater, circus, medicine show, or any other morally suspect activity.

Circuit Chautauqua's comparison of itself to churches and schools tapped into assumptions about and histories of the importance of churches and schools to newly established rural communities dating back to the mid-nineteenth century. As the frontier gave way to European American settlements, there were few cultural institutions to knit communities together. Those that were there acted as proof that a community did indeed exist. In *Kinship with the Land*, Burns notes: "Family, farm, church, and school stood as the dominant institutions within the culture."[70] This particular arrangement was prized as unique to the United States. Iowa was often held up as the representative state, the one that most characterized all that the rural life should be. Burns continues: "Folk culture, wherever it might appear, was considered to be genuine expression of American culture. In rural Iowa [for example], the organization was informal and local, centering on the family, farm, church, and school."[71] Obviously at the heart of that life was home, church, school, and, hopefully from the Circuits' point of view, Chautauqua.

Churches played a much more daily role than simply as weekly places of worship. They "provided consolation, celebration, and explanation . . . [and] were . . . major recreational centers in rural America. . . . Churches everywhere underscored neighborhood efforts to regulate behavior," David Danbom notes.[72] In identifying themselves with the church, the Circuits recalled these various functions. Religion itself, in fact, was often compared to agricultural labor. "Ministers conquered souls, just as farmers subdued the soil."[73] The correspondence of souls and soil, churches and farms, was unquestioned and demonstrates how central the agrarian ideal was in the United States. The Circuits evoked existing communal ties and commitments to remind their audiences of their unassailably moral and respectable offerings for rural Protestant audiences. Ministers, both local and as part of the talent, were a reliable presence on the Chautauqua platform. Advance agents usually sought out ministers to help secure their contracts, believing that the ministers would then urge their parishioners to attend.

Like churches, schools were a symbol of an established community, and Circuits were assiduous on extending that understanding to include themselves. Public school education was not widely available until after the Civil

War, in part because citizens had to tax themselves to provide it.[74] But those costs came to be considered essential as, for example, "school activities such as declamations and spelling matches focused community pride and loyalty."[75] Between 1900 and 1920 an unprecedented number of rural communities did levy taxes on themselves to create or better their schools. Schools were ubiquitously seen as a central way to "improve their communities."[76] Additionally, taxing themselves meant that communities retained governance of their institutions. Burns argues: "While farmers valued education, they wanted to maintain it at a very local level, where they exerted control to ensure it inculcated rural values and remained uncontaminated by urban influences."[77] Circuits capitalized on the fact that people had made collective financial sacrifices for the greater communal good, reminding people that improvements did not come without selfless commitment.

In their advertisements and programs, the Circuits were careful to emphasize the connections between the missions and purposes of churches and schools and Chautauqua. On a sheet of suggested text for advertisements, Lyman Abbott, respected minister and regular Chautauqua speaker, affirmed that Chautauqua "was next to the church and the public school system among the forces that are making for the elevation and ennobling of the American people."[78] In the same vein, Charles Horner declared in his 1925 program: "The Chautauqua is determined to be the constant ally for these four great ideals of human achievement; the *Church*, the *School*, the *Home*, and the *Government*. No community can come under the lectures of this program without becoming more American, more law-abiding, more healthful and progressive."[79] In this typical program and advertisement rhetoric, the Circuits share purposes and effects with other communal institutions, specifically the improvement and uplift of people for personal and civic enrichment.

In the 1920s the "ironclad" contract became less and less popular, and booking agents had to work harder and harder to get communities to sign one. To combat growing audience resistance, the Circuits redoubled their emphasis on identifying Chautauqua with the church and the school. Paul Pearson, managing the small and struggling Swarthmore Chautauqua (which would be run by his creditors in 1930 and finally bring him to bankruptcy in 1934), produced a long and detailed pamphlet outlining specific arguments for his sales staff to employ as they tried to secure the towns vital to structuring a reasonable Circuit.

> Take the matter of the public schools as an example. Before the present system was adopted, and each family had the right to determine whether or not they should educate their children, it was found that an amazing

percentage of them made very inadequate or positively no provision for such education. Hence it was found necessary to take so vital a thing as education out of the control of parents and make it a public function. . . . Experience had demonstrated that so obviously good a thing as the public schools would not function properly without authoritative public control.

Neither is the church left to the chance support as such as might voluntarily contribute toward its necessary operating expenses. . . . In the ordinary church congregation the responsibility for seeing that this is all done usually falls upon a few sober-minded and good men who have the interests of the church upon their hearts.[80]

Taxes and tithes were unremarkable; from them, Chautauqua hoped that it was a small leap to contract guarantees.

These comparisons were intended to bind communities closer to their Chautauquas. Churches and schools, almost more than any other civic and public institutions, signified a permanent cultivation of the landscape and the movement from pioneer to farmer or businessperson. No longer wilderness, untouched and uncivilized, the landscape was organized around human, European American institutions. That intervention was recent enough in both historical and personal memories that invoking it allowed the Circuits to bridge their outsider status by connecting their labor and institution to those at the heart of community effort, investment, and history. Solid and dependable, Chautauqua wanted audiences to embrace the idea that the labor of building communities could stand as a metaphor for the contributions of rural communities to America. Chautauqua's role was to link the two parts of the metaphor.

Chautauqua, the metaphoric process implied, was as perfect as the community and the institutions in it. Churches and schools, however, were permanent buildings (or at least were housed within them) that a community's citizens passed regularly as they navigated their landscape. Occupying a physical site, these buildings were constant spatial reminders of the many and complex roles the church and school played in the community. Tents, on the other hand, were not structures generally thought to be permanent, a seeming contradiction to the Circuit's assertion of itself as solid, reliable, and familiar. Chautauqua came once a year, brought all its own materials, and removed all traces when it departed. Citizens might point to an empty field or pasture, but there were no continuous physical signs of Chautauqua.

The physical reality of Chautauqua may have been temporary, but the effects of Chautauqua were, as Truman Talley wrote in 1921, understood as "an established and immovable institution in American life as vital as democracy itself."[81] This kind of characterization transformed impermanency into permanency. Talley adds:

> This tent, with all its appurtenances . . . is a transient affair, come but a short time ago and due to fold and depart a few hours hence. Yet it will all come again. And through the apparent transience of it all there is a pervading air of permanence. The chairs, at least, are firmly held, for in every one of them sits a man or a woman or a child. Around the fringes, leaning on or holding to tent poles and ropes, or standing grouped at the back of the main aisle, there are more people. They are all intently listening.[82]

Chautauqua, like the spring, will return and bring with it growth and sustenance. The permanence, however, is not so much in its material appearance or properties but in its cyclical nature. It had been there before and promised to be so again.

Audiences were what made Chautauqua permanent. Their desire for "uplift" and their need for Chautauqua to support their efforts at maintaining community in the face of political and historical changes placed Chautauqua firmly in the community landscape. One observer noted in 1919: "Well, the tent went away and the talent vanished, but the spirit of Chautauqua remained. I saw what Chautauqua had done for our community. I heard men in the corner groceries discuss the lectures. I heard children repeat the games and stories taught and told them that week."[83] While Chautauqua could not always be seen, outside of the few days of the year when the tent was actually present, during the time when Chautauqua was there the community was able "to realize itself at its best." The tent would leave, but the audiences would stay. If the Chautauqua was indeed "firmly held" by its audiences who remained, then Chautauqua was never truly absent, and its tangible and visible effects, "what it has done for the community," would endure.

Chautauqua may have claimed that it was strengthening the community and ensuring the community's continuation, but it was simultaneously hiring the community's young people to go on the road with the Circuits. Brothers Richie and Eben Schultz's lives were intertwined with Chautauqua. They attended their first Chautauqua in 1909 in their hometown of Canton, Missouri. Richie Schultz's son wrote: "Chautauqua made a lasting impression on the Schultz brothers. After completing their education and having taken teaching positions in academia, they were intrigued with the spirit of adventure that Chautauqua offered and the opportunity to supplement their professional salaries. In 1918 both of them signed with the Redpath-Vawter system to spend their summers as Chautauqua superintendents. For Eben it was a portentous decision because it was on Chautauqua that he met his future bride." When the Circuit on which Eben was superintendent came through Canton in 1921, the town "experienced one of its most exciting and successful Chautauqua seasons." Similarly, the Canton newspaper enthusiastically reported in an article titled "Canton Boy Pleases" that Richie had been lauded in the Geddes, North Dakota, paper. Whenever one of the Schultz brothers' outfits came to Canton, their mother, Laura, could be counted on to "put on a big spread for the Chautauqua staff and performers."[84] The Schultzes lived the metaphoric connection of small towns to America. They proved Canton's ability to make national contributions. Few other Canton residents had probably ever been to Geddes, but Richie Schultz symbolically linked the two towns as part of America.

For Richard Oram, who grew up in Mentone and Warsaw, Indiana, life in a small town and Chautauqua were inseparable. "Mentone was such a tiny town but everyone had to have Chautauqua."[85] Some of his earliest memories came from Chautauqua. He remembered being in a "little wedding" in 1919 when he was a very young boy. He also remembered that they did a lot of singing, especially popular religious songs like "Jesus Wants Me for a Sunbeam." After high school he was working for his father's insurance agency when Bob Hanscom asked around town if there was a young actor to join his troupe. Oram laughed as he recalled that moment in his life. "To have someone suddenly stand in the doorway and say, 'how would you like to go into the theater,' I, you know, the heavens opened up and the cherubs sang!"[86] Performing in Chautauqua eventually gave him the courage to try his luck as an actor in New York City.

For future journalist and author William L. Shirer, who grew up in Cedar Rapids, Iowa, and as a child attended Chautauqua on the grounds of Coe College, Chautauqua seemed as dependable and long lasting as small towns themselves. Shirer worked in Vawter's office one summer and then for two summers, in 1920 and 1921, went out as one of the tent crew on the Circuits. "It was a wondrous, romantic interlude in my young life, and largely made up for all the emptiness of the highschool [sic] years."[87] Shirer could be one of the young people who Vawter boasted about in his programs. For Shirer, Chautauqua did make life "brighter and happier," as the 1909 program had claimed. In fact, he could not imagine that there would ever be a time when Chautauqua would not exist. "I was finishing my junior year in college [1924] and working on a daily newspaper and had no idea that Chautauqua was doomed."[88]

Looking at the tent nestled in a rural landscape or joining the crowds as they showed their tickets at the box office, the metaphoric relation of the countryside, America, and Chautauqua must have seemed enduring. Inside the tent, however, a different story was starting to be told. Chautauqua promised to put the world on the platform. It largely kept that promise, but the contradictions between the tent's location and the world it tried to represent within the canvas walls were becoming more and more obvious.

Parades were the most obvious way that Circuit Chautauqua both announced its presence and began the process of temporarily changing the town into the setting for Chautauqua. These are examples from Columbia, Minnesota; Tipton, Indiana; Alma and Flint, Michigan. These photographs are undated, except for the Flint parade, which took place in 1915. Iowa.

Auto Parade
Alma (Mich) Chautauqua

Street corners, fences, storefronts, and store windows were also fair game for Chautauqua advertising. Iowa.

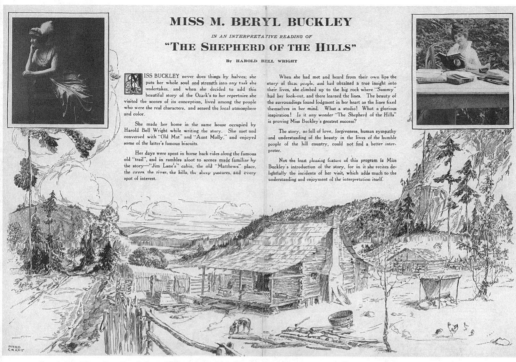

MISS M. BERYL BUCKLEY

IN AN INTERPRETATIVE READING OF

"THE SHEPHERD OF THE HILLS"

By HAROLD BELL WRIGHT

MISS BUCKLEY never does things by halves; she puts her whole soul and strength into any task she undertakes, and when she decided to add this beautiful story of the Ozark's to her repertoire she visited the scenes of its conception, lived among the people who were the real characters, and sensed the local atmosphere and color.

She made her home in the same house occupied by Harold Bell Wright while writing the story. She met and conversed with "Old Mat" and "Aunt Molly," and enjoyed some of the latter's famous biscuits.

Her days were spent in horse back rides along the famous old "trail", and in rambles afoot to scenes made familiar by the story—"Jim Lane's" cabin, the old "Matthews" place, the caves, the river, the hills, the sheep pastures, and every spot of interest.

When she had met and heard from their own lips the story of these people, and had obtained a true insight into their lives, she climbed up to the big rock where "Sammy" had her look-out, and there learned the lines. The beauty of the surroundings found lodgment in her heart as the lines fixed themselves in her mind. What a studio! What a glorious inspiration! Is it any wonder "The Shepherd of the Hills" is proving Miss Buckley's greatest success?

The story, so full of love, forgiveness, human sympathy and understanding of the beauty in the lives of the humble people of the hill country, could not find a better interpreter.

Not the least pleasing feature of this program is Miss Buckley's introduction of the story, for in it she recites delightfully the incidents of her visit, which adds much to the understanding and enjoyment of the interpretation itself.

That The Shepherd of the Hills *celebrated rural life could not have been made any clearer in Beryl Buckley's promotional materials. Iowa.*

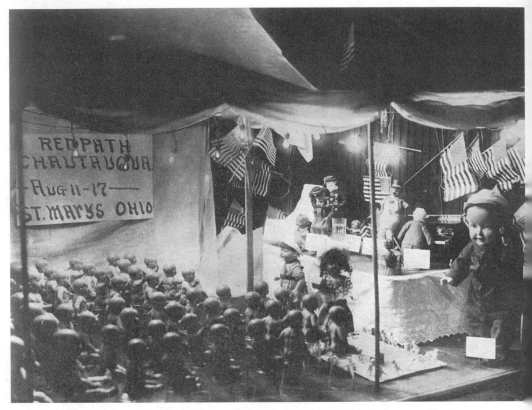

W. A. Ewing created such an elaborate window for the St. Marys, Ohio, August 1915 Chautauqua that Lyceum Magazine noted it the following month. Ewing used more than a hundred dolls and depicted talent, junior Chautauqua, and audience at the moment when the local committee agrees to renew their annual contract for the coming year. The performers on the platform are the Ben Greet Players. Iowa.

Otis T. Wingo. Iowa.

Evening Star Circuit Chautauqua understood
very clearly that the program's function was to
evoke the utopia promised by the very idea of
Chautauqua. Iowa.

The Redpath tent in Asheville, North Carolina, bore little resemblance to the sylvan idyll promised by the program. Iowa.

Midland Chautauqua Assembly
ø ø 1901 ø ø

THE Executive Committee of Midland Chautauqua take a pardonable pride in presenting this, the preliminary prospectus of the attractions for the 1901 assembly. On account of the many high-grade lecturers, artists and entertainers the program for the coming session will cost not far from one thousand dollars more than any other program ever given in Des Moines or Iowa. Believing that the best is none too good, the committee have proceeded regardless of expense, and trust to the good judgment of the patrons and citizens of the Midland territory, who they believe will stand behind them in this undertaking.

Every arrangement possible is being made for the care and accommodation of the people who attend the Assembly Meeting, and it is the desire of the management that all may feel at home on the grounds. The grounds are nicely located, upon a beautifully shaded camping spot, at night brilliantly illuminated with colored globes and abundant lamps. Chautauqua Park is easy of access, being located upon three street car lines. With the splendid facilities for handling large crowds, the Des Moines Street Ry. Co. is prepared to transport, within twenty minutes, four or five thousand people with the greatest ease.

The management, in their endeavor to build up in Central Iowa a Chautauqua Assembly second to none in America, invite the support and patronage of all who are interested in politics, religion, business, art, literature, music, science, high-grade entertainments which are both elevating and pleasing in their effects and of lasting benefit to society. The social functions at Midland Chautauqua will prove delightful to those who participate. Never before has there existed such a general desire to unite all Des Moines under the great auditorium roof into a Chautauqua circle for the pleasure and profit of all.

In preparing this program the greatest care has been exercised to preserve the proper balance between instruction and amusement. To this end some of the best entertainers in the country have been secured as well as the best of lecture talent. The musical features are of the highest quality, and are plentifully interspersed. The departments display the strongest array of talent ever presented in an Iowa Chautauqua. While especial attractions have been secured for some days, it has been the aim of the committee to make a program that will have no weak spots, and each day of which will be so good that one cannot afford to miss it.

Come and see! Trust thine own eyes.
—*Schiller.*

A program for the 1901 Midland Chautauqua Assembly in Des Moines, Iowa. Iowa.

Redpath-Vawter, 1909. Iowa.

144

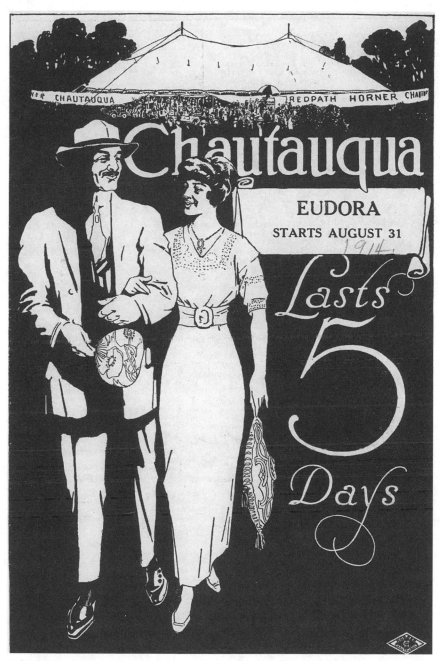

Chautauqua

EUDORA
STARTS AUGUST 31

1914

Lasts 5 Days

Redpath-Horner, 1914. Iowa.

Redpath-Vawter, 1915. Iowa.

CHAUTAUQUA

Souvenir Program
1916

TENTH
ANNIVERSARY
Redpath-Vawter
Chautauqua
System
1907 ~ 1916

Canton, Missouri
July 29 to Aug. 4

Redpath-Vawter, 1916. Iowa.

Evening Star, 1917 and 1918. Iowa.

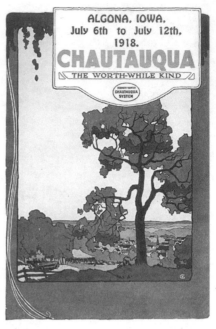

Redpath-Vawter, 1918. Iowa.

Standard Chautauqua, 1918. Iowa.

Redpath-Horner, 1918. Iowa.

SWARTHMORE
CHAUTAUQUA

1924

Swarthmore, 1924. Swarthmore.

Redpath, 1929. Iowa.

Within the illustration:

A CHANCE FOR CULTIVATION

HOME   CHURCH   SCHOOL   LYCEUM   CHAUTAUQUA

LET THE SON CONTINUE THE FATHER'S WORK THE GREATEST INHERITANCE IS AMBITION·

THE PIONEER

Colby

CULTIVATION MAKES A GARDEN OF THE JUNGLE.

"CULTIVATION has changed the jungle into the garden. Cultivation has changed the bramblebrush into the Beauty Rosebush. Cultivation has changed the election by bullets into the election by ballots on the other side of the Rio Grande. STOP CULTIVATION and we revert to the jungles, brambles, bullets and bullfights."

"A Chance for Cultivation," Lyceumite and Talent, 1913. Iowa.

A Militant Force

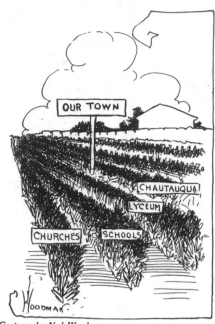

Cultivate or Degenerate—Which Shall it Be?

"Our Town," Lyceum Magazine, 1914. Iowa.

The Sower

"The Sower," Lyceum Magazine, 1919. Iowa.

Whenever possible, the Circuits tried to live up to Chautauqua's reputation as pastoral. The New York Chautauqua's location on Lake Chautauqua made water a desirable feature in the Chautauqua site. In Manchester, Iowa, they were able to achieve this goal. Iowa.

CHAPTER FOUR

Performance on the Platform
Oratory

No single figure is more identified with Circuit Chautauqua than William Jennings Bryan. His politics, character, moral values, oratory, and even blind spots and failures found their truest expression and most sympathetic reception on the Circuits. The political battles he waged were on behalf of the citizens who comprised Chautauqua audiences, and he articulated their hopes for the future of America. The morals he preached confirmed values and a worldview that were no longer quite in vogue. His extraordinary oratorical ability masked the reality that the age of oratory, when gifted speakers like Abraham Lincoln and Henry Ward Beecher were also great men, had passed. The art that had been so defining in the eighteenth and nineteenth centuries was reduced to the suspect art of elocution, and even that, by Bryan's death in 1925, was on the wane. If for many Americans he was Chautauqua itself, it was not simply because of his politics and values. It was also because in his Chautauqua presence and career can be read all the complexities, difficulties, and challenges of performance in the context of Chautauqua and Chautauqua in the context of performance.

Bryan began speaking on independent assemblies about 1894, but his strongest ties were to the Circuits, and his career was intertwined with them. He lectured the first year of the Redpath Circuits in 1904.[1] Five years later Charles Horner became his personal lecture manager, further intertwining Bryan's identity with Chautauqua. His final appearance was in 1924, the penultimate summer of his life, the summer before the infamous Scopes trial would make him ridiculous and hasten his death in the summer of 1925. He kept a punishing schedule, cramming in so many appearances that even seasoned Chautauqua talent and management, used to brutal schedules and incredible personal discomfort, wondered at his stamina and dedication. He was unfailingly kind and courteous to all he met. Anecdotes abound about his humility and genuine interest in everyone from the tent crew to the leading citizens of each town. There was no more powerful attraction than Bryan, no one in the history of Chautauqua who drew a bigger crowd or made more money doing so. Bryan was so reliable a presence that manager J. Roy Ellison described him as good for "forty acres of parked Fords."[2] He was the only speaker for whom, as fellow lecturer Richard T. Ely remembered, "the railroads ran excursion trains and . . . if it was a week day business was virtually suspended."[3] During the thirty years he epitomized Chautauqua, in the relationship of the man and the movement can be read a struggle over the value and role of performance in American life. Ultimately, for both, the struggle proved to be their undoing.

Bryan's effect on his audiences was profound. Those who heard him speak averred that it was impossible to listen to him and not be swept away by his incredible voice. It was said to have, as Victoria Case and Robert Ormond Case have described it, "the quality of a great musical instrument in that it aroused feelings and responses in the listener that were not inherent in the instrument itself. . . . Ecstacy, unexplainable in terms of reason, gripped his audience."[4] Bryan himself was aware and wary of this impressive ability. Mary Baird Bryan, his wife, wrote in Bryan's memoirs (which she completed after he died) that in 1887, when he was still an unknown Nebraska lawyer, he returned home early one morning after an all-night political gathering. Obviously worried about something, he woke her and said, "I have had a strange experience. Last night I found I had power over an audience. I could move them as I chose. I have more than unusual power as a speaker. God grant that I use it wisely."[5] He could not have uttered anything more truthful about himself, and he was to spend the next thirty-eight years making a public life for himself based on that power.

It was that power that catapulted him to national fame. A single speech before the Democratic national convention in 1896, his Cross of Gold speech assailing the gold standard central to the Republican platform, transformed him from an obscure delegate from Nebraska to an influential national leader. His voice rang out in the hall, mesmerizing all who were there. Even those who disagreed with his position were entranced and cheered as the speech concluded with the most famous lines he ever spoke: "You shall not press down upon the brow of labor this cross of thorns, you shall not crucify mankind upon a cross of gold."[6] Bryan was never able to parlay this national influence into the presidency—he lost in 1896 and 1900 to William McKinley and in 1908 to William Howard Taft—and he never held elected office after 1895. It is easy to see Bryan as on the losing side of history—with, as scholar Gretchen Ritter summarizes, his "vision of a mixed-agrarian industrial economy, regionally organized and dominated by small and medium-sized producers"—and the rise of contemporary corporate culture as inevitable.[7] Even though that agrarian vision had limited political suasion into the twentieth century, it was because of a broad range of forces, most of them outside a single party's control, not because Bryan and his allies were promoting a hopelessly naive view of American society, politics, and economics. Those on the side of urban large producers had done their best in 1896 to link Bryan to "anarchism, communism, treason, and revolution."[8] Much of that mud stuck, but his ideas were influential despite the attempts to discredit him. Theodore Roosevelt, for example, learned from Bryan's successes, and his conversion to Progressivism can be attributed less to its limited influence within the Republican Party and more to, as Elizabeth Sanders posits, the "massive support for Bryan's agrarian progressivism within the interior of the country."[9] But it was not simply Bryan's political positions that made him influential and controversial; it was the way he articulated them. An old friend of Bryan's (who was also one of McKinley's aides) had predicted prior to the 1896 convention that if Bryan could get the opportunity to speak, he would undoubtedly secure the nomination. That was precisely what happened.[10] His voice created his career, and it was his voice that everyone remembered long after he was gone. By the end of his life and career, the voice was all that remained; Bryan's national stature, political influence, and impressive ideals had all been expended.

People willingly paid extra to be in the audience when Bryan spoke, and a typical crowd could reach 30,000 or more.[11] The atmosphere in the tents was intense, and audiences ignored great physical discomfort to hear him speak. One journalist visiting the Circuits to witness the phenomenon for himself observed, "As the witching hour of eight approached an infectious whisper ran among the audience, 'He is coming, he is coming.'"[12] This would be the high point of the Chautauqua, or even a lifetime, for most audiences, a chance to see one of the few public figures from the reform era who seemed to remain true to their principles. Charles Horner, as Bryan's Chautauqua manager, often escorted him to speaking engagements, and those experiences brought home to him the magnitude of Bryan's presence. "Conveying Bryan through a little sea of friendly faces lit by shining eyes was like the passage of the hosts of Israel as they walked between the walls of parted water of the Red Sea."[13] Given Bryan's religious convictions and his determination to live them out in his public life, such comparisons must have seemed all too appropriate.

On the Circuits, Bryan was not really a political speaker but an inspirational one. His most popular speeches were "The Prince of Peace," about the importance of religion over all other institutions, including government; "The Value of an Ideal," about the privileges and obligations of citizenship, with an emphasis on the obligation of each citizen to improve life for all; and "The Price of a Soul," a cautionary speech that warns of the dangers of greed and overreaching for both individuals and governments. Everyone wanted to hear these speeches; audiences cherished them year after year, bringing friends and then their own children to hear the man who was their standard-bearer. Redpath manager Harry Harrison remembered: "All over the nation solid citizens put everything aside to hear *The Prince of Peace* on Chautauqua Week's 'Bryan Day.' Did its content hypnotize them or was it the voice, big and easy and golden? They sat dead still in their seats as long as it sounded. If Bryan smiled, they smiled. If he frowned, they frowned. Babies could cry, trains roar by, thunder and rain shake the tent, but absorbed men and women just sat still and listened."[14] Audiences were mesmerized by him. His speeches—while they were predictable, or perhaps because they were—connected Bryan with the audience through his respect for his listeners and their mutual resistance to change and critique.

A Bryan performance was both dependable and repetitive. As one biographer describes it: "Bryan's usual practice was to speak with one hand resting on a block of ice, then to wipe his brow with that hand. The other hand held a palm fan, which he kept in motion; for many Americans, Bryan's palm fan was as much a part of his normal appearance as his simple alpaca coat and string tie."[15] This image was burned into everyone's mind. He was always visibly suffering from the heat but, like the audience, enduring it for the sake of their mutual mission. A contemporary observer noted in 1922: "He is enormously concerned for prohibition, world peace, godliness, and homliness [sic]. To hear those causes argued skillfully, earnestly, these Chautauqua folk will welcome Mr. Bryan until he and they are no more."[16] There was a sense among all present that Bryan and Chautauqua audiences were bound together through a set of waning belief systems. "He belonged to them; he knew it and they knew it. He was 'the Great Commoner.'"[17]

Bryan was so popular his imitators on the Circuit came as close as they dared to impersonating the Great Commoner. To those who could not see Bryan,

R. H. Cunningham offered himself as the next best thing. "For ten years Mr. R. H. Cunningham has followed the great COMMONER. . . . He has studied the messages of Mr. Bryan, analyzed his platform work, dissected his popular lecture 'THE PRINCE OF PEACE,' until today its philosophy is a part of Mr. Cunningham's being; its phraseology a part of his vocabulary, and its spirit a part of his soul. He has given this lecture until it has been burned into him by the hot fires of forensic experience so that its delivery is an art and its effect a sermon."[18] Cunningham never claimed to be Bryan and never claimed that Bryan was a role to be acted. His performance, however, highlighted Bryan's unacknowledged theatricality. Chautauqua and Bryan ignored this paradox, but ultimately it came to define both of them.

William Jennings Bryan was Chautauqua in many ways; he lent his name to it, he trumpeted its virtues repeatedly in public address and print, and he continued his association with it even when he was fiercely criticized for doing so while serving as secretary of state from March 1913 to June 1915 in Woodrow Wilson's administration. His most obvious contribution, however, was his oratory, as a biographer notes. "During the nineteenth century, the central position of speech-making in politics and religion produced great orators. Bryan's star rose toward the end of that tradition; unquestionably he ranks among the very best."[19] Oratory was at the heart of Circuit Chautauqua. While it was also known for music and, later, drama, Chautauqua was identified to the end with lectures of various kinds. Bryan's presence and talent brought luster and credibility (in the eyes of some) to oratory on the platform. His manager stated emphatically: "I think he was the greatest speaker in Chautauqua, and . . . he did more to enliven and extend [that] movement than anyone else."[20] This position was hardly surprising, as throughout the nineteenth century oratory and democracy were inseparable for most Americans; in fact, oratory was understood as the means through which democracy was both created and honed.

Oratory's place in democracy was troubled, however, by changing political practices, emerging technologies, and evolving audience expectations. Even Chautauqua audiences, renowned for their stubborn nostalgic embrace of older cultural traditions, were looking for more daring forms of performance. Great public oratory was on the way out and being replaced, especially on the platform, by elocution, which itself was being radically challenged and revised, and by theater. Audiences were increasingly receptive to openly acknowledged theatrical performance. William Jennings Bryan is emblematic of the path of oratory in the United States. He and Chautauqua were both engaged in the struggle over performance's, especially highly theatricalized performance's, contradictory relationship to national identity. Although his work is silent on the subject of theater, it is not hard to imagine that Bryan shared his audience's distrust of the form. Yet he was embedded on the platform in one of the oldest types of suspect entertainments in the United States, the variety show. These contradictions clashed on the platform, radically altering who and what were presented and how they were seen.

"American nationality was largely created through the pulpits and platforms of the land."[21]

Integral to the complicated relationship between oratory and nation was one unshakeable belief. In no other country than the United States, as Yale University rhetoric professor Chauncey Allen Goodrich wrote in the early nineteenth century, was "the power of impressing thought on others through the medium of language so controlling in its influence as here."[22] Certainly pioneering American studies critic and scholar Constance Rourke thought that was so. Performance was central to her definition of American culture. One of her first works to reach a wide audience was a serious appreciation of vaudeville published in the *New Republic* in 1919. Rourke's first book turned to "popular expression" (her term) as the site of what was essentially American. In 1927, at the tail end of Circuit Chautauquas, Rourke published *Trumpets of Jubilee*, focusing on a signal foundational trait: "Words—the popular mind was intoxicated by words; speech might have provided liberation; sheer articulation apparently became a boon."[23] What for Rourke was a practice that had since passed in the nineteenth century was only beginning to wane on Circuit Chautauqua. By 1927 oratory, in its nineteenth-century form, had mostly disappeared from the national scene, and the Circuits were barely limping along; Chautauqua, however, was providing oratory's last stronghold.

Public speaking had not been simply an expression of opinion. For most nineteenth-century Americans, it was the means through which patriotism's agenda could be articulated. If the "great public speaker has ever been a tremendous force in American affairs," as the 1925 Redpath-Horner program claimed, it was because that speaker articulated "in words the hopes, aspirations and ideals, which patriots have later wrought in deeds."[24] Oratory provided a means for the nation to define itself, testing and refining how citizens might see themselves as American. Speakers who "proclaimed the ideals of America and debated her problems" were working with their audiences to formulate what the United States could and should be.[25] Charles Horner himself said, "I have always been very much interested in the power of the spoken word."[26] He believed the Chautauqua platform to be more effective and authentic for representing and debating public opinion than any other venue, including political campaigns and rallies.

Oratory put the author and audience in direct contact with one another. It was a fundamental public ritual, common at almost every type of event, "the face-to-face encounter of speaker and audience sealing the democratic pact," as theater historian Benjamin McArthur proposes.[27] Respected speakers sharing information, advice, opinion, anecdotes, and observations were expected fare because that was what Americans did when they gathered, especially, as the nineteenth century closed, those who lived outside urban areas. The *New York Times* intoned in 1926: "The single art which is fully appreciated by rural Americans of all classes is the art of public speech."[28] This nineteenth-century ritual survived well into the twentieth century on Chautauqua platforms removed from the changes occurring more rapidly in urban centers.

If democracy, and thus the United States's fate, was dependent on each citizen's participation, then Chautauqua functioned as a place where that citizen could participate in the oratorical culture that undergirded democracy. In 1919 one observer warned: "The fate of the democratic experiment lies in the hands of Everyman, and Everyman needs to have his judgements tried in the fires of common counsel."[29] Chautauqua's boast was not idle, and certainly millions of Americans heard ideas and news they would not have otherwise (particularly before the advent of radio). Communication scholars Frederick J. Antczak and Edith Seimers propose: "No assessment of Chautauqua can be complete without taking into account its involvement of ordinary people in discussions of public policy in matters of real public import. . . . Chautauqua generated, and to some extent maintained even to the end, an oratorical culture that was substantively ambitious and publically influential."[30] These discussions of public policy kept rural citizens feeling involved in and vital to the larger nation, one that, as has already been discussed, seemed less and less interested in them and their concerns. When Robert La Follette, Champ Clark, Jacob Riis, various governors, and secretaries of departments like commerce or agriculture spoke on the Circuits, audiences experienced a direct link with the larger world and, by extension, themselves as important participants in that world. But participation alone was not sufficient to make a citizen. A person had to be worthy of the honor, and being worthy meant having a moral character equal to the many responsibilities of citizenship.

Circuit Chautauqua did not struggle over the role of performance in morality, citizenship, and democracy because it was Chautauqua—or, rather, not simply because it was Chautauqua. The question of the role of performance in those discourses was prevalent across the United States. The other large and popular Circuit variety entertainment, vaudeville, may have been Chautauqua's despised rival, but it, too, had to envision itself in terms of prevailing national and cultural issues.

Vaudeville's promotion of itself as an agent of democracy, unlike Chautauqua, had less to do with what occurred onstage and more to do with the accessability of the stage itself. One of vaudeville's founding figures, impresario Edward F. Albee, regarded vaudeville "as very democratic because it offered something for everyone."[31] This understanding is less about enabling democracy's function, as Chautauqua viewed its mission, and more about functioning within democracy's principles. But this articulation of democracy is no less valid than Chautauqua's. Vaudeville served a cross section of the population, and its popularity demonstrated that it did so effectively. It could also say, as Chautauqua did, that in looking out from the stage one saw America. In a 1918 "how-to" manual for would-be vaudeville managers, Edward Renton cautioned his readers that "it should never be forgotten that the theater draws people from all sorts and conditions; in particular does the vaudeville house draw from both the classes and the masses."[32] But even vaudeville knew that representing America was more than just having a range of people in the audience. It was also morality and respectability, that is, being worthy of democracy.

An audience member might be excused for being occasionally confused about the boundary between vaudeville and Circuit Chautauqua. Both could fall under Robert W. Snyder's definition of vaudeville as "a series of acts strung together."[33] An argument could be made that both shared some historical roots. Sociologist Richard Butsch notes: "Variety, a bill of entertainment composed of a series of unrelated acts or bits of entertainment, has a long history. Early American theater bills resembled variety, offering miscellaneous entertainments between acts of a full-length play and a comic skit after the play. The bill included whatever might divert the audience: dancing, singing, juggling, acrobatics, demonstrations of scientific discoveries."[34] Many of the acts in the two venues were, in fact, the same. Reciter S. T. Ford, discussing the materials in his Chautauqua act, observed offhandedly, "It is a good joke anyhow and the people . . . will never know that it was originally a vaudeville gag."[35] Most performers were not overly worried about drawing many distinctions between what they did in vaudeville versus Chautauqua. One performer, Richard Oram, admitted that while touring, "every once in a while I would sit back and think, we were doing vaudeville."[36] William Jennings Bryan, for all his moral rectitude, could have looked to some like he was on the vaudeville stage. Since Bryan rarely booked his Chautauqua appearances early enough to appear in the program (especially after 1910), it is not always possible to say with certainty which acts might have appeared on every bill with him. But it is almost certain that the same yodelers, birdcallers, impersonators, ethnic singing groups, and comic lecturers that populated the rest of Chautauqua framed Bryan when he lectured.

Refinement and respectability were important concerns of every performance form of the time. While Chautauqua appeared to be detracting from Bryan's prestige, vaudeville used Chautauqua-like strategies to increase its own standing, as Allison Kibler demonstrates in *Rank Ladies*. "The leading vaudeville magnate, B. F. Keith, voiced a philosophy of cultural uplift . . . that depended largely on attracting respectable female patrons and highbrow performers, from Shakespearean actors to learned lecturers."[37] Benjamin Franklin Keith, who is credited with the creation of big-time vaudeville with its constant infusion of new and high-quality acts, wanted to ensure that middle-class audiences thought of his theaters in conjunction with respectable entertainment. Anyone who appeared in his theater knew that she or he would have to present material appropriate for the "refined audience who are characteristic of Keith's." This desire for respectability dated back to the middle of the nineteenth century, when "variety halls adopted strategies of legitimate theaters to attract a family clientele."[38] The raucous audiences such performances attracted could not generate the revenue brought in by middle-class audiences. This movement toward the "family" audience "set the precedent for marketing to women, which Tony Pastor and others further developed in the 1870s."[39] In the late nineteenth and early twentieth centuries, managers like Sylvester Poli (a contemporary of Keith's and Albee's) continued the trend. "Poli tried to differentiate his shows from rowdier, lewder variety halls, burlesque theaters, and concert saloons, thus reinforcing a cultural hierarchy that equated culture and civilization and 'refinement.'"[40]

While vaudeville would have liked its history to be an unbroken movement toward increasing respectability, it was more like a tug-of-war between owners who wanted to please certain types of audiences and others, including performers, managers, and some audiences, who wanted racier fare. By the second decade of the twentieth century, certain admirers of the form thought that vaudeville, in its attempt to play it safe, was also condescending to audiences who would have thrived on more challenging material. At the same time, however, critics thought that vaudeville was losing its battle for decency and that it was less and less appropriate for family audiences. In addition to questions of morality was the fact that vaudeville often mocked the very respectability it purported to offer.

Vaudeville always subjected "the cultural hierarchies it endorsed" to "self-reflexive critique."[41] Its "multilayered publicity and variety acts onstage upheld the ideal of a genteel culture cordoned off from the working classes but also mocked that refinement."[42] This was alien to the Chautauqua stage. Bryan believed in the Chautauqua mission and spent his entire life embodying it. Those performers who did not share this zealous mission were advised to keep their opinions to themselves. On the platform, successful performers limited themselves to material, habits, and beliefs congenial to their audiences. Allen Albert, for example, cautioned in 1922 that the lecturer "imperils his service in any cause by any unnecessary attention whatsoever to card-playing, to dancing, to sex, to non-Christian religion, to any theory of any philosophy that threatens the security of property."[43] From that perspective, there was no confusion at all about the differences between vaudeville and Chautauqua.

For some audiences, vaudeville could never dissociate itself from its less-refined and immediate origins, as Kibler remarks, "nineteenth-century popular theater, namely, the tradition of 'aggregate' entertainment: the heterogenous offerings in the minstrel show, the concert saloon, the variety theater, and the dime museum."[44] In addition, most Chautauqua audiences would not likely have had access to big-time vaudeville, which tended to be more reputable. They would have seen small-time vaudeville, and "lively audiences and rowdiness seem more prevalent in small-time compared to big-time vaudeville."[45] Not only did those roots determine vaudeville, but vaudeville was also troubling because it addressed "multiple perspectives on urban life."[46] Urban and dissolute were traits enough to damn vaudeville for rural Chautauqua's supporters.

The differences of setting and origins, however, did not absolve Chautauqua of its own struggle around respectability. Nonetheless, unlike vaudeville, it did not focus solely on the performance material. Circuits went to great lengths to assure that Chautauqua performers lived the ideals they performed on the platform. Dr. William Sadler, speaking at the 1923 conference of the International Lyceum and Chautauqua Association (ILCA), reminded those present that the "lack of moral character and ethical understanding may not always seriously handicap an actress, entertainer, or musician on the American stage today, but such a lack of moral worth is, and I believe will always be, sufficient cause for disbarment from the platform of the American Chautauqua."[47] In 1914 the Star Chautauqua System program read: "THE STAR CHAUTAUQUA SYSTEM is distinct in that it refuses to place on its programs anything than what the best Christian people can endorse and the most cultured enjoy. . . . No member of talent is placed on the program whose personal habits are offensive in any way."[48] The management had to be able to guarantee morality in order for audiences to trust that this was indeed Chautauqua, where such a concern was a priority.

Journalists, too, let the public know that this was the case. *Collier's* described in 1923: "Chautauqua's managers realize their responsibility to the millions and take it very seriously indeed. No lecturer is ever employed until he has been heard in public by an official representative of the organization; no performer is ever engaged until it is known that he is a solid respectable citizen."[49] As the experiences of Gay MacLaren and Fern Donahue demonstrated and the numerous letters in business files indicate, these standards were rarely met.[50] While performers were not always as morally upright as Chautauqua demanded, they were urged to be seen to have reformed themselves for the summer at least. "As a general rule a discreet entertainer anxious to avoid harming the institution he represents, will be very careful about admitting he smokes, dances, or plays cards; and especially that he has ever consumed alcoholic liquor."[51] Even in the 1920s, when many of these prohibitions were falling away in the larger culture, Chautauqua understood that its audience clung to older standards of behavior. But the Circuit's emphasis on the personal conduct of performers was only part of the strategy for ensuring respectability and morality.

While B. F. Keith may have put "learned lecturers" in vaudeville as a play for respectability, they were by no means standard or popular fare on that venue. For Chautauqua, lectures were, conversely, the source of its unique identity. Of all the kinds of lectures on the Circuits, the essential lecture, the backbone of the movement, was the inspirational lecture. Paul Pearson pointed out as early as 1906 that "special pleaders for great moral and political reforms are always in demand."[52] That demand was part and parcel of the desire for uplift of respectability so promised by Chautauqua. Harry Harrison remembered humorously: "These lecturers 'inspired,' and culture hungry rural America devoured their cheerful words. Wheat growers in the Dakotas, western cattle men, corn and hog farmers in Iowa, dairymen in Wisconsin, cotton planters in Tennessee, one or all might disagree violently with a political lecturer, or dispute business facts, but none was crass enough to object to 'mother, home, and heaven.' None sold virtue and honesty short."[53] If uplift and entertainment was the rallying cry of Chautauqua, the inspirational speaker was to be the fulfillment of its promise.

Bryan's only competition for the most revered speaker on the Circuits was Russell Conwell. One journalist wrote in 1924: "Dr. Russell Conwell's famous oration, Acres of Diamonds, is the ideal toward which all inspirational lecturers strive."[54] Conwell did not set out to be a lecturer. He had followed several careers, but he studied theology and in the early 1880s was offered the ministry at the Grace Baptist Temple in Philadelphia. In a few short years that church had one of the largest congregations in the world.[55]

Grace Baptist was primarily known for its dynamic preacher, who could hold crowds spellbound with his message of Christianity, Populism, hard work, and free enterprise. His fame and message spread beyond Philadelphia through his "Acres of Diamonds" speech. In forty years Conwell gave this speech over 6,000 times, most of these deliveries occurring on Chautauqua platforms. He used the proceeds of his lecture work to fund the various institutions he founded, including Temple University.

The speech's message was simple: being poor was sinful, being rich was a sign of inner goodness. "You have no right to be poor."[56] In true Progressive spirit he emphasized that wealth had to be earned and not inherited. "I pity a rich man's son. . . . A rich man's son cannot know the very best things in human life."[57] Inheritance, Conwell reiterated, sapped the will and divided the rich from their communities. He assured his listeners that the opportunities to become affluent, that is, to find their own "acres of diamonds," were right there in their own backyards, and there was no need to leave home to seek them.

Adults who had heard the speech when they were young brought their children to hear Conwell speak. Like Bryan, he was important enough to inspire imitators. Swarthmore Circuit Chautauqua founder Paul Pearson discovered his own approach to the platform in 1897, years before he began his Swarthmore Circuit. In that year "the idea of the 'lecture-recital' crystallized, and this distinctive format that was new to the platform was to be Paul Pearson's trademark for the rest of his life. Thus, for some thirty-nine years he delivered hundreds of these inspirational lectures that were combined with poetry readings."[58] Amos Elwood Reynolds remembers that when he attended the Swarthmore Chautauqua during the second and third decades of the twentieth century, "Dr. Pearson would give the Acres of Diamonds lecture once a week all summer."[59] Performance gave audiences access to Conwell even after his death in 1925.

Conwell's "massive power, his strength as a preacher and lecturer, did not lie in ideas, but in inspiration."[60] This was the template for inspirational speakers. Content, other than the appropriate moral certainties, was not important. Emotion and audience experience were. George C. Aydelott, for example, began as an impersonator in 1908, but after 1912 he "devoted all his energies to that great work [of inspirational lectures]." His lecture "The Man For Today" demonstrated, Chautauqua assured its audiences, that Aydelott "knows folks and it is about them and to them that he speaks. He speaks with amazing power. His lectures are inspirational, but they contain a world of real thought and sound philosophic truth. They glow with wit and humor, but they teach the deep and sincere. He has been called 'The man whose heart is as true as steel and as pure as gold.'"[61] Occasionally, the Circuits did not even bother mentioning content and went straight for the lecture's effect. Redpath-Vawter presented Dr. George R. Stuart in 1909, whose "power over an audience is nothing short of marvelous. One moment the people are convulsed, the next moment they are in tears. One moment they are lost in self-condemnation, [the next] they are lifted to the heights of moral vision that makes it absolutely impossible to descend to the old planes of common and sordid living."[62] The task facing an inspirational lecturer was daunting, as *Everybody's Magazine* pointed out in 1915. "Your real inspirational lecturer takes firm hold of all science and all Art and of all History and of all everything else and concocts from them a blend of profuse information and of homely wisdom and of rugged humor and of dauntless optimism which braces your courage and unlimbers your kindliness and sends your ambitions soaring upward out into the blue night over the white tents to the stars which you look at with a dominating eye as you walk home."[63]

This formulaic approach did not go unremarked. Those who looked at Chautauqua with skepticism pointed out, as Gregory Mason did in *American Mercury* in 1929, that the "lecturer must be more than merely informative or entertaining; he must also have a Message. The messianic delusion of the lecturer, plus the self improvement complex of the audience—there is your Chautauqua equation."[64] Additionally, Roland W. Baggott and Philip McKee argued in 1931, content could bring people to think but could not be thought-provoking. "The lectures, however, were safe and uplifting. Not one word in any of them departed at all from the fixed channels of orthodox thought and belief, as charted by the combined Baptist and Methodist clergy."[65] Lecturers were often booked because their position jibed with that of the Circuit managers. In preparing for the 1929 season, for example, Crawford Peffer of New York–New England Redpath wrote Keith Vawter suggesting that lecturers be chosen to speak on "American ideals" in order to "uphold the Administration of standing by the President. Already it seems to me there has begun in the metropolitan area of New York, a reaction on the President; nothing pronounced in the Republican newspapers, but insidious and artful references which have a discrediting import."[66] This letter leaves no doubt that the platform was being manipulated to support a specific political perspective. It is not surprising, then, that others believed that the commercialism of the Circuits had "degraded the quality and spirit of many Chautauqua organizations."[67] As that observation was published in *Outlook* in 1927, many had begun to turn away from Chautauqua.

The inspirational lecture was the most popular form of oratory on the platform, and it is easy to situate it within a specific tradition of oratorical performance. Elocution, the art of graceful and mannered public speaking that emphasized gesture, vocal command, and delivery and whose texts tended to be drawn from literature, is very difficult to define more than in a broad and general way. Certainly, experts and amateurs alike during Circuit Chautauqua's time disagreed vehemently about what constituted elocution. But the stakes were high because almost everyone agreed that the fight went to the very heart of morality, citizenship, and self-improvement.

"Mere literature will keep us pure and keep us strong."[68]

In *Democratic Eloquence: The Fight over Popular Speech in Nineteenth-Century America*, Kenneth Cmiel stresses: "The nineteenth century debate over language was a fight over what kind of personality was needed to sustain a healthy democracy."[69] Chautauqua had participated in that debate since its founding in 1874, and the Circuits in particular are evidence of its vitality into the early part of the twentieth century. Speech had been singled out in that debate as critical evidence of an individual's respectability and refinement. These two values, popular belief had it, were central elements of education and fitness for citizenship because, as Cmiel observes, "an educated people guarded the republic and an educated people were an articulate people."[70] Self-improvement, so valued by Chautauquans, was concomitantly community and national improvement. Whatever improved one improved the other. The nation was the citizen and vice versa, "eloquence and republicanism flourished and perished together. . . . Learning rhetoric . . . was both a personal and public good."[71] The way most people learned rhetoric, particularly those outside the professions of law and the ministry, was elocution. By the time of the Circuits, elocution had largely come to mean the oral recitation of literature. Literature was the ground on which much of the fight over American culture was fought. Future president and Circuit supporter Woodrow Wilson's unqualified belief that literature ennobled and nourished people prefaces this section as the epigraph. He wrote those words in 1893 while a professor at Princeton University, where he was known as a champion of "humanistic and inspirational themes," an approach to literary study that resonated outside the academy.[72]

Many of these belletrist professors participated in projects that made education popularly available. Whether it was "Dr. Eliot's sixty inches of printing" or the "[sincere supposition] that 'culture' is generated in 'courses' and proceeds as by nature from the lecture platform," as two journalists wryly described the situation in the late 1920s, these experts most commonly recommended encounters with great literature.[73] Universities were confident that literature was fundamental to training a person, as Paul Edwards's study of literature and performance in the United States put it, to be "a responsible member of society."[74] Undergirding even popular approaches to elocution was the assumption that, rhetoric scholar Nan Johnson wrote in 1993, the "dramatic reader benefits intellectually and morally from both the study and the performance of the work, and the audience is similarly improved by experiencing the actual performance and by being exposed to the subject and the rhetorical qualitites of the work."[75] That elocution, the intersection of literature and performance, could produce morality and citizens was the very foundation of Circuit Chautauqua.

Despite this certainty, an argument had to be made in defense of elocution's value. In an era that saw public and verbal self-presentation as commensurate with private and moral character, elocution promised to produce the type of speech that identified a person as educated and respectable. Proponents of elocution emphasized that speech separated those worthy of respect and advancement from those without potential. No one who mastered the lessons of elocution could be seen as "ill-bred," a sure sign that one was failing morally. Nan Johnson observes: "Popular elocutionists stressed the relationship between the study and practice of elocution and the development of 'well-bred' qualitites by pointing out that the practice of correct speaking through dramatic reading and conversation elevates the mind in the same way the study of great orations enhances the powers of expression."[76] A contemporary elocution textbook made the case in absolute terms. "The value of the study of spoken language can scarcely be overrated. The human voice is a great power among men. It is human nature to want to hear truth presented in the most interesting and, if may be, the most vivid manner; and although the daily papers have become the medium of conveying to the masses current news and general information, it is still the province of the public speaker *to convince men and move them to action*. This can be done through the living voice and manner."[77] Chautauqua seized on this message in its embrace of oratory: proper speech can effect moral action. That embrace was not without cost, however, as elocution's place and value were very much under examination during the turn into the twentieth century.

Philosophers since Aristotle have debated rhetoric's theory and practice, but developments in the eighteenth century directly influenced its evolution in the United States. Specific training to improve oratorical "delivery" emerged about 1750 in the United States.[78] By the end of the eighteenth century it was a respected and influential part of the curriculum in higher education. Every university and college, especially those that prepared students for the law or the ministry, required proficiency in elocution, and that proficiency was the hallmark of an educated person.

Even as elocution was advancing in the academy, it was also emerging as an influential popular movement. Nan Johnson notes: "The most successful and widespread branch of popular rhetorical education in the nineteenth century was the elocution movement, which was supported by the general public's keen interest in oratorical skills and the popularity of the practice of rhetoric in the public forum and the parlor. Interest in oratory and elocution was especially intense, encouraged by numerous and varied occasions for oratory and elocutionary performance serving a variety of political, cultural, and social functions."[79] School children learning to read, for example, were evaluated according to "pronunciation and voice," and elocution was also part of adult education outside universities and colleges.[80] Two authoritative popular texts were L. T. Townsend's *The Art of Speech* (1885) and Adams Sherman Hill's *Our English* (1888). Both volumes began as Chautauqua lectures. "The books were used in the Chautauqua reading course, reaching some sixty thousand people every year."[81] Unlike volumes for those engaged in professional training, these popular texts, and others by Alexander Melville Bell, Merritt Caldwell, and J. H. McIlvaine, encouraged people to be self-taught or taught by teachers without formal credentials.

Ordinary people without links to either the professions or the academy could practice elocution at home and with friends. Texts were readily available with "selections for . . . the public . . . , especially . . . appropriate material for performance at social events and in the home."[82] When Chautauqua actor Bob Hanscom was traveling on the Circuits, he fell ill and remained in one town for several days, recovering. His doctor took great interest in him and in conversation accurately identified Hanscom as a novice performer. Surprised, Hanscom acknowledged his inexperience. The doctor, Hanscom remembered, "had done readings himself and they were his favorite form of entertainment."[83] He suggested some selections to Hanscom. "He recommended 'The Pencil Seller' by Robert Service and 'Boots' by Rudyard Kipling . . . [and] through the years my reputation as an impersonator was built on those two poems."[84] Popular elocution kept the public's interest in it keen for many years, even after some academics had dismissed it as superficial.

The two movements, popular and academic, were not synchronous, however, and elocution enjoyed its academic dominance until the 1870s, when it began to fall out of favor in higher education. Many academics did not see elocution as a "branch of study based on philosophic or scientific principles," two speech historians noted in 1954.[85] By 1873, for example, the University of Texas School of Oratory included a "disclaimer in [its catalog] to the effect that [its] objective was not to train elocutionists."[86] But the growing discomfort about elocution within the academy was not reflected popularly. Local schools, usually run by women, thrived into the 1930s, and popular interest in oratory survived well into the twentieth century.

One thing everyone from the amateur enthusiast to the seasoned platform performer to the university professor adamantly agreed upon was that literature was central to any venture into self-improvement. By choosing material from "written works, which (collectively) 'are the *best expression* of the best thoughts of men,'" the performer could help audiences move closer to the mutual goal of morality and respectability, as Margaret Prendergast McLean affirmed in the early twentieth century.[87] This connection was unquestioned. Two early theorists of the oral interpretation of literature declared: "There can be no doubt that through the creative and appreciative experiences, the individual may enjoy a richer and fuller life, and that through this enjoyment his personality may be greatly cultivated."[88] No Circuit hesitated to assure spectators that its speakers would move the audience toward that goal.

Katharine Ridgeway's entire career was predicated on the uplift of literature spoken in performance. Sometimes called the "Queen of the Platform," she emphasized in a 1910 interview that her aim "was to read something that would prove a lesson and an inspiration to her audience." Ridgeway was "considered to be the most eminent of the interpreters of miscellaneous programs by many managers as well as other readers."[89] She began performing in 1896 and continued to do so until the early 1930s. Her program was always about two hours long, and she offered changing excerpts from prose, poems, and plays, among which were *Suppressed Desires* by Susan Glaspell and *The Finger of God* by Percival Wilde, to musical accompaniment, often original compositions written for her. It was not simply her skill and talent that made her so appropriate for the platform, it was also because her life was seen as "an inspiration in itself."[90] The daughter of an impoverished Civil War officer, she moved with him to Washington State, where she taught in lumber towns, usually sharing a bed with her pupils, until she discovered elocution and moved to Boston to train for a career in the field. Chautauqua went to great lengths to ensure that its audience knew it was presenting only the most appropriate performers. Morality could be produced in the audience through performance but only by performers who possessed it themselves.

Lucille Adams, for example, who did selections from *Little Lord Fauntleroy*, *Peg O' My Heart*, and *Such a Little Queen* by Channing Pollock, was another performer who capitalized on an intersection of moral art and life as her identity. In a testimonial for her, Frank Gunsaulus, a respected minister and inspirational lecturer, affirmed: "Miss Lucille Adams' work is beautifully conceived and splendidly executed. She is one of the first women on the platform to interpret really fine representations of human feelings and thought in the best literature. She is a woman of high character and is realizing excellent ideals."[91] Gunsaulus sounded every major theme: Adams's work is the "best literature," her moral character is "high," and she offers "excellent ideals." Like Ridgeway and many of the other women on the Circuits, it was very important to remind audiences that performers were living the ideals that they preached.

Speech scholars Frank M. Rarig and Halbert S. Greaves note that despite their suspicions about popular elocution as "too much the performer's art [that] did not meet the needs of the students who were being trained for the professions," "many of the pioneer speech educators were also entertainers."[92] Robert Maclean Cumnock, who founded the School of Oratory, Speech, and Performance at Northwestern University, was greatly admired for his delivery of material in a Scottish accent. Cumnock especially was highly respected at Chautauqua, both as a platform performer and as an adviser. His presence at Chautauqua served not only to bolster his personal reputation but also that of Northwestern and helped attract students. Also at Northwestern from 1909 to 1941 was James Lawrence Lardner, well known for his readings of Shakespeare, Dickens, and Browning.[93] Samuel Silas Curry, considered by many to be the most important teacher and theorist of his time, founded the School of Expression at Boston University in 1888 and was a dependable presence on the New York Chautauqua platform. Solomon Henry Clark, an influential teacher and theorist at the University of Chicago, also appeared regularly at the Chautauqua Institution. Even his peers found Clark impressive. Maud May Babcock, from the University of Utah, wrote: "There is no difficulty in keeping the characters distinct when one hears Mr. Clark read The Melting Pot or The Servant in the House, and yet the messages of both plays are greater and more impressive than would be the case did he impersonate and attempt to embody the outside rather than project the soul of his man and woman."[94] Performing was important for these academics not only because "presentations . . . on the Chautauqua circuit inspired many youthful spectators to test their own histrionic powers and brought new talent to the reading field" but also because academics felt strongly that their presence elevated and challenged popular elocution, which many feared was, as one academic put it, "rubbish."[95]

Since the 1890s academics had been gradually disowning popular elocution: they founded professional organizations that excluded popular practitioners; relabeled what they did as suggestion, reading, or oral interpretation; and inveighed against popular practices at every opportunity. Thomas Clarkson Trueblood, from the University of Michigan, for example, would not be called an elocutionist, insisting, "Let us get rid of that abominable name 'elocutionists' that is down in the mud. We have tried for fourteen years to pull it out of the mud and it will not pull, it is there—not 'elocution,' but 'elocutionists.' Let us get it out."[96] Maud May Babcock epitomized those views in a paper she delivered in 1915. An elocutionist, she argued, had no higher aspiration than to entertain, a goal unworthy of the field.

> It would be hard to say just why readers desire to exploit themselves as impersonators or imitators of bells, bugles, birds, or beasts, or accompany their work with music, or costume it, unless it be to surprise the audience with the startling and extraordinary, the unusual and marvelous. Since they cannot convey the author's purpose so well, and since impersonation defeats the end in literature, it must be for personal display. Real literature will not lend itself to such imitative treatment, and there are few, if any, opportunities in things of literary worth to exploit one's ability as an entertainer.[97]

Babcock called for "suggestion" as a more appropriate focus than "the imitation of bugles, bird notes, bells, moaning, groaning, tremolos—all this rubbish which has brought our profession into disrepute with the thinking public."[98] She protested that she was not against the very existence of those who would do "birds, beasts, or musical instruments" but that those forms of imitation were inferior and must not aspire to be more than what they were. "The objection is, therefore, not to the *doing* of such stunts, but to the doing of them under the *misnomer* of elocution, reading, interpreting, public speaking, and reciting."[99] It was Babcock who so praised Clark for his readings of Israel Zangwill and Charles Rann Kennedy, and this raises questions about what exactly literature was and how it might be delineated from "rubbish."

When Babcock dismissed the "rubbish," she was dismissing some of the more beloved Chautauqua attractions. She was probably thinking of someone like Elma B. Smith, "reader and impersonator," who was credited in 1905 with being "unquestionably the greatest imitator of children and birds now before the public. Her imitations of birds, babes and children are a unique feature of her work. Her bird warbling is the best on the platform to-day. Her imitations of children are so real and lifelike that they are the talk of the Chautauqua for days after her departure."[100] More than ten years later the same kind of work was still a staple on the platform. Tom Corwine was billed in 1916 as a "Polyphonic Imitator and Fun Maker. A unique figure among America's entertainers. Possessed of an acutely developed faculty for imitation, working upon lungs, mouth and lips he imitates everything from a bumble-bee to a sawmill or a Mississippi River steamboat. If you want to laugh, and laugh, and laugh, hear Corwine."[101]

Lew Sarett was another prominent Chautauqua performer on the Northwestern faculty, but his work probably fell far short of the standards Babcock shared with so many of her colleagues. Sarett recited his own poetry, often dressed as a Chippewa Indian.[102] In 1917 Redpath-Vawter proclaimed:

Sarett will wear the costume of the wilderness guide and will tell tales in the dialect of the French-Canadian. He will sing the songs of the Chippewas, rollicking squaw dance songs and the plaintive lullabies of Indian mothers. He will play Indian music and dance the weird dances of the medicine men. He will impersonate, with remarkable realism, the Chippewa chiefs as they deliver with aboriginal power and naive humor their council talks at tribal pow wows. Throughout the address Mr. Sarett will introduce several of his original wilderness poems.[103]

Sarett may have represented a less-elevated form of elocution and Chautauqua performance, but many wanted to follow in his footsteps. In 1922 Sarett offered a course at Northwestern titled "The Lyceum and Chautauqua Lecture-Recital" in response to the keen interest many students displayed for going on the Circuits.[104]

Clearly, the category of literature was more elastic than one might assume. While there were plenty of elocutionists offering readings from Shakespeare, Dickens, Tennyson, and Poe, and few would dispute characterizing those authors' works as literature, there were many more performing works like *The Little Shepherd of Kingdom Come*, *The Darky and the Boys*, and *Peg O' My Heart*. These titles are more appropriately categorized as popular literature, not a genre that critics of elocution recognized as literature at all. That Clark, who told the extremely successful platform artist Gay MacLaren in no uncertain terms that "I was nothing but an actress—that I knew nothing of the reader's art of suggestion. I had better go to New York and 'join a theatrical troupe'—there was no place for such a performance on the Chautauqua platform," was celebrated for reading a play like *Servant in the House* or *The Melting-Pot* seems absolutely paradoxical.[105] What haunted these attempts to distinguish among types of readings was the way in which theatricality colored and shaped notions of performance.

Literature was more a front, a distraction from the real issue. While there was great agreement that contact with literature was morally and intellectually improving, there was no strong disagreement over how to apply the term literature. The disagreement, as Babcock's paper makes abundantly clear, was really about performance. If William Jennings Bryan was considered a great orator and moral influence, it was not because of the content of his speeches, which even fellow Chautauquans thought "so full of generalities that little of it . . . actually stayed in the listener's mind."[106] Instead, it was because, as one biographer analyzed, when "Bryan spoke on the Chautauqua circuit . . . he seemed to extemporize. He delivered the same speeches over and over, honing the delivery, sharpening the metaphors, testing new phrases, and discarding those that failed to provoke the desired response."[107] In short, he was an excellent performer. He could make a tired old speech seem fresh and new each time he delivered it. Audiences shared the belief in the moral value of literature, but they wanted great performance as well. They were still wary of theater, but they were more than ready for the theatrical.

Some invoked theater more directly by performing it as much as the content of the text. Gay MacLaren was the most renowned performer in this vein. Her work as an elocutionist, or as she called herself, a "dramatic artist," was to perform theatrical productions.[108] As Harry Harrison described, "She needed to listen to a Broadway hit only five or six times, without ever having seen the script, before she took it on the road. She created each character, imitating the styles and voices of the stars who played the New York leads."[109] MacLaren would attend several performances of the same production and subsequently be able to re-create the entire production in performance. Everyone who remarked on her was taken with her ability to remember and reproduce.

The reaction of Glenn Frank, president of the University of Wisconsin and former editor of the *Century* magazine, was worth quoting at length in her publicity materials.

> "I'll be interested to see how she *interprets* these characters," I said to my friend, "for I saw the original production. I wonder what she will make of 'Jimmy.' Will she have the same conception that Frank Craven had when he created the role?"
>
> "Oh," said my friend, "You miss the point. Miss MacLaren doesn't create or interpret any character. You see she isn't just a 'reader' of plays. She reproduces the original performance with all the accuracy of a Victrola record. It isn't Miss MacLaren's 'Jimmy' you are about to see; it is Frank Craven's 'Jimmy.'" . . .
>
> I can only say that the illusion was perfect. It was not a reading. It was not an impersonation. It was a re-creation. The original cast lived and acted again.[110]

Frank's testimony provided a narrative of experiencing MacLaren's work for the first time, illustrating the movement from polite interest to incredulity to enthusiastic supporter. Most of the testimonials she collected from famous people repeat that narrative form. This was important because it "proved" that MacLaren faithfully reproduced a text, rather than inventing one herself. She was not a theatrical actress but an impersonator and had not sacrificed her moral respectability or community standing in order to perform. This allowed her to escape the opprobrium attached to the theater and remain morally untainted safely within the Chautauqua fold.

Many of her peers were trying to do the same thing in their own way. An acknowledged theatrical illusion was palatable, even welcomed. A 1912 season program described Arthur Kachel in the *Music Master* in glowing terms: "The distinctness of the various characters, each portrayed with an appreciative understanding of human nature and showing the finest touches of interpretation, makes them seem to be separate actors in a moving drama, and the audience forgets that but one man occupies the stage."[111] Probably the most notorious in this line was M. C. Hutchinson, who had in her repertoire plays including *What Every Woman Knows*, *The Importance of Being Ernest*, and *Rebecca of Sunnybrook Farm*.[112] She was known for her exuberant performances in which she enthralled audiences by "changing her voice, making love to herself, responding, breaking in as a great blustering villain, resuming as a mild shrinking maid, creating and maintaining the illusion to the last curtain—and finally taking her bow, alone, on behalf of 'the entire cast.'"[113] While to twenty-first-century sensibilities the distinction between MacLaren, Kachel, and Hutchinson, on the one hand, and theater, on the other, may seem virtually nonexistent, in the world of Chautauqua it was believed to be a wide and unbridgeable gulf indeed.

"The old time medicine show is gone—the worst of the street carnivals are nearly gone, not because of any tirade or campaign against them, but because the Chautauqua has led the people away from such coarse horse-play."[114]

Keith Vawter's claim was ironic. Even if Chautauqua could take credit for such a triumph (from the Chautauqua perspective), much of what had been eliminated in those venues was sneaking in the through the flaps of the brown tent. Chautauqua did not so much lead "people away from such coarse horse-play" as give the horseplay a new look and present it on the platform. Some people, usually those who already thought little of Circuit Chautauqua, were not fooled.

When William Jennings Bryan appeared on Chautauqua in 1915, one poster advertised: "TEN BIG DAYS. AFTERNOON AND NIGHT—TWENTY RICH ROYAL SESSIONS—LITERARY, MUSICAL, ENTERTAINING, INSTRUCTIVE,

DEVOTIONAL, INSPIRATIONAL, AND LIFE BUILDING—UNDER THE GREAT PAVILION OUT IN THE OPEN—NEXT TO NATURE'S HEART. . . . COME ONE, COME ALL."[115] The fact that Bryan continued to speak on Chautauqua after he became secretary of state made him the object of much criticism in the national press. "No previous Secretary of State has 'chautalked,' they complained."[116] Defenders were quick to point out the special mission of Chautauqua and that President Wilson himself had approved Bryan's appearances. The greatest cry was that Bryan was staying in touch with ordinary citizens. But even Bryan's biographers did not always understand the distinction. One wrote censoriously in 1969: "He should have given up Chautauqua at least during his first year in office . . . for his billing as part of commercial enterprise comparable to a vaudeville show lessened his personal dignity as well as that of his office."[117] While Chautauquans would have been horrified at Chautauqua being mentioned in the same sentence as vaudeville, the luster that Bryan brought to Chautauqua was at the expense of his own reputation.

Chautauqua may also have cost Bryan the sharpness of his intellect. William Shirer, working on the Circuits in the early 1920s, was thrilled to see his idol speak in person. But he was quickly disabused of the notion that what he was seeing was the Bryan of the 1896 Democratic convention.

> He had become, it seemed to me, an empty shell, a vain and foolish old man. But if, more than any other person, he had made chautauqua, it was obvious by 1920 and 1921 that chautauqua had destroyed him. It stifled his mind, deadening him against the reception of new ideas as the world continued to change. . . . His eloquence remained unimpaired, as did his magnetism at the tribune. But even as he continued to sway the masses with his repetitious oratory, he retreated more and more from reality, perhaps unaware of the banality, the triviality, of the haven he had found under the chautauqua tents.[118]

Shirer's harsh portrait points out something very important. As Bryan's political oratorical talents had faded, his oratorical performance had stayed as sharp as ever. This is the heart of the paradox about Chautauqua and performance. While from the distance of a century it may seem that the lines between political oratory and elocution are clearly drawn, a closer examination reveals that the two were intermeshed and that the distinctions dear to Chautauqua's heart do not exist. This had important implications for Chautauqua's identity as the embodiment of oratory as a signal democratic tradition.

Oratory generated controversy not simply because of an ongoing feud between popular and academic practitioners. It created controversy because it was so embedded in the battle over respectability, literacy, and morality.

Elocution was about being a citizen: "Republicanism was government by discussion as opposed to force of fiat. Speech was more important to a republic than any other kind of polity," as Kenneth Cmiel argues.[119] Citizenship was not a static experience, as the Circuits emphasized repeatedly; it was achieved and reachieved through relentless self-improvement, and elocution was at the heart of that process. Chautauqua's experience, rather than its rhetoric, implied that theatricalized performance was an essential component of citizenship.

Audiences, managers, and performers alike all believed some version of the idea that "the state of mind of the speaker can be inferred from tones and inflections of the voice, movements of the body, and expressions of the face."[120] There were a great many contradictions to be sure—performers were sometimes less than morally scrupulous, managers made decisions based on profit at the expense of other concerns, and audiences resisted challenges to their belief systems—but all engaged in Chautauqua truly believed that by performing from a state of moral rectitude, the performance would have a greater effect on the audience. In a history of women's elocution schools in Dallas, Texas, Judy Baker Goss observes about all such enterprises: "Much of what underlay their commitment was a belief that an appreciation of literature and moral character were intimately linked."[121] Even if literature was a highly qualified category, its presence seemed to elevate Chautauqua above other performance forms like vaudeville. But the very theatricality the Circuits tried to evade was animating the presentations.

The superiority of oratory and elocution was an article of faith in Chautauqua. Theater, its nearest competitor, was seen as falling short of elocution's ability to uplift audiences. On the platform, as Bahn and Bahn describe, the "reader . . . stands alone without special costuming or scenic effect. . . . [B]y his choice and his action he must so vividly convey both characters and scenery that the spectator forgets the reader and lives in the world of his characters."[122] Even Gay MacLaren, presenting the suspect theater on the platform, was noted for her ability to disappear. One reviewer noted, "Those who are familiar with Mrs. Fiske forgot the young lady who was giving the presentation and saw again their old favorite."[123] Circuit Chautauqua believed that elocution was of greater quality because it connected the spectator more directly with ideas and democracy. The reader was invisible, elocution's champions claimed, while the actor was the entire focus in the theater. Most were confident that theater would never appear on the platform. But in 1913 all that changed.

In 1904 an unknown photographer took a series of pictures while William Jennings Bryan delivered one of his typical addresses. These four images give a sense of Bryan's expressive range in performance. Nebraska.

R. H. Cunningham

In an evening's entertainment presenting the
Hon. William Jennings Bryan's masterpiece

"THE PRINCE OF PEACE"

R. H. Cunningham presented himself as an expert in "presenting in form, tone, gesture and purpose the great messages of others." Bryan's "Prince of Peace" lecture seems to have been the one for which Cunningham was known. Arizona.

This billboard, from the 1910 Maryville, Missouri, Circuit Chautauqua, trumpeted the feature attractions of the week. Iowa.

Russell Conwell was young Harriette Kohler Smith's favorite lecturer. When the Swarthmore Circuit came to town, he stayed with her family, and she remembers being very proud to have such an important figure at her house. Iowa.

Those who knew him described Paul Pearson as an exceptionally charismatic manager and performer. Iowa.

Modern Lectures
Modern America
by
GEORGE C. AYDELOTT

George Aydelott claimed that his authority as a speaker derived from "his vast knowledge of life through his intimate relationship with men and their problems." Iowa.

INTERSTATE PLAYERS Present **The Music Master**
Starring BOB HANSCOM, Character Actor, Supported By An Excellent Professional Cast

BOB HANSCOM

Bob Hanscom saw little difference between elocution and acting; in fact, he thought of himself as an actor. Iowa.

THE KATHARINE RIDGEWAY
CONCERT COMPANY

Direction:
Redpath Lyceum Bureau
Boston and Chicago

THE COMPANY:
MISS KATHARINE RIDGEWAY, Reader
MISS AGNES C. YARRALL, Pianist
PERC GEORGE W. JENKINS, Tenor

Katharine Ridgeway was noted for the special care with which she selected her elegant costumes. She epitomized for many the ideal lady, and Harry Harrison said her "soft voice" was a large part of her appeal. Iowa.

182

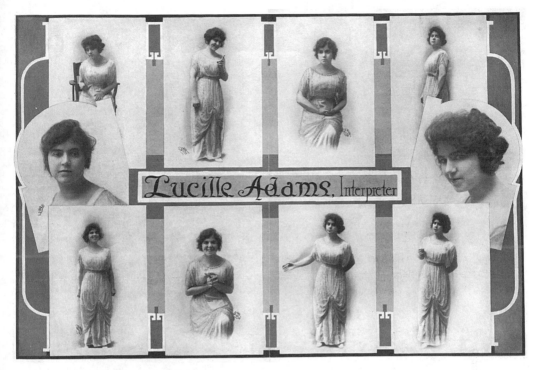

Lucille Adams's publicity materials emphasized her range as a performer. Iowa.

Lew Sarett did not reference his work as a college professor; instead he focused on his hearty outdoor identity as America's "Foremost Woodsman/Poet." Iowa.

Lew Sarett

The
Woodsman-Poet

From her childhood as a spectator to her entire career as a performer, Gay Zenola MacLaren's understanding of performance was shaped by the demands of the Chautauqua platform. She used her publicity materials to emphasize the ways in which she changed herself for each new character she portrayed without losing sight of her elegant and refined offstage identity. Iowa.

Like MacLaren, M. C. Hutchinson was known for presenting entire plays. One of her specialities was the works of Shakespeare, and she had five of his plays in her repertoire. Iowa.

For those near the back of the tent, the speaker would be very small indeed. Iowa.

CHAPTER FIVE

Performance on the Platform Theater

In 1913 the Redpath Bureau sent the Ben Greet Players out on Circuit Chautauqua. They opened the week of May 18 near Albany, Georgia, and toured for almost fifteen weeks, closing near Pittsburgh.[1] They had two plays in their repertoire—*Comedy of Errors*, "with every tart Elizabethan phrase that might wound soft sensibilities" excised, and a similarly bowdlerized *She Stoops to Conquer*.[2] This booking was a daring choice on the part of the Redpath Bureau. It had no wish to squander its reputation as a desirable community venture, but it did wish to further its commercial success. Theater seemed an obvious choice for audiences who, as Harry Harrison commented dryly, "wanted the thrill of the drama, the fun of make-believe . . . performers who for a rapturous hour could transport them out of a drab, mud-bound world into fictional far places and other, better times."[3] The challenge was to include theater as a demonstration of Circuit Chautauqua's conformation to community values, albeit an unusual one that chanced being viewed as a loss of respectability.

Most of the rural (Protestant) churchgoing audiences thoroughly believed that theater was, according to one Chautauqua memoir, "big city evil" and "the handiwork of the devil."[4] Managers were understandably apprehensive because they were violating a long-standing taboo against theatrical production. Their patrons' distrust and dislike of theater as an immoral, urban, and vulgar practice were well documented. Paul Pearson noted simply, "As Chautauquas were sponsored by the churches, and organized by ministers, drama was unthought of."[5] Harrison knew full well audiences "did not want actors. They had seen what they called 'actors' in that disreputable free medicine show last year and all the other tawdry outfits that straggled into town to corrupt impressionable youth."[6] Yet, with their hearts in their mouths, Redpath managers elected to send the Ben Greet Players out on the Circuits, even though the introduction of theater risked the distinctions they had made between "disreputable" entertainments and the respectability Chautauqua had established and the trust it had earned.

Other Chautauquas had tried to introduce theater with little success and much uproar. Soon after the New York institution's founding in 1874, for example, the Reverend J. M. Buckley inveighed against theater, claiming that those attending a national touring production of Gilbert and Sullivan's *H.M.S. Pinafore* were "selling out their whole Christian influence."[7] Buckley "expressed his sense of shock at learning that a church choir from Philadelphia had gone out to act it [*Pinafore*] 'all over the country.'"[8] When the New York Chautauqua subsequently produced *Pinafore*, it was as a concert, not a full-fledged production. Buckley's denunciation was typical of the Chautauqua Institution's stance on theater. Even as late as 1910 Max Eisenstat, manager and director of the Cleveland Playhouse who eventually ran the Chautauqua Institution's theater programs, noted that Chautauqua "shared the opinion, then common among many church-going people, that there was something inherently sinful in the production of plays and in the acting profession."[9] Integrating theater loomed as a risky departure for Chautauqua.

The enormity of this venture was not lost on Redpath and Harry Harrison. They recognized that this could be a turning point for Chautauqua audiences if handled carefully by the managers. Harrison wrote Greet: "You know Mr. Greet I believe in putting on good plays with good people. I mean good both off and on the stage. They will do much to bring the church and the stage together and away from the prejudice that is now in the minds of most of the better thinking people."[10] Introducing theater was not done naively, and there was more than a whiff of missionary intent behind what would turn out to be a sound business decision.

The introduction of theater to Chautauqua did not go quite as Redpath and Harrison expected. "With hands cupped to ears Redpath waited for the reaction. The storm of moral indignation that had been feared did not materialize. Instead came shouts of praise. By the time the company reached [the end of its tour] crowds were gathering at the big brown tent two hours before the program."[11] Rather than protests or outcry, Chautauqua found that audiences willingly welcomed the theater. Harrison says simply, "People liked both the play [*Comedy of Errors*] and the players," suggesting that it was a combination of Shakespeare and Ben Greet's specific approaches to production.[12] The theater succeeded beyond their greatest hopes. Charles Horner noted later that the "experiment was so successful after the first attempt at play producing, almost every Chautauqua program included a drama of some sort and often more than one. . . . Plays were so popular and drew so well, that when we had begun to offer them there was no way to stop."[13] Redpath set the pace, and other managers and Circuit companies quickly joined Redpath in the presentation of fully produced plays. Theater was a success, and in the late 1920s it would be the primary draw for audiences.

As chapter 4 demonstrated, Chautauqua performance was contested terrain, even without theater. Chautauqua was founded as a rejection of evangelical Protestantism, which bequeathed a mixed legacy: an embrace of spectacular public emotion and performance and a simultaneous horror at its expression. This contradiction would ultimately be used to redeem theater, the very enterprise that so many evangelical Protestants distrusted. Ben Greet, his work, and his reputation proved pivotal in that redemption, as will be explored more fully later in the chapter. As theater solidified its position on the Circuits in Greet's wake, managers continued to defend theater's presence long after its successful integration. This ongoing, and probably unnecessary, struggle illustrates the Circuits' inability to relinquish the belief that theater had no place on Chautauqua.

"And the [Chautauqua] Assembly was totally unlike the camp-meeting. We did our best to make it so."[14]

Chautauqua's disdain for camp meetings and its distrust of theater were in many ways the same position. Camp meetings and theater both licensed overt displays of emotion, and both depended on the illusion of spectacle to sway audiences. There were differences between the two forms to be sure. Chautauqua never saw revivals as anything but morally correct, even if they were a public display of unrestrained irrationality. Theater, on the other hand, was both immoral and irrational. There was no place for either camp meetings or theater in the ordered Chautauqua universe.

Camp meetings had been a part of evangelical Protestantism since the eighteenth century. Revivals could draw tens of thousands and, as religion scholar Nathan O. Hatch depicted them in 1989, were "awesome spectacles indeed, conjuring up feelings of supernatural awe in some, 'the air of bedlam' in others."[15] The evangelism of nineteenth-century Protestantism was less a matter of theological indoctrination by scholarly experts and more a concern of improvised performance both on the part of the preacher and the congregation. Writing on democracy, literature, and performance, Alessandro Portelli comments: "In camp meetings and revivals, the event was as much in the collective emotions of the crowds and in their physical and musical expressions as in the sermons that were preached. Indeed, the preacher's success began to be measured on their [sic] ability to excite these reactions."[16] Just as revivals were becoming more predictable, more people were finding this kind of worship distasteful. By the mid-nineteenth century "wealthy and fashionable Methodists were turning their back on exuberant revivals."[17] But wealth and fashion were not the only reasons some Protestants were rejecting the revival form.

Chautauqua itself was born out of a rejection of revivalism and its emotional extremes. Both of its founders expressed a distaste for and a distrust of revivals. In 1872 cofounder Lewis Miller attended a session at the Ohio State camp meeting. He was joined by two women from his hometown of Canton, Ohio, who taught Sunday school. A 1974 history of Chautauqua relates: "They sat a great distance from the crowd, since none of them had a taste for revivalism. The ladies were surprised when Miller asked, 'Girls, wouldn't it be a good idea to have a Sunday School Camp Meeting?' They questioned the proposal, but Miller explained that what he had in mind would not be a camp meeting in the familiar evangelistic sense."[18] What he had in mind was something that harked back to eighteenth-century investments in expertise and rationalism that had shaped early camp meetings.

Bishop John Vincent was of the same mind as the two women. In fact, he was very wary of Miller's idea.

> At first Dr. Vincent did not take kindly to the thought of holding his training classes and their accompaniments in any relationship to a camp meeting or even on a camp ground. He was not in sympathy with the type of religious life manifested and promoted at these gatherings. The fact that they dwelt too deeply in the realm of emotion and excitement, that they stirred the feelings to the neglect of reasoning and thinking faculties, that the crowd called together on a camp meeting ground would not represent the sober, sane, thoughtful element of church life—all these repelled Dr. Vincent from the camp meeting.[19]

Vincent objected to revivals for almost the same reasons he objected to theater—both were uncontrolled and unrestrained displays of emotion that could lead to dangerous moral choices. At a time when one's outward behavior was understood as a indicator of one's inward worth, making public feelings that were assumed to be more properly private flew in the face of bourgeois respectability.

When Chautauqua opened its New York gates, Rebecca Richmond's 1943 history of the New York Chautauqua reports, "there were many . . . who were expecting to find the familiar features of a camp meeting; they were indignant when they learned that exhortation and a call to sinners to repent had no place on the program and that voluntary and spontaneous gatherings were not permitted."[20] Their indignance was not unreasonable, as historian Jeanne Kilde succinctly observes, "although Chautauqua was not precisely a camp meeting, it was located on a former camp-meeting site."[21] In fact, Miller and Vincent had searched for a name for the gathering that would not call to mind "a revival camp-meeting style religion with its sapping emotional hysteria" but indicate its distance from it, Circuit Chautauqua performer Irene Briggs Da Boll and her husband, Raymond F. Da Boll, recalled.[22] Chautauqua was, however, still a product of evangelical revivals, even if only in its rejection of them. Vincent and Miller were both devout Methodists (Vincent, of course, was a bishop) and embraced the Methodist commitment to spreading the word. As with camp meetings, the natural, rural setting was central to Chautauqua philosophy. Chautauqua sprang from an evangelical culture. Religion scholar Mark A. Noll observes that in Chautauqua, as in many other institutions in the United States at that time, "much of the visible public activity, so great a proportion of the learned culture, and so many dynamic organizations were products of evangelical conviction."[23] Even the Circuits, with their roots in New York and Lyceums, were also products of Methodism's circuit-riding belief that a traveling preacher could knit a congregation together. In this case, however, the congregation was a nation.

Protestants might be divided over appropriate revival practices, but there was more unanimity around objections to theater. Most antitheatrical rhetoric oscillated between two characterizations of theater. The first was that theater itself was inherently evil and thus impossible to redeem or recuperate. The other view of theater was that it was not evil or immoral, in and of itself, but that evil and immoral behaviors, people, and actions had been associated with it, making it a dangerous and threatening enterprise by association. It was this second understanding that the managers capitalized on and which ultimately allowed them to make a case for the acceptance of theater.

For many people in the late nineteenth and early twentieth centuries, immorality was constituent of the very nature of theater itself. What theater meant was clear and unequivocal. "'Theater' meant painted women and dissolute men. . . . It meant cheap vaudeville and the cancan and chorine hussies who not only displayed ankles but brazen knees to the public gaze."[24] Like many other Methodists, the Reverend Buckley, who had so objected to *Pinafore*, was absolute in his condemnation of theater. He summarized his objections in 1904, the year the Circuits began, as not about content but "the general effect, general character, general associations, and the relation of the whole institution to the progress of Christianity."[25] Theater's impurities contaminated all those who came in contact with it, as Jonas Barish summarized the antitheatrical attitudes that emerged from the eighteenth century. "Any traffic with the Theater, whether as participant or spectator, must enroll a man in the legions of the damned."[26] These characterizations of theater offered no hope, because they implied that theater's immoral nature was transcendent and unchanging. As *Lyceum Magazine* put it decisively in 1919: "The difference, then, between the platform and the stage is a moral one."[27] Religion played a key role in promoting these attitudes toward theater, and many ministers were influential voices against theater. Chautauqua's Christian grounding, as well as the support from churches that it heavily relied on, did not allow it to take this critique lightly.

Bishop Vincent, when asked about theater, said that he put it on his "'Better Not' list."[28] His attitude was typical of many religious leaders. "Methodists, Baptists, and Presbyterians alike rallied against it."[29] Methodists, who were most closely allied with Chautauqua, were the most sweeping in their condemnation of theater. In 1887 they established the Methodist Amusement Ban, as theater historian Benjamin McArthur explains, which "stated that a member could be reproved or even expelled from membership for patronizing certain amusements, including the theater."[30] Despite this draconian measure, there is a good body of evidence that large numbers of Methodists attended theater by the end of the nineteenth century and that few churches actually enforced the ban. The theater community was fully aware of the Methodist ban. As he was founding the School of Oratory at Northwestern University in 1878, Robert Cumnock considered leaving academia for the more lucrative legitimate stage. In a history of Northwestern's School of Speech, Laura Miller Rein narrates: "A backstage visit to the McVickers Theater in Chicago swiftly dissuaded him from making a serious move when he confronted actor James O'Neill, who sneered, 'Well, here's one of those ——— ——— Methodists from Evanston who wants to act.' That insult, combined with the generally bohemian backstage atmosphere, discouraged the proper professor from attempting commercial acting."[31] While the ban was not yet official policy,

O'Neill, father of playwright Eugene O'Neill, clearly recognized Methodism as a leader in the religious objections to theater (he also may have been expressing a typical actor's opinion of elocution). The ban was remarkably hardy and divisive. Despite annual debates, it was not repealed by the General Conference until 1924.

New York Chautauqua was not immune to the controversy. Francis Wilson, a prominent comedian and singer, was one of the leaders of the artists' fight against the Syndicate. His first appearance in Chautauqua was in 1900 when he spoke on the journalist and children's poet Eugene Field, who had recently died and about whom Wilson would publish a memoir the following year. Wilson's lecturing experience was a successful one, and "an instantaneous regard sprang up between him and his audience." Given that he was also known for his large library and commitment to learning, it is not surprising that he organized a Chautauqua Literary and Scientific Circle (a guided-reading course that provided year-round instruction) in his acting company. He returned to the New York platform often after that initial visit and could be counted on to "plead for the actor's calling as legitimate and useful." In 1910 Wilson staged a one-act play, The Little Father of the Wilderness, by Austin Strong (in which he had premiered on Broadway in 1906), as part of a pageant of Chautauqua history and "astounded the audience by denouncing the Methodist ban."[32] Wilson's direct action had little effect on the presentation of theater on the Chautauqua platform. Neither New York nor the Circuits changed their practices, perhaps because Wilson was arguing with those who thought theater essentially corrupt. It was a different understanding of theater that would ultimately allow for redemption and change.

The other position late-nineteenth and early-twentieth-century Circuit managers could take was that theater was immoral only by association. Theater itself was not evil, this approach argued, but because of practices connected to it, it had, inevitably, become disreputable. In 1911, for example, young women were warned that theatrical managers were often "white slave traders" who used theater's glamorous lure to entice their victims, as Susan Harris Smith describes in her study of the place of drama in considerations of American literature. Many saw theater as a disruptive, masculine enterprise where "rowdy behavior and prostitution prevailed."[33] These contexts made theater unthinkable for those who claimed social or religious respectability. The editor of the Chautauquan warned readers that "in close proximity to every theater there are saloons and gambling rooms."[34] Tellingly, news about the theater was often in the same newspaper sections as sports and crime reporting, offering through juxtaposition a judgment on the activity itself.[35] Circuit audiences combined a wariness of theater with an antipathy toward medicine shows, circuses, and revivals, as well as racier forms like burlesque. Nor were audiences totally wrong. Burlesque, for example, often lived up to Chautauqua audiences' fears. One such theater, in Independence, Missouri, where Bob Hanscom's company played in 1926, "was musty and evil smelling and many of its seats were broken. The floor was filthy, and rats scurried around beneath the customers' feet. The theater enjoyed a doubtful reputation of being an excellent spot for unrestrained loving. There were generally a dozen or more couples locked in amorous embrace who never glanced toward the show. We played there, however, to packed houses each week—partly because of our show, and partly because of the necking privileges."[36] The line between character and context was obviously a fine one. Whether Hanscom's anecdote demonstrates that people are openly sexual because performance is morally bankrupt or that performance is morally bankrupt because people are openly sexual is ultimately unknowable. Circuit managers, however, had the historical changes happening in theater on their side.

There were historical antecedents to audience objections to theater, as theater historian Faye Dudden documents: "The woeful reputation of the early [American] theater as a place of sexual dissipation was in effect confirmed by the presence of prostitutes in the third tier of boxes."[37] By the period of Circuit Chautauqua, however, most of these offensive elements, particularly prostitution and theater rowdies, were distant memories, as theater managers had worked hard from the 1830s through the 1850s to eliminate barriers to middle-class and female spectators.[38] But these efforts were sporadic and intermittent and reached fewer rural audiences than they did urban ones. There were other changes, however, that would help bring theater onto the platform. Theater had been largely a local endeavor in the first two-thirds of the nineteenth century. While there were touring performers and companies, most audiences attended theater performed by their local stock companies. In the 1870s "first class stock companies declined precipitously" and were replaced by combination companies, as theater historian John Frick notes.[39] Combination companies were essentially a package deal: rather than a touring star performing with a local company in its production, as had been common practice, the touring star brought an entire production complete with actors, sets, costumes, and repertoire. Small towns would get one night of performance only, and larger towns and cities could count on a longer run. Antitheatrical prejudices did not condone building theaters, but it was the rare small town that did not have an opera house or academy of music in which to present these popular combination companies.

Ministers who themselves began to argue for theater's redemption through reform probably had more impact on audiences than combination companies, available spaces, and changing audience practices. The Reverend Charles M. Sheldon was a Congregationalist minister who was renowned for *In His Steps* (published serially in 1896 and then as a book in 1897), which founded the approach later summarized as "What would Jesus do?" The book was immensely popular; in fact, it was a best seller for over sixty years, and Sheldon was approached many times about dramatizing it.[40] He declined because he was unsure that Christianity could be properly presented on the stage. Ultimately, however, in 1901 he called for a Christian theater because "this desire to picture life upon the stage is a desire that will always be a part of the human being's life."[41] The question for Sheldon was transformed from "is theater moral?" to "how can theater be made moral?" He commented that, as a minister, he could not attend theater because "I am not able to avoid the conclusion that at least half the plays which are at present put upon the stage in the great cities are not helpful to the Christian life of those who attend them."[42] If the theater should become Christian, Sheldon concluded, its influence and importance would be "wonderful." This kind of argument opened a space for the Circuits to make their case for theater, a case they very much wanted to make despite their reservations. During the life of Circuit Chautauqua, entertainment would "become one of the largest industries in the country," as theater historian Thomas Postlewait argued in 1999, and Chautauqua would not be able to resist this larger national trend.[43]

"Mr. Greet has been doing important missionary work for the stage for some years."[44]

This one sentence from about 1911, two years before his work appeared on the Circuits, illustrates how well suited Philip Ben Greet was to be the first to bring theater officially to Circuit Chautauqua. He did not just appear in or manage the theater, he improved it. Such an attitude, that theater was in need of reform but also was capable of being reformed, fit neatly into the developing Chautauqua argument. A man of the theater who had a long-standing reputation for working actively to make theater morally upstanding was just what the Circuits ordered. Greet's company had been touring in the United States since 1902 under Charles Frohman's auspices, including a highly acclaimed performance at the White House for President Theodore Roosevelt. The Ben Greet Players were among Frohman's many British imports. One of the most powerful theatrical producers of his time, Frohman dominated the

American stage for more than twenty years by introducing new works, faces, and productions to the American stage. Greet's outdoor productions in the United States were popularly received as a return to the production conditions of Shakespeare's time.

Greet, who had worked with William Poel and was greatly influenced by him, was opposed to the theatrical conventions that dictated heavy and impressive scenery.[45] Both men believed that contemporary production practices, elaborate box sets, and lengthy scene changes did a disservice to the plays. Greet shared Poel's conviction, as Robert Speight analyzed in 1954,

> that [Shakespeare's] fellow-Elizabethans could not adequately be contained within the limits of the proscenium stage; that they were harmed by realistic scenery; and that the rhythm of the plays was destroyed by the intervals that those accessories imposed. He had come to see, and was now incessantly to preach, that Shakespeare the poet was his own scene painter and electrician. He believed that although Shakespeare had indeed written for all time, he had not written out of time; that as he had seen the world through Elizabethan eye, so must we recover that vision if we wish to do him justice.[46]

Poel's first attempts at historical authenticity did not meet with great favor, but his work eventually set the standard. He and Greet collaborated on an outdoor production of Everyman in 1901. It was the most successful of all Poel's productions and formed the basis for the work that Greet and Frohman toured in the United States. Poel's legacy to Greet was work that struck "a note of adult education and sober self-improvement," and this was the perfect approach to introduce theater to Chautauqua.[47]

Crawford Peffer, manager of New York–New England Redpath, who was known for presenting the "ablest lecturers, musicians, and entertainers," was the first to connect Chautauqua with Greet by contracting him to provide a company of players for Peffer's Lyceum circuit in 1910.[48] Peffer believed Greet's company to be the "natural selection" to bring theater to Circuit Chautauqua because, as Alan Hedges makes clear, "[Greet's] reputation as a Shakespeare scholar was already established in America . . . and . . . his repertory primarily consisted of plays by Shakespeare, an author Chautauqua audiences found it hard to disdain."[49] Peffer shared the Chautauqua emphasis on education, seeing his productions as a way to enrich the lives of ordinary people.[50]

Part of the prepartion for theater, especially Greet's approach to it, had been made coincidently by lectures that repeatedly emphasized Shakespeare's genius. Most of the lecturers were university professors supplementing their salaries by taking their expertise on the road. Truman Joseph Spencer of

Connecticut State College and F. C. Tilden of Depauw University were only two of those who exhorted Shakespeare as relevant to audiences' lives in the years before 1913. Frederick Koch of the University of North Carolina, who himself would go on to be central in the development of community and educational theater, spoke on "Shakespeare and His Relation to Modern Life" in 1915.[51] Such lectures were also sometimes a way to sneak actual actors from the legitimate stage onto the platform. When Richard Mansfield's acting company folded after his death, Mansfield's leading man, Walter Howe, created a combination lecture and dramatic reading both to describe and demonstrate Shakespeare's dramatic work.[52] While this programming had not been part of an overt effort to create a context for producing theatrical works, it must have contributed to audiences' willingness to attend and support theater once it appeared.

Audiences who were still wary of theater's power to deceive often focused on production values such as costumes, scenery, lighting effects, and makeup as marks of the iniquity of theater. Harry Harrison observed that one reason readers were accepted on the Circuits was because "their 'stage' was an empty platform; scenery they manufactured out of the air."[53] This was an acceptable mode of performance, while fully realized productions had not been. Redpath reassured those concerned about theater's dissembling by emphasizing the benefits of the lack of scenery. Greet's approach, Redpath promised, "shows what effect can be produced by a good play, interpreted by capable and well-trained players, even with the barest possible stage."[54] Greet, too, offered assurances. He promised audiences that in She Stoops to Conquer, "scenery is simple and will be composed on screens painted to represent an Old English Home of the Period."[55] Even production values are recuperated. They become less a sign of falsity and more a convenience to provide context. Theater was becoming less and less threatening.

Programs deliberately downplayed the presence of theatrical elements, directing the audience's attention instead to Greet's expertise.

> Mr. Greet is considered today one of the greatest living authorities on the English drama and is world-famous for his remarkable productions of Shakespearean plays and old English comedies. He has been connected with the stage for thirty years and has taught many actors; perhaps more than any other living man today.
>
> For twenty years Mr. Greet has been prominent in England for performances in which his splendid companies have acted each year in London, Cambridge, Stratford-on-Avon, and other places in "Shakespeare's England."[56]

Greet was primarily positioned as an educator rather than a theater practitioner. In fact, as early as 1911 when his work was being booked on the Lyceum, this was precisely how it was received. The *New York Evening Post* reviewed one production in those terms. "This is the real educational theater in which the constant aim [is] to familiarize its audiences—especially the budding playgoers of the rising generation—with acknowledged masterpieces of literature and drama, and thus enable them to discriminate between solid worth and beauty and the merely luxurious, sensational, and meretricious."[57] Greet's personal authority on the subject made it imperative for Chautauqua audiences to see his company perform. Greet's approach promised to improve their understanding of an author they already revered; consequently, uplift and entertainment would be served. Greet may not have appeared with his companies, but they were "personally directed by him from his New York studio and an occasional visit to where the players are appearing."[58] It did not hurt, either, that the program made a slight attempt to elide Shakespeare and Greet—Greet apparently dwelled in "Shakespeare's England," a neat historical trick.

Newspaper responses indicated that Circuit spectators approved. In one clipping sent to the management after a performance in Indianapolis, Indiana, the reviewer wrote warmly, "The plays given by him are given in pure fashion with the minimum stage effect. There is nothing to detract from the play itself."[59] Hedges emphasizes that in Greet, "Peffer found an actor who . . . was exhibiting presentations of the irreproachable plays of the Bard of Avon in surroundings that suggested almost nothing of the undesirable associations of theaters."[60] These practices on Greet's part made him an excellent fit with Circuit Chautauqua's needs. Greet's work, Chautauqua seemed to be promising, was a natural and unremarkable extension of oratorical practices.

"The play was in!"[61]

Chautauqua talent had always included professional actors who made their living in the theater, legitimate and otherwise. The managers were practical businessmen who realized that trained and experienced actors would give excellent performances. Harry Harrison, who convinced many theater professionals to tour the Circuits, noted that managers were determined to book the "finest readers they could find," and "if some of these readers happened to be Broadway actors and actresses, out to make an honest summer dollar, so much the better, provided the folks out front could learn the horrid truth gradually. Instead of hackneyed recitations from elocution books, these artists brought fresh materials and methods to the tents."[62] Arthur Row, who performed on the Circuits in the early 1920s in *It Pays to Advertise* and *Crossed Wires*, reflected the theater's bafflement at an arbitrary and artificial boundary. "The actor in Chautauqua is a comparative novelty, in fact only a few years ago the idea was treated with utmost scorn by the powers that rule the 100 percent American institution known as Chautauqua. Actors are born and trained to entertain, but for some inscrutable reason the combination of actors and Chautauqua was deemed impossible and something not to be considered."[63] Actors, whether they were acknowledged as such or not, saw the Circuits as simply another performance opportunity and made little of the issues around morality and improvement that so preoccupied Chautauqua.

Some came from less legitimate venues. Bob Hanscom recalled with humor how in the mid 1920s he secured a Chautauqua contract for his small theater company for the following summer while members of his company were earning their living in a burlesque house. "Out of burlesque a Chautauqua company was born. That should make the culturists turn over in their graves."[64] His humor turned to concern one evening in 1926, however, when he realized that his Circuit manager was in the burlesque audience. "[I] looked right into the eyes of Dr. E. J. Powell, my circuit manager for the summer. He was laughing uproariously at the antics of his cultural performers. He never mentioned, during succeeding days and years, that he saw me on the boards of burlesque, and I never found out how he happened to be in the obscure theater."[65] Obviously, both were bound to silence because neither could admit that he was in a burlesque house.

In 1915 the Redpath managers tried again to see if they would have the same luck with contemporary drama as they had with Ben Greet's Shakespeare. "Again we waited. In spite of a good start this adventure might have a sad ending. But again it did not. . . . Small-town America was ready to pay hard-earned half dollars, and finally dollars, to see high class, decent plays, ready to accept the haunting odor of greasepaint."[66] The play that clinched Chautauqua's move into theater was Charles Rann Kennedy's *The Servant in the House*.

The play had opened on Broadway in 1908 and had enjoyed much success in various productions around the country. Set in a single day, the play follows the difficulties of an English vicar as he struggles knowing that "God and Mammon are about us, fighting for our souls."[67] His family is in disarray, and his church is literally disintegrating. The family eagerly awaits his long-lost brother, the bishop of Benares, who is rumored to have built the richest, most successful church ever. It turns out that the bishop is already there, masquerading as the butler. The real masquerade in this modern morality play is that the brother/butler is actually Jesus Christ, who intones to the vicar and his wife: "Now let me tell you exactly why you have sent for me here. There is a strange and wretched turmoil in your soul: you have done wrong, and you know it—but you don't know all! You would keep what little miserable right you have by bolstering it up with further wrong."[68] With his help, they commit to transforming their lives, and the play ends on a triumphal note. Kennedy's work may also have been reassuringly safe to the Circuit managers for a reason other than content. He and his wife, the actress Edith Wynne Matthison, who played the vicar's wife on Broadway, had performed with Ben Greet's company in the tours of the United States that Frohman had organized. While not involved in the 1913 Greet/Chautauqua venture, the Kennedys' connection to Greet could only have made this play seem the perfect vehicle to bring contemporary theater to the platform, although there are no surviving records that make this connection.

It did not take long for theater to become touted as one of Chautauqua's leading attractions and services. "The most popular feature of the whole Chautauqua program is the play. Those who deplore the combined influence of the movies and high railroad rates in destroying traveling theatrical companies, should not overlook these productions which give ten million of our fellow citizens their only contact with the spoken drama from one year's end to the other."[69] This 1924 argument, that Chautauqua is theater, is an astounding one given the decades that Chautauqua spent differentiating itself from theater. In fact, after all that struggle, Chautauqua often received national attention because of its theater.

Perhaps because of Circuit Chautauqua's relentless focus on the moral issues surrounding theater and its wariness of most production values, at first little attention was paid to the work as theater. Contemporary commentators, expecting the worst, often found that the performances were compelling. "The entertainment provided is good. I have seen—believe it or not—magnificent acting on the Chautauqua platform, passages from Shakespeare in which the actors sounded deeply the depth of that great master. And I have seen modern comedies delightfully performed. The reason for this, I think, was that the Chautauqua players did not enjoy the advantages of the best costuming, scenery, staging, and lighting. Whatever effect they produced had to come almost entirely from within themselves."[70] This opinion, from 1931 at the end of the Circuits, marks how adept they had become at touring theater.

The Circuits did not throw caution to the winds, however. Theatrical productions in the first few years were performed in the mornings, and evenings were still reserved for oratory and music. This put theater in the weakest performance slot and the one most likely to have the smallest audiences.[71] By the

1920s, however, plays had become so important to the Circuits that their productions began to appear on the covers of the programs. Rather than depicting the pastoral idyll of Chautauqua, some programs featured the casts of the plays themselves. White and Myers's 1922 program featured an image of a demure young woman and her horse to introduce *Polly of the Circus*, Margaret Mayo's play, which had premiered on Broadway in 1907 and was later adapted into a novel.[72] Redpath put photographs of two productions, *Nothing But the Truth* and *H.M.S. Pinafore*, on its 1920 program cover, giving audiences a choice of performances.[73] Theater was also moved to the evening in the 1920s, promoting it to the most coveted and influential spot in the production. It was this move, more than any other, that cemented theater's permanent presence on the Circuits.

Even though the Circuits trumpeted the virtues of rural life over an urban one, they could not escape the national trend that used the imprimatur of the large city, usually New York, to guarantee the quality of their theater. *Friendly Enemies* "played on Broadway for two years," one Circuit promised.[74] "Ran two years in New York, one year in Chicago" was the assurance that accompanied *It Pays to Advertise*.[75] *The Bubble* had a "strictly New York cast."[76] The shift from local stock companies to combination companies not only denied local communities their theatrical autonomy, it also participated in the further centralization of cultural activity in the city. John Frick argues: "New York's reputation as a theatrical center, which prior to 1870 was due to the quality of its first-class stock companies and its ability to influence theatrical tastes, came to depend on its role as the principal supplier of America's entertainments."[77] One of the many ways theater transformed Chautauqua, although not one of the changes that the managers anticipated or discussed, was to ally it more closely with the urban industrial culture that the Circuits were supposed to be resisting.

By 1924 a spectator would have been hard-pressed to tell the difference between Chautauqua theater and other itinerant theater forms. Even though throughout the 1920s the age of touring was coming to a close, there were still a lot of live performances for rural audiences to choose among. In the second decade of the twentieth century, as the Circuits introduced theater to the platform, tent entertainments were growing in numbers and traveling the nation to perform in small towns. One of the most popular types was the tent repertoire. In the history of one such organization, Robert Lee Wyatt III writes: "Tent Repertoire as an art form developed primarily for the rural areas of the country. It flourished in the Midwest and the Southwest. At the height of the art, almost seven hundred companies performed full seasons."[78] While tent shows had started out with dependable chestnuts like *Uncle Tom's Cabin*, they soon developed their own traditions and forms. The most popular invention of the tent repertoire was the Toby and Suzy genre. Brooks MacNamara, popular entertainment historian, reveals: "As they were usually originally presented, they featured Toby, a freckle-faced country boy of indeterminate age, and his girlfriend Suzy, both uneducated rural characters. . . . Usually, they were cast in plays in which rural and urban values and characters were contrasted—with rural standards eventually emerging as more satisfying and long-lasting."[79] Chautauqua, no matter how much the Circuits might deny it, had to compete with these shows for the diminishing entertainment budget of rural audiences. Adding theater, with the imprimatur of New York, was one obvious way to trump its competitors, but paradoxically it also diminished the difference between Chautauqua and its competitors.

Very little of what appeared on the Circuit Chautauqua platform was anything but light comedy or sentimental drama. "Comedies or dramas with simple moral messages are most popular. Heavy stuff does not go over at all, and anything bordering on the risqué is strictly taboo," remarked one theater historian in 1932.[80] After theater's inclusion had become unremarkable, the choice of plays was dictated less by the treatment of a particular idea or politics and more by what had already demonstrated its broad popularity. One contemporary observed: "The modern drama, if it really treats of the essential truths of life, would [not be tolerated]. I like to picture the average Chautauqua audience's reaction to 'Strange Interlude'—it would be cataclysmic, but it would be gorgeous."[81] Needless to say, Eugene O'Neill's *Strange Interlude* never appeared on the Circuits. Most of Chautauqua's dramatic offerings came directly from Broadway, with permission from those holding the rights to "Chautauqua-ize the script," as Harry Harrison described it.[82] A play may have been advertised as coming straight from a Broadway run, but almost all plays went through heavy editing to produce a script appropriate to Chautauqua sensitivities.

As theater became more central to Chautauqua and the Circuits were relying heavily on it to continue to draw large audiences, the spectacle moved away from the bare stage of Ben Greet to one that more closely resembled conventional theater of the time. At Crawford Peffer's request, William Keighley had left managing the Greet company to produce plays for all the Redpath Circuits out of the Knickerbocker building in New York City.[83] By 1926 Harrison knew they were dealing with a considerably more sophisticated audience than they once had. He wrote Keighley: "Regarding the drapes for scenery: They will be O.K., providing you give us good showmanship, and, if you can work out any lighting effects, do so. What we want is a good city show and no hick-town stuff."[84] This is a sea change from their hesitancy in 1913 to include most of the trappings of theater. Now, as much as possible, the goal was to produce dramatic literature in such a way as to be indistinguishable from professional theater.

That goal was already running Chautauqua and bringing real challenges to the managers. One manager documented how the spare scenery had become a liability.

> Personally, I am of the opinion that poor scenery, poor draperies, and short casts are rapidly putting the play off the Chautauqua platform. Our receipts are not as good as they used to be. Two of the most successful plays were "Give and Take" and "Friendly Enemies." In both of these we had scenery which produced the proper atmosphere for the plays. The play that drew the best in the last few years was "The Meanest Man in the World." The scenery on this was terrible. It was one of the plays in which we changed the pictures on the wall and made ourselves believe that we had changed rooms. Since then, the receipts have fallen off an average of $40.00 a night on plays.[85]

He continued in a reversal of the argument that had brought theater to Chautauqua—namely, that full scenic effect was instrumental in getting audiences to enjoy the play. "With people who are not accustomed to the theater, the scenery is a big thing in the play. To those who have seen the plays produced in New York, the play is a failure without the proper atmosphere. We fooled ourselves into thinking that a small percentage of our people are unacquainted with the theater."[86] Thirteen years had obviously made quite a difference. The Circuits now worried about matching the sophistication of their audiences instead of how to educate their audiences beyond their simple limitations.

"The whole history of the drama shows how important a part it has played in the development of civilization, and there is no reason to believe that it may not under proper guidance and influences continue to be a most important factor in the cultural development of the United States."[87]

Circuit Chautauquas had found a place for theater on the tent platform, and there should have been little continuing concern about its reception. Communities had embraced theater, safely contextualized by Chautauqua. One only had to look around the tent during a performance to be reassured that the shift in programming was not controversial. Victoria Case and Robert

Ormond Case, writing from their extensive interviews with manager J. Roy Ellison, argue: "The conscience of the most devout churchgoer was soothed by the fact that this was Chautauqua . . . and by the further fact that the minister . . . and the deacon's wife . . . were laughing as heartily as the unwashed flock."[88] Community standards were upheld by the presentations, and those who might have been expected to protest offered no resistance. The very presence of civic and religious leaders, in fact, was read by fellow community members and others as a sign of the acceptability of Chautauqua's theater. Despite these promising signs, however, managers continued to worry about what it meant to put theater on the Chautauqua platform and how that might change Chautauqua, theater, and the community in which the two were presented. Audience acceptance did not seem to diminish the Circuit's fears about theater's presence. The managers found various ways to address these anxieties, from rehearsing them in the pages of their professional journals and the popular press to lecturing audiences directly to accept what they had already embraced.

Managers consistently used religion as a way to justify theater on the platform. In placing theater in a familiar setting, they also turned to an approach that had been used successfully elsewhere: that theater could be reformed by religious conversion. Chautauqua saw "missionary possibilities in the development of theater" and argued that Chautauqua could be perhaps "a factor in the birth of a new and true American drama" that was "cleaner and artistically more earnest" than what was usually found on the stage, as an anonymous *Lyceum Magazine* article reasoned in 1922.[89] Critics of the theater outside Chautauqua had articulated similar approaches to rehabilitating theater. One critic proposed in 1912 that literature possessed the power to save the theater. "Literature is to theater as Christianity was to paganism, that is a conversionary and purifying force."[90] This extension of Chautauqua's progressive zeal made the case that Chautauqua was rescuing theater, much as it had preserved democracy and advanced good citizenship.

When contemporary drama, through the play *Servant in the House*, was introduced into the Chautauqua repertoire in 1915, the Circuits contended: "In the beginning the drama was the handmaiden of the church. Since then it has wandered afar. . . . The church today recognizes its power and force for good when rightly directed and looks forward to the time when it will come into its own. The introduction of this play by Redpath this season is, we believe, a long step in the right direction."[91] Hedging their bets against audience disapproval, the brochure reversed the usual objections to theater. Rather than endangering religious standards and practices, theater was essential to maintaining them.

Redpath conveniently sidestepped the fact that it was the Catholic church that had employed theater as part of the liturgy, a fact that would have been unacceptable to Protestant audiences. The only possible conclusion was that the inclusion of theater supported a respectable community's religious, social, and cultural morality rather than threatened it.

Circuit Chautauqua iterated and reiterated that theater's best work had been when it was associated with the church. The break with organized religion was the moment when theater became dangerous. If theater's value and intent are shaped by its context, as the Circuits argued, then a religious context would produce a theater that promoted appropriate values and standards. Hugh Orchard followed this line of reasoning in his authorized volume on Chautauqua. Theater, he explained, "was born of the church and was kept entirely within the control of the church up to the time of the Puritan revolution. At that time the theater became commercialized, and was handed down to us in a somewhat demoralized condition, discredited by religious thinkers and workers." Orchard used this argument to demonstrate that what his contemporaries knew as theater was a perversion and that "the drama should be reinstated in its pristine purity, and given back to the whole people for their enjoyment."[92] Theater's potential for rehabilitation continued to reassure managers that it had a place on the Circuits.

Even as late as 1929 Crawford Peffer recapitulated this argument. He offered a version of theater history that traced the downfall of theater from its rightful place within religious expression to its current restoration by the Circuits. Theater was central to society in ancient Greece and Rome as "the means of the expression of some of the greatest solemnities of their religious thought."[93] Theater went into a decline, he argued, but was revived during the Middle Ages by the church. With Shakespeare, and the playwrights who followed him (Peffer mentioned, among others, Richard Brinsley Sheridan, Oliver Goldsmith, and George Bernard Shaw), theater emerged as a great literary endeavor. Peffer draws two conclusions: theater has a "religious origin and . . . the greatest literary men of every period have contributed to it." Peffer's inclusion of literature in his argument gestures toward Chautauqua's other form of theater: elocution. It was in elocution that the improving qualities of literature were firmly touted. Literature and religion juxtaposed was a powerful connection between two quintessentially American approaches to uplift and self-improvement.

Chautauqua generously redeemed theater by assimilating its literature and removing it from offensive contexts. What occurred within the canvas walls of the brown tent, everyone agreed, would never be a threat to morality. The opinions of popular commentators ran in the same direction. Journalist G. S. Chance declared in 1924: "It was a great day when the drama was introduced into Chautauqua. . . . Humanity has an instinctive love for good drama. This is particularly true when there has been no distortion by panderers with the cheap and vulgar article. The fifty millions and more of good Americans who live outside our large cities have not had their taste corrupted to any extent, and few realize how easy it would be to develop their taste for sound and wholesome dramatic art."[94] Chautauqua theater was superior not simply because of its context, proponents of rural life reminded readers, but also because its audiences were morally superior to those usually found in urban theaters.

These arguments were not confined to the pages of journals. They were also laid out on the platform for audiences in the tent. In 1916 Redpath's Seven-Day Deluxe Season booked the Parish Players, headed by Harold Heaton. Heaton, "prominent in connection with the 'little theater' movement, and Chautauqua lecturer on matters pertaining to drama, will give a brief introductory address on this theme ["the value of drama, rightly directed, in community life"] upon which he is an authority."[95] The Parish Players presented three unnamed one-act plays and an excerpt from School for Scandal. Heaton made the argument for theater simultaneously with doing theater and put theater in an educational context. Theater was transformed into an example for a lecture, firmly tying the two forms together.

Peffer, Orchard, and the others who wrote about theater from the Chautauqua context struggled valiantly to define and justify theater. Their repetitive attempts demonstrate that they were never able to do so to their satisfaction. This failure suggests that theater was too complex a cultural practice to be recuperated in a single effort. In the years that followed 1913, Chautauqua managers and practitioners continued to assert the difference between what they did and "the brass and tinsel of the 'theater.'"[96] Professional theater was not much more enchanted with Chautauqua than Chautauqua was with professional theater. The commercial theater was largely silent on the issues Chautauqua raised, probably because the Circuits were originally little threat and later a significant financial opportunity as Broadway hits were licensed to play Chautauqua. The burgeoning little theater, or art theater, movement was another matter, however. It found Chautauqua as distasteful as Chautauqua had at first found theater.

Little theaters were an American adaptation of the changes that were sweeping European theater at the end of the nineteenth and beginning of the twentieth centuries. Exasperated with commercial and state theaters that resisted innovation and experimentation, European directors and playwrights had begun to create small subscription theaters that catered only to those audiences interested in a new kind of theater. In the context of the United States, this also merged with an interest in community work. Little theater participants and commentators saw themselves as struggling toward a new future that would challenge the status quo of theater (particularly Broadway) and in doing so move the emphasis from the business of theater to its artists. There was also an echo of Progressive politics—little theaters hoped to break the stranglehold of commercial monopolies that dictated what people could and would see. Instead, audiences were to determine for themselves what they could and would see, as well as how they would see it. Commercial theater came to mean large, impersonal, and simplistic entertainment, while little theaters meant local, communal, and challenging art. Circuit Chautauquas disrupted this neat division of meaning—they were large but believed they should bring entertainment and enlightenment to those who would not otherwise have it, and they were commercial but focused on communities.

Walter Prichard Eaton, writing in 1922, believed that the commercial theater system of tours and stars was being replaced by a new mode of making theater no longer dependent on the choices of managers in distant cities. In place of commercial theater and its tours, Prichard enthused, "a totally new and different theatrical system is springing up, a new and different attitude toward theater is apparent: the people themselves are producing drama, not professionally, not as commercialized entertainment, but as a means of community enjoyment and self-expression. This fact is, today, the most significant thing in American theater."[97] Eaton focused on communal self-determination and concomitantly rejected profit-making. In this "totally new and different theatrical system," the audience was to control repertoire, and commercial theater was seen as an exploitative enterprise prohibiting such advancement.

Keith Vawter took issue with Eaton's grand, and to Vawter, uninformed claims on behalf of little theater. Eaton had argued that little theater provided "those who witness . . . a chance—often the first and only chance they've ever had—to enjoy good plays."[98] Vawter took the time to dispute Eaton's argument and make a stand on behalf of his commercial enterprise. He wrote *Scribner's* that "it is to be regretted [that] the one writing such an article as this should not be better posted on kindred lines within the territory he is attempting to cover." Vawter pointed out that in 1922 his Circuits "furnished" 375 towns with productions and in 1921 500 towns.[99] Vawter was fighting a losing battle, however. Little theater advocates were never convinced that Chautauqua had anything to offer, despite their shared investment in community. Kenneth Macgowan, who was an active practitioner in little theaters (particularly the influential Provincetown Players) and a widely respected commentator on them, mentioned Circuit Chautauquas in *Footlights across America*, his 1929 survey of contemporary theater. His contradictory assessment was less than complimentary. On the one hand, he praised the Circuits for their service to "even the most out-of-the-way places," which evinced "America's hearty appetite for the spoken drama." On the other hand, he cautioned that "the level of play and performance has been very low," leaving the impression that the Circuits fell well short of the achievements of little and university theaters.[100] Chautauqua supporter Hugh Orchard may have defended theater's presence with the idea that "circuit Chautauqua might be styled a 'Little Theater Movement' to restore the old time drama in a refined form."[101] Little theater and subsequent movements found nothing in Chautauqua that was useful or innovative. It is ironic that after all the years that Chautauqua had resisted including theater, once theater was included, the Circuits came to be seen as the type of theatrical practice that needed to be abandoned in order to reform theater.

Some Chautauquans were never convinced that theater had a place on the platform. They observed that "frequently the receipts of the plays pay the deficits of other attractions," but L. Verne Slout, a theater practitioner who worked on the Circuits, cautioned Chautauqua managers not to lose their "high ideals" when including theater.[102] Slout's 1923 *Lyceum Magazine* article had a conflicted view of theater. He worried that managers used theater merely as a "deficit dodger" (as indeed many were) and not as "something worthwhile in the drama."[103] His real concern, however, was that the distinctions between Chautauquas and other tent shows were diminishing. "The main trouble with [making Chautauqua productions from Broadway hits] is that it has a strong competitor in the traveling repertoire shows under canvas. . . . The day is coming when these same 'Broadway plays' [on Chautauqua] with their too often shabby mountings . . . will not induce the public to part with their [money]. Why? Because many traveling repertoire shows . . . are giving better mounted productions of pleasing plays." Slout ended his article with a strongly worded caveat: "What of the future? The hand-writing on the wall indicates 'Danger! Go slow!'"[104] Slout believed that theater was changing the nature of the Circuits.

Charles Horner was similarly conflicted. He commented that the "play gave a tint of commercialism, without a doubt."[105] While he was not alone in this, the balance of opinion was that theater was a productive addition to Circuit offerings. In 1926 the *New York Times* blithely observed: "This season's plays have drawn larger audiences than other program items. Religious opposition to the drama has ceased in rural America and the growth in the appreciation of good music and plays during the last ten years has been phenomenal."[106] Richard Oram saw it as an aggregate process. "It peeled a little off of vaudeville, it peeled a little off the music world, and it peeled a little off the dramatic world, so it was an important bridge" from the past when entertainment was "wicked" to a future where people embraced "higher cultural things."[107] Case and Case sum up theater's introduction to the Circuits as a tidy, evolutionary process.

> First came the impersonators and dramatic readers. Who could object to them? Then came lecturers reading extracts from great plays in resounding, musical, frightening voices. This was still above reproach, but with each passing season the dramatic offering—always reflecting an increasing public demand—came closer to the crumbling walls of prejudice. Soon there were bits of opera and Shakespearean excerpts; and finally, without squirming, Chautauqua audiences were sitting through a real play in which up to a dozen actors appeared, and the curtain actually rose and fell between acts. . . . These were the successive steps whereby the stage reached the cornbelt.[108]

Case and Case's account implies that the managers had always intended to introduce theater to the platform. In light of their anxieties about theater, this assumption is highly improbable. What is striking about this description is that it absolutely contradicts what the managers thought and said at the time. While they were not unaware of the deep connections between oratory and theater, they saw the two forms of performance as opposed to one another despite shared characteristics. Lectures and elocution did not simply fill the programming gap until theater could arrive. Instead, they provided Chautauqua with its American oratorical identity. Circuit Chautauqua saw itself as theater's antithesis, but by the mid 1920s the balance on the program tilted away from lectures to music and theater. It is more than coincidental that theater's successful integration came at the end of Chautauqua's existence and popularity. Theater's reform and redemption revealed that the Circuits were no longer the dominant performance of American identity. They were a worn holdover from a previous era, unable to incorporate what it now meant to be American.

Sir Philip Ben Greet. Iowa.

This illustration of a camp meeting and its potential emotional and physical excesses depicts just the kind of unpredictability the Chautauqua founders so disliked. It is interesting to note, however, how closely the original Chautauqua grounds resemble this typical camp meeting arrangement. Old Dartmouth.

Francis Wilson as his character Père Marlotte in Little Father of the Wilderness. *Because of his reputation as a comedian, Wilson saw the serious role of the beloved priest as a huge challenge, but, as he notes in his autobiography, "I found myself so stirred and carried forth by the story . . . that I never once thought of [laughter]." Author.*

Long before his work appeared on the Circuits, Ben Greet had built his reputation on pastoral productions of Shakespeare. The 1904 performance at the White House by his company captured the nation's attention and imagination. Iowa.

While Greet was quick to capitalize on the success of Everyman, William Poel was never comfortable with the mass audiences the production attracted. Iowa.

A publicity photograph for She Stoops to Conquer. Iowa.

Publicity photographs, like this one for It Pays to Advertise, usually relied on pictures from professional productions, often from New York, and gave Circuit audiences little indication of what the production they would see actually looked like. Iowa.

While The Servant in the House's script never overtly identified the bishop as Jesus Christ (second from right in both pictures), acting and design choices left audiences in little doubt about the real identity of the character. Iowa.

CHAUTAUQUA
PROGRAM
1922

DIRECTION
of
MORELAND BROWN

Polly of the Circus

GAGE, OKLA.
AUGUST 2, 3, 4, 5, 6

WHITE & MYERS
AMERICA'S PIONEER
CHAUTAUQUA SYSTEM
SAS CITY

White and Myers, 1922. Iowa.

Audiences routinely overflowed the tent, but their interest in Chautauqua was so keen that they willingly sat far from the platform. Iowa.

Richard Oram during the time of his Chautauqua career. He played many leading roles in plays such as Smilin' Through, Sun-Up, and an adaptation of A Tale of Two Cities. Courtesy of the Oram family.

The Palimpsestic Platform

As the black-and-white movie begins, a huge crowd waits at the train station. Men have their jackets slung over their shoulders, children run excitedly, and all those gathered fan themselves in the noonday heat. A train whistle is heard in the distance, and immediately the band begins to play, while the crowd's enthusiastic exclamations can be heard over the music. The narrator's deep, authoritative voice speaks over this charming small-town scene.

> 1927. Will Coolidge choose to run again? Will Dempsey beat Sharkey? Is Babe Ruth going to hit sixty homers this year? Lucky Lindy had just flown the Atlantic. Janet Gaynor had just won the first Oscar. Al Capone was scaring Chicago. But the really big event in thousands of towns like Radford Center, Iowa, was the traveling Chautauqua troupe that was coming to town with its silver-tongued orators and exciting entertainers. There was one man who held the dizzy troupe together. He was the manager. He wore a white suit and when he stepped down off that big train on a hot summer's day a town looked different. It somehow CAME ALIVE.[1]

The narrator's voice crescendos with these last two words, and the manager comes out of the train car. He stands on the car's steps, smiles, and begins shaking the many hands thrust in his direction. As he appears, the picture snaps instantaneously from black-and-white to color.

Who is this powerful Chautauqua manager who can quite literally transform drab, gray, small-town existence into exciting, vivid Panavision Metrocolor? Who else could that Chautauqua manager be but Elvis Presley?

The Trouble with Girls, Presley's penultimate movie, was released in 1969 and received terrible reviews. The plot, which lacks any real focus, ostensibly follows the attempt of Chautauqua manager Walter Hale (Presley) to solve the murder of Wilby (Dabney Coleman), the thoroughly despicable local pharmacist, and to free his unjustly accused tent crew man from jail. Along the way he plays touch football, pursues and is pursued by several women, and joins a gospel choir onstage for a few numbers. The movie has quite a few well-known actors in small roles; John Carradine, Vincent Price, and Joyce Van Patten all have cameos. When the movie is remembered at all, it is largely for Presley's excellent gospel singing.

It had the potential to be a much better movie. Presley had stepped into a script written for someone else (Dick Van Dyke), but Colonel Tom Parker, Presley's manager, had suggested that the producers "cash . . . in on the Bonnie and Clyde craze or utilize . . . some of the great old-time talents he [Parker] wanted to put them in touch with." The producers did not take these suggestions, and "instead, they just blundered along on their own, creating neither a believable story nor a believable setting for their star—though he looked good in a white suit that didn't seem to match up particularly with the period and long, black muttonchop sideburns."[2] Unlike other Elvis vehicles, The Trouble with Girls has never been accorded cult status and is largely forgotten.

The movie was based on the novel Chautauqua by Day Keene and Dwight Vincent, published in 1960. Keith Vawter died in 1937, so he could not have read the novel. It is likely, however, that this novel, which uses a cynical view of Chautauqua to tell a story of adultery and murder, would have received the same scathing assessment he gave to a similar 1935 novel. "I have little patience with the artist who can find nothing but human derelicts and human wreckage in models in painting and I haven't any use whatever for a writer of the Sinclair Lewis type that takes a few of the human derelicts of the neighborhood and try [sic] to present them as the leading citizens. I look on Tom Duncan's 'O Chautauqua' as the Elmer Gantry of the Chautauqua movement."[3] Perhaps fortunately from Vawter's point of view, there were few Circuit Chautauqua novels at all.

It is amazing that the biggest Hollywood treatment of Circuit Chautauqua is in an Elvis Presley movie, a fact that continues to amuse me and never fails to surprise anyone with whom I share this information. This 1969 movie was at the start of a small revival in Chautauqua nostalgia, which culminated in

1974, the hundredth anniversary of the founding of the New York Chautauqua. The U.S. Postal Service issued a commemorative stamp in 1974 that echoed the many souvenir program covers; it depicted the tent, centered and surrounded by trees, and horses and buggies around it. It is an ironic image, however, since the anniversary being celebrated was that of the New York Chautauqua (founded in 1874) and not the "Rural America" so clearly spelled out on each stamp. There was a spate of articles as well. *Newsweek*, for example, gave one page to Chautauqua in its "Ideas" section. In keeping with Chautauqua's contradictory status as important cultural icon and gauche relic, the magazine could not decide what tone to take. It ultimately characterizes Chautauqua humorously, with more than a touch of embarrassment, as a "sedate survivor" populated by "Middle American" "culture seekers." The article concedes at the end that "there is something to be said in these times of severe cultural confusion for keeping Chautauqua's rich cultural subsoil of tradition undisturbed."[4] This is a fairly thin selection of examples, not to mention uninformed and condescending, for such a tremendously influential national phenomenon. As former Redpath manager C. E. Backman wrote James S. Smoot in 1953 when Smoot was conducting research for his dissertation on Chautauqua: "Everyone who has tried writing about the Chautauqua movement . . . has found it difficult. It is one of those things that continuously flows away from you."[5] As these examples attest, it is not only in writing about Chautauqua that it "flows away." They simply demonstrate, as I argued in the introduction, that Chautauqua has largely disappeared from the community landscape and national memory.

Circuit Chautauqua's ending was actually quite swift. Just as it had only taken a couple of years for the Circuit idea to catch on, it only took a couple of years for it to disappear almost completely. W. S. Rupe had been buying Redpath Circuits since 1926, when he bought out Keith Vawter. Rupe took over the White and Brown Circuit in 1927 and between 1927 and 1929 gradually bought out Harry Harrison as well.[6] His consolidation was ruthless. He homogenized offerings even more than they had been and increased the amount of novelty acts (especially animals) and drama on the program. By 1929–1930 there was not much left of Rupe's Circuits. The Ellison-White Circuit (J. Roy Ellison himself had sold out to C. Benjamin Franklin, head of the Cadmean Circuit, in 1925) and Crawford Peffer's New York–New England Redpath were in a minority that tried to survive the public's waning interest. Ellison-White's 1928 program faced the challenge head-on and optimistically claimed: "Chautauqua is keeping pace with the metamorphosis that has been changing the world into a new and better one in recent years."[7] Crawford Peffer, the last of the Redpath managers to run his own Circuit, was willing to adapt to whatever the audience demanded to keep his Circuit viable. He wrote Eben Schultz: "They would rather see their money spent on the entertainments than on the lectures, so we are going ahead on that basis."[8] But these measures made little difference, and by 1933 neither Circuit was still in business.

Crawford Peffer's secretary, Anne Lauers Matthews, remembers how striking the tent for the last time in September 1932 affected all who stayed to watch. "They stood in prayer-like silence as they watched the big tent slowly, quietly lowered to the ground. No one spoke while the sections were unlaced, folded, and put in the dray wagon to be taken to the waiting baggage car. Each walked slowly away to his home."[9] That evening in New Hampshire, it is generally agreed, marked the last time anyone saw a genuine Circuit Chautauqua tent in the United States. Its passing, as Matthews described, was not without pain. Richard Oram witnessed the same set of emotions when he saw his last tent folded away. "Bob [Hanscom] kept lamenting that this was the end of an era. That the tent Chautauqua was no longer."[10] The process of forgetting was less difficult. When she began writing *Morally We Roll Along* in the mid 1930s, Gay MacLaren found that "various bureaus were discarding their pictures and data, and the story of one of the most valuable and significant chapters in the social history of our country was in a fair way towards being lost."[11] As communities had outgrown their desire for Chautauqua, it got remembered as naive, old-fashioned, and superficial. Cultural imagination almost did not want to admit that it had been so taken with the idea in the first place.

There is little disagreement among contemporary observers about why the Circuits came to an end. Harry Harrison joked: "The world had changed; the hinterland had disappeared. . . . Youths who had never ventured beyond the second station up the line had come back from France saying *mercy bo-koo* and *toot sweet*. The popular song, 'How you going to keep 'em down on the farm, after they've seen Paree,' was based on fact. Hard roads and movies and the car standing at the back door were too inviting."[12] In a similar vein, Charles Horner remembered: "The final and direct blow to the Chautauqua came from the radio and talking movies."[13] Keith Vawter echoed the same themes. "In later years," Vawter told an interviewer, it was increasingly difficult for the Circuits to "reach the young people." He noted in particular that the "roadside dance hall was a factor," as was the "fading away of civic pride."[14] Audiences concurred on the reasons for the Circuit's demise. One former spectator wrote about his Circuit memories to historian Harrison John Thornton: "We had a Greene County Chautauqua from 1901 to about 1930. Before the days of radio, movies, paved roads to pleasure resorts—*it was well patronized.*"[15] A man from Cresco, Iowa, recalled that

> the local business men became tired of sponsoring the institution and assuming whole responsibility financially with a written guarantee, and the chautauqua began to wane, it kept dwindling until there was little or no interest, and the last one was held in 1923 with a small attendance and financial loss. . . . Our county fair was re-organized in 1924 and well patronized which took the place of the Chautauqua, not by comparison of course, but so in the minds of the people, and the fair has been run successfully each year since.[16]

The world had most assuredly changed, and Chautauqua had not been able to change with it.

Audiences no longer were as dependent on entertainment coming to them via the rails. They could hop in their cars and drive greater distances in a few hours than their parents and grandparents had covered in days. The Model T was introduced by the Ford Motor Company in 1908. In a time when the average car cost $5,000 and was available only to the very rich, the Model T could be purchased for $850. By 1925 the price had decreased to $360, and in 1927 Ford announced that 15 million cars had been sold to date.[17] The millions buying Fords were the same millions attending Chautauqua, only now those Fords gave them more options. Similarly, radio and talking movies gave them choices Chautauqua could not. Radio meant you did not have to wait for one week a year to get news, information, ideas, and entertainment. It also meant that you could listen in the comfort of your own home. While many people saw their first silent movies in a Chautauqua tent, the advent of sound brought an expansion in the number of movie theaters, which provided almost as much comfort as home and considerably more comfort than a Chautauqua tent. Radio and film reached millions effortlessly, on a daily basis. This was the true mass entertainment, which Chautauqua had only been able to anticipate.

Not only was technology changing what people wanted and expected from information and entertainment, people themselves were changing. The pervasive public oratorical culture was dead, and audiences no longer wanted to listen for hours to a single lecturer. Radio, especially, but also the whistle-stop tours of politicians, built the desire for and expectation of a more intimate public discourse, one where the speaker seemed to be addressing you directly and conversationally. The late-nineteenth- and early-twentieth-century models of citizenship based on service, responsibility, and reform seemed outmoded and were gradually being replaced by notions of the citizen as consumer.

Paul Pearson observed in notes titled "Causes for Collapse" for a book on Circuit Chautauqua, which he never wrote: "Women who sold tickets now active in clubs. Men who sold tickets and walked up the street with the distinguished lecturer, now finds his pride in shooting golf."[18] Pearson traced a shift in rural America from frontier life to suburban status in his progressive narrative of collapse. He labeled those who originally championed the Circuits as the "pioneer generation." They had few opportunities for education and "were faithful attendants." They were the ones who ensured Chautauqua's community success. "Their eager acceptance of [Chautauqua] as a means of acquiring some culture made them season ticket subscribers or guarantors."[19] The next generation benefited from their parents' sacrifices, were better educated, and had more opportunities. They "prefer the country club, the bridge club, the woman's club or other select or exclusive groups."[20] The democratic ethos of Chautauqua, one that prided itself on bringing everyone regardless of social status under the tent, no longer held any cultural sway. The loss of that ethos was, in Pearson's view, the most significant reason for Chautauqua's end. Finally, he emphasized that "culture cannot be purchased, or passed on like currency, but this older generation had a desire to learn and they learned, from a youth spent in a bookless wilderness, or on a prairie where they built the school houses for their children they turned to [Chautauqua] in their grey haired semi-leisure, or less strenuous work to find some substitute for travel, and schooling."[21] Pearson made these notes while his Circuit was being seized by creditors and he was declaring personal bankruptcy. The best days of Chautauqua must have seemed distant but halcyon to him, and the sense of loss and nostalgia that pervades these notes is understandable. But even taking his argument skeptically, his sense of zeitgeist change is compelling. The United States was no longer a pioneer nation, and its citizens no longer thought of themselves as supplicants grateful for knowledge about the wider world.

In 1906 Paul Pearson recalled that President James A. Garfield had observed: "It has been the struggle of the world to get more leisure, but it was left for Chautauqua to show us how to use it."[22] Twenty-three years later President Herbert Hoover echoed Garfield's sentiment: "This civilization is not going to depend so much on what we do when we work as what we do in our time off."[23] Leisure, historically never a problem before, had become one in the twentieth century. Technology and labor politics combined to shorten working hours and make many tasks less onerous. Providing options for "what we do in our time off" would become a multimillion-dollar business and remains so to this day. Like Circuit Chautauquas, one significant aspect of that industry is based on selling the United States back to its citizens. Whether "visiting" colonial

America by walking on the very streets their forebears are said to have walked on at Colonial Williamsburg or strolling down the bland simulation of "Main Street USA" at Disney World, U.S. citizens are still invested in and compelled by representations of their communal landscapes. Circuit Chautauqua helped to create a precedent and appetite for such activities.

In many ways Chautauqua ensured its own demise. The Circuits were largely successful because of an absence of a shared national culture. Chautauqua was instrumental in promoting the idea that such a culture existed and never failed to remind its audiences that it was America that the platform and its audiences were creating together. Having contributed to a national identity, however, it could not sustain it. Chautauqua was predicated on an absence of national connection, not dependent upon it. The middle-class culture that it had helped to bring into being had no interest in communal efforts of uplift. Instead, there was great excitement about "individual freedom and the pursuit of pleasure."[24] Even the continuing Depression did not bring about a return to "island communities" but a greater sense of how interdependent the nation as a whole had become. The performances this awareness seemed to translate into on a national scale were either escapes into the romance and adventure of Hollywood movies and Broadway or the more radical political experimentation like that of the Group Theater or the "Living Newspapers" of the Federal Theatre Project (FTP).

Circuit Chautauqua had shown that the American version of a national arts enterprise was not one located in a single capital city, as in the European model, but one that was federated across the entire country, an idea to which the FTP was indebted.[25] The Circuits demonstrated beyond the shadow of a doubt that America could be defined by connecting communities across the continent and insisting on each one as a significant part of the whole. Additionally, the thousands of people who were its talent and personnel did not disappear along with the Circuits. In many cases they kept performing: some at the independent Chautauquas, some in other performance venues like theater or movies, and some as solo performers for women's clubs, universities, schools, churches, and other social and civic organizations. The experience they garnered on the Circuits stood them in good stead.

The New York Chautauqua survived and exists today as a vibrant, thriving organization. That it does so is in large part due to the leadership of Arthur Bestor, who became the third president of Chautauqua in 1915. While the period during and following World War I had been a good one for the New York Chautauqua, its debts and infrastructure needs began to outpace its income. In 1933 it was forced into receivership. Three years of relentless fund-raising, debt restructuring, and reorganization culminating in a last-minute gift from John D. Rockefeller (secured by Anna Pennybacker) were successful, and by the end of 1936 the institution was on the secure footing it continues to enjoy. It is not, however, the only current example of the Chautauqua legacy. There are others—descendants of New York, independent assemblies, and the Circuits—that continue to engage with their communities on matters of local, regional, and national significance.

In Boulder, Colorado, the Chautauqua founded as a joint effort with several University of Texas at Austin professors provides cultural and intellectual programming. The New Paisa Chautauqua in Missouri continues as a residential community. Chautauquas in Ocean Park, Maine; Ocean Grove, New Jersey; and Lakeside, Ohio, strive to make vital community contributions. Others, like the Waxahachie Chautauqua in Texas, are inspired by the fact that Chautauqua existed in their communities historically and are members of the Chautauqua Network.

The Chautauqua Network is organized out of the New York Chautauqua as a way to keep Chautauqua organizations across the country in touch with one another. Its mission statement declares that it is "a group of organizations and individuals committed to the communication and implementation of the chautauqua concept of building community by supporting all persons in the development of their full potential intellectually, spiritually, emotionally, and physically."[26] Maureen Moore and Kirk Hunter loved the beautiful Chautauqua building in the middle of Getzendaner Park in Waxahachie, Texas. After a visit to the New York Chautauqua in 1999, they were inspired to revive Chautauqua in Waxahachie. Working with others in the community, they created an annual one-day event in September. The goal of the organization is to "continue the Chautauqua legacy that was begun here in 1900."[27] "The American West: An Idea That Became a Place," the 2003 program, included lectures on the buffalo soldiers, Cabeza de Vaca, Katherine Ann Porter, and frontier fashion. There were also three different musical groups. While Hunter and Moore no longer run the Waxahachie organization themselves, they are still very involved with it and hope it has a long and fruitful life in Waxahachie.

Another way the Chautauqua has survived is a new incarnation, sometimes called the neo-Chautauqua, a public education initiative largely (although not entirely) funded by the National Endowment for the Humanities (NEH) and its state affiliates. It was called Chautauqua, Andrew Rieser points out in his book on New York Chautauqua, because "officials believed [it] . . . would strike a balance between populism and elitism."[28] Chautauqua reemerged in 1975 when the North Dakota Humanities Council sent scholars out to small towns to perform composite characters of the Old West. Described by George Frein, the dean of Chautauqua scholars and performers, as "entertainment with a touch of history," the events were very like the sort of elocution performed by impersonators and readers on the Circuits.[29] Quickly, however, the format shifted to the one that is now common: a scholar performs a forty-minute monologue impersonating a historical figure, followed by an hour of questions, which the scholar answers first in character, then later as herself or himself. In the 2003 Great Plains Chautauqua, which traveled to Oklahoma, Kansas, Nebraska, South Dakota, and North Dakota, the theme was "From Sea to Shining Sea: American Expansion and Cultural Change, 1790–1850," and among the figures performed were William Clark (Jeffrey E. Smith of Lindenwood University), Dolley Madison (Kris Runberg Smith of Webster University), John Jacob Astor (D. Jerome Tweton of University of North Dakota), York (Charles Everett Pace of Centre College), and Tecumseh (Jerome Kills Small). Previous Great Plains themes have included "The American Renaissance" (1991), the "Gilded Age" (1994), and "Early 20th Century American Visionary Voices" (2001). Billed as education, neo-Chautauquas, based in states including North Dakota, South Dakota, Oklahoma, Nebraska, Colorado, Kansas, and California, borrow many of their emphases, devices, and theory from the earlier forms of Chautauqua. This incarnation is a significant departure from the original Circuit vision because this Chautauqua's unifying narrative is not about the nation's present but about its past. As Susan Savage, the mayor of Tulsa, Oklahoma, said when she opened the city's 1993 Chautauqua: "Enjoy and participate in history."[30] Her historical counterparts would have been more likely to enjoin their constituents to participate in Chautauqua as a vital way to understand their present rather than their past.

At these Chautauquas, representations of important historical figures serve as the basis for a series of events, including lectures, discussion groups, and workshops. "Have breakfast with Isadora Duncan and Gertrude Stein" and "go on a pub crawl with Ezra Pound and learn the great art of insult" are possible things an attendee might do. All of these Chautauquas offer about three to five days of programming, and audiences are provided with free programs, pamphlets with further information, and access to the authors' works through libraries and bookmobiles.

The literature produced by current Chautauquas adamantly states that they are not theater. Despite the fact that history is presented through performance, grant applications go to great lengths (as do promotional materials) to define Chautauqua as education, not representation. One grant application passage assured the NEH that "we do very little in the way of acting." The application goes on: "Chautauqua fellows are not actors. The costume and first-person portrayal is [sic] merely a device to present a 'text' for discussion."[31] The word "text" is used throughout to differentiate Chautauqua from theater, foregrounding the idea that the representational mode is merely "a device" offering the material to audiences to facilitate their discussions. The implication is that theater is trivial and deludes people by offering illusion rather than substance, fiction rather than fact.

The president of the Great Plains Chautauqua, Everett Albers, writes:

> It is the prospect of finding, finally, a way to do the humanities that brings a "text" which all can read and appreciate, a "text" which seems to compel questions and alternatives, discourse and dialogue. People astonish their neighbors with their insights in the Chautauqua tent following the presentation of the first-person characterization, the "text." There's no question about whether or not those who gather have "read the text." They heard it presented in such a way that they want to know more.[32]

The question this approach raises is: what is the text? The literature argues that it is confined to the words uttered by the scholar, which are in turn based on an immersion in the work of the historical personage. One cannot help but point out that the presentations are not unmediated: the scholars make choices in their research, writing, and rehearsal; the Chautauqua boards choose specific themes and figures; and the scholars/performers have authority vested in them that authenticates their work. These other texts are elided behind the notion that the purpose of the humanities is to enlighten and educate: "We play our characters for questions. As humanities scholars we want questions above all else. We do historical characterizations because they give the audiences the texts they need to ask good questions."[33] The basis for the questions comes not from first-hand contact with the works themselves but from another's reading, a reading that is represented as authoritative, accurate, and authentic.

A third, much less established, revival of the Chautauqua idea was created by Jim Hightower, the National Public Radio (NPR) commentator, author, and former Texas agriculture commissioner. In 2002 he inaugurated the "Rolling Thunder Chautauqua Tour," intended to forge bonds among existing progressive organizations and create local and national political coalitions in the atmosphere of a festive community gathering. As the Web site exhorts: "As we nurture the civic side of our community, let's also relish the cultural side, interspersing the event's agenda with some of our best musicians, comedians, artists, satirical troupes, and other performers. . . . Think of it like a county fair, where citizens come together to learn, participate, celebrate and enjoy."[34]

Hightower's choice to style the tour a Chautauqua emerged from a sense of Chautauqua not unlike Pirsig's in *Zen and the Art of Motorcycle Maintenance*. In a brief history of Chautauqua on Hightower's Web site, the emphasis is on Chautauqua's civic, social, and educational aspects. "At the turn of the century, Traveling Chautauquas were first introduced, and the Chautauqua Circuit was organized to spread the opportunity for the American people to share information and join in the discussion of ideas."[35] Clearly Hightower's organization has seized not on the actual historical Chautauqua but the Chautauqua ideal. "At the turn of the 20th century, Theodore Roosevelt was so taken by the democratic value of the original Chautauqua Tours that he said, 'The Chautauqua is the most American thing in America.' Let's reclaim it as our own."[36] While one could quibble with some of the historical accuracy of the Chautauqua history being represented here, it is clear that Chautauqua, when it is remembered, occupies a powerful place in the national imagination. All of these Chautauqua approaches indicate that oratorical struggles around how to employ performance are far from settled. Instead, they are as much a lively part of U.S. culture as they were a hundred years ago. While the stakes have changed, performing nation and community is still a highly charged endeavor.

At the end of *The Trouble with Girls*, Presley's character gets "the girl" underhandedly. Charlene (Marlyn Mason) has told him she does not want to continue with Chautauqua or their relationship. He seems to accept this and gives her severance pay. In the next scene, with a huge grin, he accuses her of theft to the town police. The police, in turn, force her into the police car to throw her out of town on the conveniently available Chautauqua train. The final images of the movie are the police, with a great deal of slapstick, loading her resistant body onto the train and into Elvis's waiting arms. As this happens, the narrator's deep, authoritative voice returns to close the movie.

> This is almost the end of our story and it was close to the end of Chautauqua too. By 1934 the tattered, big, brown Chautauqua tents were folded, stored for the last time. Chautauqua trains chugged out of town, never to return again. The victim of the radio, phonograph, pictures that talked, the Model A, hard roads, and sophistication. Chautauqua is gone now but something has endured, something more than a memory because no one who ever saw Chautauqua will ever forget its excitement, its fun, its joy. In its time it was the most American thing about America, and we're not saying it, President Theodore Roosevelt said it. Nowadays we're just saying it was the end.[37]

The end of the movie suggests that Circuit Chautauqua's legacy can be found in the memories of its participants, evidence of a utopic moment in American history when citizens gathered to negotiate their concerns in open democratic discussion.

This image is a tempting one with which to end this study. It is also not entirely inaccurate. Communities did find that Chautauqua knit them together in ways that nothing else could or did. Some version of that memory survived into the end of the twentieth century, spawning the Chautauqua Network and the neo-Chautauquas as attempts to restore something lost by the end of the 1920s. But this memory forgets significant parts of Chautauqua history. It forgets the ambivalent tone of Chautauqua's dismissal of the Klantauqua, a tone that allowed the Circuits to authorize virulently racist speakers like Belle Kearney and James K. Vardaman as reasonable representatives of a legitimate point of view. It forgets the significant sexism that left women who resisted the Circuit's patriarchal approach silenced and frustrated. It forgets the number of young men and women, like Richard Oram and William Shirer, who saw Chautauqua not as a way to make the small town more palatable but as a way to get out of the small town that they experienced as narrow-minded, judgmental, smug, and ignorant. Finally, it forgets that Circuit Chautauqua was an unabashedly capitalist enterprise. Part of Chautauqua's "success" is that the managers were able to correlate community values and needs to profit so exactly.

To embrace a more complicated view of Chautauqua, one that remembers both positive and negative aspects simultaneously, and to use that view to create contemporary versions are worthwhile goals. Like many American institutions, Chautauqua's legacy is one that deserves to be both judged as wanting and celebrated as empowering. The goals of community support, informed critical thinking, popular education, and public performance and discussion that Chautauqua espoused are legitimate ideals to continue to try to realize, even if the original incarnation fell far short of doing so. "Chautauqua is an opportunity for all the people of the town to work together to foster a sense of community that reaches out to everyone."[38] This statement, written in 1991, could be from 1901, 1911, or 1921. While live performance does not have the same (or even similar) resonance for audiences today as it did for the audiences of Circuit Chautauqua, community and nation still demand to be performed.

Elvis Presley as Walter Hale, the manager of the Circuit outfit, as seen in the 1969 MGM film The Trouble with Girls.

No one seems to have commented on the disparity between the anniversary being commemorated and the image depicted on the stamp itself. Author.

Boulder, Colorado, Chautauqua. Author.

Waxahachie, Texas, Chautauqua. Built in 1902, the building was placed on the National Register of Historic Places in the 1970s. Author.

During the 2001 Chautauqua, the Waxahachie, Texas, committee erected tents in the park to hold the various events. What had been an independent assembly historically looked like a tent Chautauqua for a day. Author.

These small schedules were sent out in advance to attract people to the Great Plains Chautauqua programming. Author.

Unidentified ticket seller. Iowa.

Notes

INTRODUCTION

1 Marian Johnson Castle, "Chautauqua: The Intellectual Circus," *Forum* 87 (June 1932): 374.

2 Ibid. Emphasis in the original.

3 Ibid.

4 Robert M. Pirsig, *Zen and the Art of Motorcycle Maintenance: An Inquiry into Values* (New York: Bantam Books, 1980 [1974]), 7.

5 Chautauqua Foundation, "The Chautauqua River School Day Trips," publicity brochure, ca. 2000. Author.

6 Kitty Crider, "Cured for Charity," *Austin American-Statesman* (September 17, 2003), http://nl.newsbank.com/nl-search/we/Archives?p_action=print. January 29, 2004.

7 Chautauqua Airlines, "Setting a Course," http://www.flychautauqua.com/WhoWeAre.asp. March 4, 2004.

8 Jeffrey Simpson, *Chautauqua: An American Utopia* (New York: Harry M. Abrams, 1999), 48.

9 Andrew C. Rieser, *The Chautauqua Moment: Protestants, Progressives, and the Culture of Modern Liberalism* (New York: Columbia University Press, 2003), 2.

10 Victoria Case and Robert Ormond Case, *We Called It Culture: The Story of Chautauqua* (New York: Doubleday, 1948); Harry P. Harrison (as told to Karl Detzer), *Culture under Canvas: The Story of Tent Chautauqua* (New York: Hastings House, 1958); Charles F. Horner, *Strike the Tents: The Story of Chautauqua* (Philadelphia: Dorrance, 1954).

11 Irene Briggs Da Boll and Raymond F. Da Boll, *Recollections of the Chautauqua and Lyceum Circuits* (Freeport, Maine: Wheelwright, 1969); Warren D. Hanscom, *Pioneers in Grease Paint* (Bradenton, Fla.: Collins, 1975); Gay MacLaren, *Morally We Roll Along* (Boston: Little, Brown, 1938); Frances Perry-Cowen, *Chautauqua to Opera: An Autobiography of a Voice Teacher and Daughter of a Chautauqua Pioneer* (Hicksville, N.Y.: Exposition Press, 1978); Marion A. Scott, *Chautauqua Caravan* (New York: D. Appleton Century, 1939).

12 Jean Handley Adams, *Second Fiddle to Chautauqua* (n.p.: n.p., 1983); James R. Schultz, *The Romance of Small-Town Chautauquas* (Columbia: University of Missouri Press, 2002).

13 John Edward Tapia, *Circuit Chautauqua: From Rural Education to Popular Entertainment in Early Twentieth-Century America* (Jefferson, N.C.: McFarland, 1997); John S. Gentile, *Cast of One: One-Person Shows from the Chautauqua Platform to the Broadway Stage* (Urbana: University of Illinois Press, 1989).

14 George J. Dillavou, "The Swarthmore Chautauqua: An Adult Education Enterprise"

(Ph.D. diss., University of Chicago, 1970); Donald L. Graham, "Circuit Chautauqua, Middle Western Institution" (Ph.D. diss., University of Iowa, 1953); R. Alan Hedges, "Actors under Canvas: A Study of the Theater of the Circuit Chautauqua, 1910–1933" (Ph.D. diss., Ohio State University, 1976); Drew Allan Kent, "The Circuit-Chautauqua Produced Play: Reading Historic Plays as Cultural Scripts of Social Interaction" (Ph.D. diss., University of Texas at Austin, 1992); M. Sandra Manderson, "The Redpath Lyceum Bureau, an American Critic: Decision-Making and Programming Methods for Circuit Chautauquas, Circa 1912–1930" (Ph.D. diss., University of Iowa, 1981); Nydia Joan Reynolds, "A Historical Study of the Oral Interpretation Activities of the Circuit Chautauqua 1904–1932" (Ph.D. diss., University of Southern California, 1961).

15 Glenn Hughes, *A History of American Theatre 1700–1950* (London: Samuel French, 1950), 229.

16 Garff Wilson, *Three Hundred Years of American Drama and Theatre: From Ye Bear and Ye Cubb to Hair* (Englewood Cliffs, N.J.: Prentice Hall, 1973), 197.

17 Don B. Wilmith and Christopher Bigsby, eds., *The Cambridge History of the American Theatre* (Cambridge: Cambridge University Press, 1999), 3:397–398.

18 Joseph Roach, "Slave Spectacles and Tragic Octoroons: A Cultural Genealogy of Antebellum Performance," *Theatre Survey* 33, no. 2 (1992): 168. Emphasis in the original.

19 Richard Oram, interview by author, May 20, 1998.

20 Frances D. C. McCaskill, "Chautauqua in a New England Community," *Lyceum Magazine*, June 1919: 15.

21 Theodore Morrison, *Chautauqua: A Center for Education, Religion, and the Arts in America* (Chicago: University of Chicago Press, 1974), 31.

22 Richard Hofstadter, *Anti-Intellectualism in American Life* (New York: Vintage Books, 1963), 79.

23 Ibid., 112.

24 Morrison, *Chautauqua*, 31.

25 John H. Vincent, *The Chautauqua Movement* (Boston: Chautauqua Press, 1886), 19–20, 21.

26 Rebecca Richmond, *Chautauqua: An American Place* (New York: Duell, Sloan, and Pearce, 1943), 59.

27 Jeffrey Simpson, *Chautauqua: An American Utopia* (New York: Harry N. Abrams, 1999), 34.

28 Hugh A. Orchard, *Fifty Years of Chautauqua: Its Beginnings, Its Development, Its Message and Its Life* (Cedar Rapids, Iowa: Torch Press, 1923), 30.

29 Jesse Lyman Hurlbut, *The Story of Chautauqua* (New York: G. P. Putnam and Sons, 1921), 119.

30 Orchard, *Fifty Years of Chautauqua*, 52.

31 Hurlbut, *The Story of Chautauqua*, 361.

32 Case and Case, *We Called It Culture*, 17–18.

33 Hurlbut, *The Story of Chautauqua*, 27.

34 Josiah Holbrook, "The American Lyceum, or Society for the Improvement of Schools and Useful Knowledge," *Old South Leaflets*, vol. 6 (Boston: Directors of Old South Work, n.d.), 293.

35 James Truslow Adams, *Frontiers of American Culture: A Study of Adult Education in a Democracy* (New York: Charles Scribner's Sons, 1944), 146.

36 Charles Horner claims that he came up with the idea and that he and Vawter worked out the details together in the winter of 1909–1910, both of them putting it into practice in their Circuits that summer (Horner, *Strike the Tents*, 59–61). Orchard and Victoria Case and Robert Ormond Case credit Vawter alone, but Harry Harrison, who managed one of the Redpath Circuits, gives credit to both men (Orchard, *Fifty Years of Chautauqua*, 113; Case and Case, *We Called It Culture*, 22–31; and Harrison, *Culture under Canvas*, 81).

37 After the publication of *Fifty Years of Chautauqua*, which Keith Vawter funded, there were some arguments about who did what when. Nelson Trimble of Midland Chautauquas claimed that his was the first Circuit. Vawter, writing to Orchard about this claim, grumbled, "Trimble is not using much logic in this. I can see how this ad could have appeared in 1904 but he overlooks the fact that we ran a circuit, b'gosh, in the summer of 1904." Keith Vawter to Hugh Orchard, April 14, 1924. Iowa.

38 Redpath-Vawter Service, *Twenty Years of Chautauqua Progress 1904–1923* (1923), no page. Iowa.

39 Orchard, *Fifty Years of Chautauqua*, 92.

40 Horner, *Strike the Tents*, 94–95.

41 Tapia, *Circuit Chautauqua*, 31.

42 Ibid., 32.

43 The U.S. population in 1924 was 114,109,000. U.S. Department of Commerce, Bureau of the Census, *Historical Statistics of the United States, Colonial Times to 1970* (Washington D.C.: Government Printing Office, 1975), Series A 6–8.

44 Paul M. Pearson, "A Chronology of the Paul M. Pearsons," unpublished manuscript (1934), no page. Swarthmore.

45 All sources agree that the tents seated anywhere from 1,000 to 2,000 people.

46 *Chautauqua and Summer Assemblies and Their Managers, Superintendents, Secretaries, and Program Builders* (International Chautauqua Alliance, February 1, 1911), 516; Clay Smith, "What the Modern Chautauqua Is Doing for Music of All Kinds Everywhere in Our Country," *Etude*, August 1922, 514. These figures can also be found in Horner, *Strike the Tents*, 97. It is difficult to know how reliable these numbers are; in 1913, for example, figures vary from 1,300 to 2,930 Circuit Chautauquas. See W. Frank McClure, "On the Chautauqua Circuit," *St. Louis Daily Globe Democrat*, August 3, 1913; "Great Chautauqua Expansion of 1913," *Lyceum Magazine*, July 1913, 17; W. Frank McClure, "Chautauqua of Today," *American Review of Reviews* 50 (July

1914): 54. The two most disparate figures (1,300 and 2,930) come from the same author in two different articles.

47 Tapia, *Circuit Chautauqua*, 32.

48 *The Population of States and Counties of the United States: 1790–1990*, http://www.census.gov/population/cencounts/mt190090.txt. February 19, 2004.

49 Sheilagh S. Jameson, *Chautauqua in Canada* (Calgary: Glenbow-Alberta Institute, 1987), 16–33.

50 Harry Harrison notes about the only Circuit Chautauqua ever held in New York City, "Only a handful of persons occup[ied] a few scattered seats in a vast tent" (Harrison, *Culture under Canvas*, 49).

51 C. E. Backman to Mrs. Ralph Parlette (Gay MacLaren), September 26, 1936. Iowa.

52 Redpath-Vawter Service, *Twenty Years of Chautauqua Progress*.

53 Horner, *Strike the Tents*, 62–69.

54 Harrison, *Culture under Canvas*, 81.

55 C. E. Backman, "Bulletin to Superintendents Five-Day DeLuxe Circuit," July 23, 1920. Iowa.

56 Harry Harrison, "Bulletin to All the Superintendents," June 21, 1913. Iowa.

57 Redpath Chautauquas, contract, 1918. Iowa. All the Chautauquas followed a similar form and pricing structure in their contracts.

58 Orchard, *Fifty Years of Chautauqua*, 120.

59 Keith Vawter to underwriters, June 1921. Iowa.

60 S. Russell Bridge to Mr. and Mrs. Chautauquan, May 1915. Iowa.

61 A. M. Weiskopf to C. E. Noel, April 15, 1921. Iowa.

62 Albert Oberst to John F. Chambers, January 26, 1926. Iowa.

63 Gertrude Timmons to R. M. Kendall, June 10, 1921. Iowa.

64 O. W. T. to L. W. Phillips, August 3, 1921. Iowa.

65 Hugh Orchard, *The No Guarantee Chautauqua?* (N.p.: Redpath-Vawter Chautauqua System, 1922), no page. Iowa.

66 Hugh Orchard, *Who Said Quit?* (N.p.: Redpath-Vawter Chautauqua System, 1922), no page. Iowa.

67 C. B. Wait to Keith Vawter, August 20, 1926. Iowa.

68 Case and Case, *We Called It Culture*, 30.

69 Harrison, *Culture under Canvas*, 138–143.

70 Tapia, *Circuit Chautauqua*, 45.

71 Horner, *Strike the Tents*, 187.

72 Richard Oram, interview by author, February 15, 1996.

73 Charles M. Sheldon, "The Task of the 'Talent,'" *Independent* 91 (August 4, 1917): 165.

74 Case and Case, *We Called It Culture*, 136.

75 Scott, *Chautauqua Caravan*, 33.

76 Sheldon, "The Task," 195.

77 Tapia, *Circuit Chautauqua*, 49.

78 J. William Terry, "How About Chautauqua?" *Overland Monthly and Out West Magazine*, July 1924, 311.

79 Case and Case, *We Called It Culture*, 75–76.

80 "Lecture Season 1915–1916: Charles Zueblin," publicity brochure, no page. Iowa.

81 Charles Zueblin, *American Municipal Progress: Chapters in Municipal Sociology* (New York: MacMillan, 1902), 6.

82 Charles Zueblin to William A. Colledge, October 21, 1918. Iowa.

83 Sinclair Lewis, *Main Street* (New York: Signet Classics, 1980 [1920]), 231, 232, 233.

84 Janice A. Radway, *A Feeling for Books: The Book-of-the-Month Club, Literary Taste, and Middle-Class Desire* (Chapel Hill: University of North Carolina Press, 1997), 143.

85 Gregory Mason, "Chautauqua: Its Technic," *American Mercury* 16 (January 1929): 279–280.

86 Joan Shelley Rubin, *The Making of Middlebrow Culture* (Chapel Hill: University of North Carolina Press, 1992), 28.

87 Ibid.

88 Radway, *A Feeling for Books*, 147.

89 Ibid., 152.

90 Keith Vawter, address to the Poor Richard (Advertising) Club, Philadelphia, December 8, 1921. Iowa.

91 Ibid. Sinclair Lewis was thirty-five when *Main Street* was published. Vawter's anger at and disgust with Lewis endured. Fourteen years later he would write: "I have little patience with the artist who can find nothing but human derelicts and human wreckage in models in painting and I haven't any use whatever for a writer of the Sinclair Lewis type that takes a few of the human derelicts of the neighborhood and try [sic] to present them as the leading citizens." Keith Vawter to Edgar R. Harlan, April 10, 1935. Iowa.

92 William James to Henry James, August 15, 1896, in William James, *The Correspondence of William James*, vol. 2, *William and Henry 1885–1896*, ed. Ignas K. Skrupskelis and Elizabeth M. Berkeley (Charlottesville: University Press of Virginia, 1993), 406.

93 William James, "What Makes a Life Significant," in William James, *The Writing of William James: A Comprehensive Edition*, ed. John McDermott (New York: Random House, 1967), 647.

94 Harrison, *Culture under Canvas*, 153.

95 Case and Case, *We Called It Culture*, 73.

96 Dunbar Chautauqua Bureau to Ethel Hinton, care of Hinton Verdi Company, July 16, 1914. Iowa. The Dunbar Chautauqua Bureau billed itself on its letterhead as "An Independent Organization for Cooperation with Chautauqua Assemblies Under Local Management." An example of a reference to the Circuits as "a three ring circus" can be found in "Chautauqua and Water," *Nation* 26, no. 14 (August 1915): 168.

97 Janet Davis, *The Circus Age: Culture and Society under the American Big Top* (Chapel Hill: University of North Carolina Press, 2002).

98 Dunbar Chautauqua Bureau to Hinton.

99 Rieser, *The Chautauqua Moment*, 4.

100 Theodore Roosevelt is usually credited with calling Chautauqua "the most American thing in America," and it was one of the most repeated and quoted phrases about Chautauqua. There is, however, significant doubt about who actually said it. Alma Ellerbe and Paul Ellerbe attribute it to Lord Bryce ("The Most American Thing in America," *World's Work* 48 [August 1924]: 441). Robert Louis Utlaut credits Hjalmar H. Boyesen, novelist and professor at Cornell and Columbia universities ("The Role of the Chautauqua Movement in the Shaping of Progressive Thought in America at the End of the Nineteenth Century" [Ph.D. diss., University of Minnesota, 1972], 2). Jeffrey Simpson argues that Roosevelt actually said that "Chautauqua was typically American in that it was typical of America at its best" but that reporters "rephrased" (Simpson's term) Roosevelt's characterization (*Chautauqua*, 70).

101 Montrose J. Moses, *The American Dramatist* (Boston: Little, Brown, 1911), 13.

102 Castle, "Chautauqua," 373.

103 Harriette Kohler Smith, interview by author, February 25, 2004.

1. AMERICA ON THE PLATFORM

1 Welcome to Mooresville, Indiana, http://www.mooresville-in.com/community/index.html. February 6, 2004.

2 Lincoln Chautauquas, season program, Mooresville, Ind., 1917. Iowa.

3 Ibid.

4 David Glassberg, *American Historical Pageantry: The Uses of Tradition in the Early Twentieth Century* (Chapel Hill: University of North Carolina Press, 1990), 215.

5 Ibid., 105, 235.

6 Lincoln Chautauquas, season program, Mooresville, Ind., 1917.

7 Glassberg, *American Historical Pageantry*, 215.

8 Richard T. Ely, *Ground under Our Feet: An Autobiography* (New York: Macmillan, 1938), 79.

9 Quoted in Hurlbut, *The Story of Chautauqua*, xvi.

10 Quoted in Lee Green, "Camp Chautauqua," *American Way* 31, no. 10 (May 15, 1998): 48.

11 John Whiteclay Chambers II, *The Tyranny of Change: America in the Progressive Era 1890–1920*, 2nd ed. (New York: St. Martin's Press, 1992), 11.

12 Ellis W. Hawley, *The Great War and the Search for a Modern Order*, 2nd ed. (Prospect Heights, Ill.: Waveland Press, 1992), 10.

13 The population was actually 39,905,000. U.S. Department of Commerce, *Historical Statistics*, Series A 6–8.

14 Nell Irvin Painter, *Standing at Armageddon: The United States 1877–1919* (New York: W. W. Norton, 1987), xxxiv.

15 Matthew Frye Jacobson, *Whiteness of a Different Color: European Immigrants and the Alchemy of Race* (Cambridge, Mass.: Harvard University Press, 1998), 72.

16 Ibid., 17.

17 Chambers, *The Tyranny of Change*, 38.

18 Ibid., 160.

19 William Allen White, *The Old Order Changeth: A View of American Democracy* (New York: Macmillan, 1910), 49–50.

20 "The progressive movement that is now sweeping the country owes its strength very largely to the chautauqua" (French Strother, "The Great American Forum," *World's Work* 24 [September 1912]: 553).

21 Steven J. Diner, *A Very Different Age: Americans of the Progressive Era* (New York: Hill and Wang, 1998), 12.

22 Harrison John Thorton, "Chautauqua in Iowa," *Iowa Journal of History* 50, no. 2 (April 1952): 111.

23 Quoted in Hurlbut, *The Story of Chautauqua*, xv.

24 "The Uplift of Chautauqua Week," *Literary Digest*, October 18, 1913, 684.

25 Horner, *Strike the Tents*, 11–12.

26 Quoted in Carl D. Thompson, "Is the Chautauqua a Free Platform?" *New Republic*, December 17, 1924, 86; also quoted in Harrison, *Culture under Canvas*, 272.

27 Thomas Postlewait, "The Hieroglyphic Stage: American Theatre and Society, Post–Civil War to 1945," in Wilmeth and Bigsby, *The Cambridge History of the American Theatre*, 2:134.

28 Alan Trachtenberg, "'We Study the Word and Works of God:' Chautauqua and the Sacralization of American Culture," *Henry Ford Museum and Greenfield Village Herald* 13, no. 2 (1984): 9.

29 Glenn Frank, "The Parliament of the People," *Century* 98 (July 1919): 402.

30 George E. Vincent, "What Is Chautauqua?" *Independent*, July 6, 1914, 19.

31 Judith N. Shklar, *American Citizenship: The Quest for Inclusion* (Cambridge, Mass.: Harvard University Press, 1991), 5.

32 Clifton E. Olmstead, *Religion in America: Past and Present* (Englewood Cliffs, N.J.: Prentice Hall, 1961), 116.

33 Mark A. Noll, *A History of Christianity in the United States and Canada* (Grand Rapids, Mich.: William B. Eerdmans, 1992), 299, 243.

34 Robert T. Handy, *A Christian America: Protestant Hopes and Historical Realities* (New York: Oxford University Press, 1971), 115.

35 Andrew Chamberlin Rieser, "Secularization Reconsidered: Chautauqua and the De-Christianization of Middle-Class Authority, 1880–1920," in *The Middling Sorts: Explorations in the History of the American Middle-Class*, ed. Burton J. Bledstein and Robert D. Johnson, 147 (New York: Routledge, 2001).

36 Elizabeth Southwick and Bertha Smith Titus, *A Mother Goose Party* (Cedar Rapids, Iowa: Redpath-Vawter Chautauqua System, 1921), 16.

37 Lincoln Chautauquas, season program, Mooresville, Ind., 1917.

38 Helen B. Paulsen, publicity brochure, 1920s. Iowa.

39 Ibid.

40 Frederick Perry Noble, "Chautauqua as a New Factor in American Life," *New England Magazine* 8, no. 1 (March 1890): 100.

41 Loring Whiteside to William A. Colledge, February 11, 1916. Iowa.

42 Oram, interview, May 20, 1998.

43 Jane Addams, *The Spirit of Youth and the City Streets* (New York: Macmillan, 1910), 103.

44 Peter Levine, *The New Progressive Era: Toward a Fair and Deliberative Democracy* (Lanham, Md.: Rowman and Littlefield, 2000), 71.

45 George Ellsworth Johnson, *Education by Play and Games* (Boston: Ginn, 1907), 14–15.

46 Nina B. Lamkin, *Good Times for All Times: A Cyclopaedia of Entertainment with Programs, Outlines, References, Practical Suggestions for Home, Church, School and Community* (New York: Samuel French, 1929), 148.

47 Radcliffe Chautauqua, season program, Arlington, [no state], n.d. Iowa.

48 "Minna Mae Lewis, B.O., M.O.: Reader—Morning Lecturer, Children's Entertainer," publicity brochure, 1910s. Iowa.

49 "Have You Stopped to Think?" publicity brochure, 1927. Iowa.

50 Glassberg, *American Historical Pageantry*, 64.

51 Southwick and Titus, *A Mother Goose Party*, 4.

52 Shannon Jackson, *Lines of Activity: Performance, Historiography, Hull-House Domesticity* (Ann Arbor: University of Michigan Press, 2000), 238.

53 Southwick and Titus, *A Mother Goose Party*, 7.

54 Oram, interview, May 20, 1998.

55 Nancy F. Cott, *Public Vows: A History of Marriage and the Nation* (Cambridge, Mass.: Harvard University Press, 2000), 5.

56 Edith Williams Way, unpublished notebook, n.d. Swarthmore.

57 Ibid.

58 Levine, *The New Progressive Era*, 73.

59 Shklar, *American Citizenship*, 6.

60 Way, notebook.

61 Redpath-Vawter, season advertising brochure, 1923. Iowa.

62 Redpath Chautauquas, season program, Georgetown, [no state], 1929. Iowa.

63 Evelyn Nakano Glenn, *Unequal Freedom: How Race and Gender Shaped American Citizenship and Labor* (Cambridge, Mass.: Harvard University Press, 2002), 19.

64 Arthur William Row, "Acting in Tents in Chautauqua," *PoetLore* 36 (Summer 1925): 225.

65 Jackson, *Lines of Activity*, 244.

66 Woodrow Wilson, War Messages, 65th Congress, 1st Session, Senate Document no. 5, Serial no. 7264, Washington, D.C., 1917, 7.

67 Frank Dixon, "Appreciation of Paul M. Pearson," unpublished manuscript, January 7, 1916. Swarthmore.

68 Caroline McCarthy, "The International Lyceum Association in War," unpublished manuscript, ca. 1942. Iowa.

69 Chambers, *The Tyranny of Change*, 244.

70 Woodrow Wilson to Montaville Flowers, December 14, 1917, reprinted in all Standard Chautauqua System season programs, 1918. Iowa.

71 McCarthy, "The International Lyceum Association."

72 Chambers, *The Tyranny of Change*, 245.

73 Stewart Halsey Ross, *Propaganda for War: How the United States Was Conditioned to Fight the Great War of 1914–1918* (Jefferson, N.C.: McFarland, 1996), 2.

74 Painter, *Standing at Armageddon*, 329.

75 Ross, *Propaganda for War*, 226.

76 Chambers, *The Tyranny of Change*, 244.

77 Harry Harrison to William A. Sunday, December 24, 1917. Iowa.

78 "History-Making Plans for Coordination," *Smileage News* 1, no. 1 (1918): 3.

79 "Citizens throughout America Enthusiastic," *Smileage News* 1, no. 1 (1918): 1.

80 Smileage Book, ticket. Iowa.

81 "What Will the Soldiers See?" *Smileage News* 1, no. 1 (1918): 2.

82 *How to Conduct the Smileage Book Campaign to Provide Entertainment for Our Soldiers* (n.p.: Military Entertainment Council, n.d.), 2.

83 Harold Braddock to Harry Harrison, April 9, 1918. Iowa.

84 "The Smileage Book Campaign," *Lyceum Magazine*, February 1918, 19.

85 Lyman P. Powell, "The End of a Perfect Day," *Outlook* 120 (September 18, 1918): 103.

86 Redpath-Vawter, season program, Canton, Ohio, 1918. Iowa.

87 Tapia, *Circuit Chautauqua*, 120.

88 Israel Zangwill, *The Melting-Pot* (New York: Macmillan, 1932), 33–34. Subsequent references to the play will be cited in the text.

89 *The Melting Pot: The Great American Drama by Israel Zangwill* (Lyceum/Chautauqua, 1916), no page. Iowa.

90 Harley Erdman, *Staging the Jew: The Performance of an American Ethnicity, 1860–1920* (New Brunswick, N.J.: Rutgers University Press, 1997), 134.

91 Arthur Kachel, publicity brochure, n.d. Iowa.

92 Maureen Murphy, "Bridie, We Hardly Knew Ye: The Irish Domestics," in *The Irish in America*, ed. Michael Coffey, 141 (New York: Hyperion, 1997).

93 "The Players: The Irish Onstage," in Coffey, *The Irish in America*, 189.

94 Israel Zangwill to Theodore Roosevelt, August 25, 1908, quoted in Joseph H. Udelson, *Dreamer of the Ghetto: The Life and Works of Israel Zangwill* (Tuscaloosa: University of Alabama Press, 1990), 194.

95 Erdman, *Staging the Jew*, 137.

96 Redpath-Vawter, season advertising brochure, 1915. Iowa.

97 Redpath-Horner, season program, n.p., 1917. Iowa.

98 Powell, "The End of a Perfect Day," 103.

99 Tapia, *Circuit Chautauqua*, 135.

100 Ibid.

101 R. M. K. to Harry Harrison, April 25, 1919, quoting letter from Ernestine Schumann-Heink. Iowa.

102 Harry Harrison to T. F. Graham, February 20, 1919. Iowa.

103 Rieser, *The Chautauqua Moment*, 280.

104 Lincoln Chautauquas, season program, Mooresville, Ind., 1917.

105 This image of Uncle Sam was a new and contemporary one for Chautauqua spectators—the recruiting poster of Uncle Sam pointing to viewers and saying, "I Want You for the US Army," was created in 1917. Chambers, *The Tyranny of Change*, 244.

2. COMMUNITY ON THE PLATFORM

 1 Harrison, *Culture under Canvas*, 183. Harrison does not give a date for this event.

 2 David Mead, "1914: The Chautauqua and American Innocence," *Journal of Popular Culture* 1 (Spring 1968): 344.

 3 *14th Census of the United States*, vol. 1, *Population* (Washington D.C.: Government Printing Office, 1921), 271.

 4 Edna E. Wilson, "Canvas and Culture: When Chautauqua Comes to Town," *Outlook* 131 (August 1922): 599.

 5 Ben R. Vardaman to W. Frank McClure, January 12, 1914. Iowa.

 6 Ibid.

 7 Warren G. Harding to Charles F. Horner, December 6, 1922, quoted in Horner, *Strike the Tents*, 198.

 8 Harold C. Kessinger, "What the Small Town Must Do to Be Saved," *Lyceum Magazine*, April 1914, 11.

 9 Swarthmore Chautauqua Association, "I Am What I Am," n.d. Swarthmore.

 10 Ronald H. Wiebe, *The Search for Order, 1877–1920* (New York: Hill and Wang, 1967), viii, xiv.

 11 David B. Danbom, *Born in the Country: A History of Rural America* (Baltimore: Johns Hopkins University Press, 1995), 134.

 12 U.S. Department of Commerce, *Historical Statistics*, Series A 57–72 and A 73–81.

 13 Wiebe, *The Search for Order*, 44.

 14 Thomas Bender, *Community and Social Change in America* (New Brunswick, N.J.: Rutgers University Press, 1978), 89.

 15 Chambers, *The Tyranny of Change*, 111.

 16 Albert E. Wiggam, "Is Chautauqua Worth While?" *Bookman*, June 1927, 403.

 17 Central Community Chautauqua System, season program, Lewiston, Maine, 1916. Iowa.

 18 *Vandalia Leader*, clipping in scrapbook, n.d. Iowa.

 19 Jessie Bernard, *The Sociology of Community* (Glenville, Ill.: Scott, Foresman, 1973), 3.

 20 Bender, *Community and Social Change*, 6.

 21 Ibid., 3.

22 Benedict Anderson, *Imagined Communities* (London: Verso, 1991), 6.

23 Ibid.

24 Horner, *Strike the Tents*, 90.

25 Anderson, *Imagined Communities*, 7.

26 Redpath-Vawter, season program, Anamosa, Iowa. 1922. Iowa.

27 Ibid.

28 L. B. Crotty to J. W. Gray of the Ethiopian Serenaders, November 7, 1912. Iowa.

29 Central Community Chautauqua System, season program.

30 "T. Dinsmore Upton: Community Builder," publicity brochure, ca. 1925. Iowa.

31 Case and Case, *We Called It Culture*, 36.

32 Jacobson, *Whiteness of a Different Color*, 6.

33 Ibid., 22.

34 Harry H. Laughlin, *Immigration and Conquest* (New York: New York State Chamber of Commerce, 1939), 39.

35 Not surprisingly, there has not been much contemporary discussion of the Circuits' accommodation of racist preferences until very recently. Typically, scholars have noted that the Circuits "in the South were unlikely to risk any discussion of the Negro" (Mead, "1914," 348). Redpath Circuit manager Leo Rosencrans remembered that "blacks did not attend our Chautauquas in the South. I did not give it a thought then. I accepted it" (Eldon E. Snyder, "The Chautauqua Movement in Popular Culture: A Sociological Analysis," *Journal of American Culture* 8 [Fall 1985]: 88). There is no reason to believe that Rosencrans's attitude and experience were anything other than typical.

36 Shawn Lay, "Introduction: The Second Invisible Empire," in *The Invisible Empire in the West: Toward a New Historical Appraisal of the Ku Klux Klan of the 1920s*, ed. Shawn Lay, 3, 4 (Urbana: University of Illinois Press, 1992).

37 Wyn Craig Wade, *The Fiery Cross: The Ku Klux Klan in America* (New York: Simon and Schuster, 1987), 165.

38 Lay, "Introduction," 8. It is interesting to note that Chautauqua and the Ku Klux Klan both had their roots in the revivalist, evangelical Methodism that arose during the nineteenth century. Lewis Miller and John Vincent were active and influential members of the church, and William J. Simmons had been a Circuit preacher who was a successful and popular platform lecturer (Wade, *The Fiery Cross*, 140).

39 "Ku Klux Klan Sends Out 'Klantauqua,'" *Lyceum Magazine*, June 1924, 26.

40 "Klantauqua Cannot Supplant Chautauqua," *Lyceum Magazine*, June 1924, 32.

41 Walter Holcomb, "Famous Men I Have Met," *Success*, February 1924, 108.

42 Ibid.

43 William F. Holmes, *The White Chief: James Kimble Vardaman* (Baton Rouge: Louisiana State University Press, 1970).

44 Beth Day, *The Little Professor of the Piney Woods: The Story of Professor Laurence Jones* (New York: Julian Messner, 1955), 77, 123.

45 Redpath-Vawter, season program, n.p., 1915. Iowa.

46 Ibid.

47 Lewis L. Gould, "A Neglected First Lady," in *Lou Henry Hoover: Essays on a Busy Life*, ed. Dale C. Mayer, 68 (Worland, Wyo.: High Plains, 1994). President Hoover responded by inviting the presidents of Hampton Institute and Tuskeegee to dine at the White House on several occasions. Dale C. Mayer, e-mail message to Jessica Hester, February 7, 1998.

48 L. B. Crotty to C. E. Backman, June 24, 1929. Iowa.

49 C. E. Backman to L. B. Crotty, July 3, 1929. Iowa.

50 L. B. Crotty to C. E. Backman, July 8, 1929. Iowa.

51 C. E. Backman to L. B. Crotty, July 18, 1929. Iowa.

52 W. E. Burghardt DuBois, *The Souls of Black Folk* (New York: Signet Classics, 1969 [1903]), xi.

53 White and Myers Chautauqua System, season program, n.p., 1922. Iowa.

54 "'Mammy' Scores a Hit at Chautauqua NY," clipping, n.d. Iowa.

55 "Mrs. John McRaven Premier Presentation of the Drama 'Mammy,'" publicity brochure, ca. 1915. Iowa.

56 Harry Hibschman, "Chautauqua Pro and Contra," *North American Review* 22 (May 1928): 597.

57 George M. Marsden, *Fundamentalism and American Culture: The Shaping of Twentieth-Century Evangelicalism: 1870–1925* (New York: Oxford University Press, 1980), 12.

58 Andrew F. Walls, *The Missionary Movement in Christian History: Studies in the Transmission of Faith* (Maryknoll, N.Y.: Orbis Books, 1996), 228.

59 Quoted in Hurlbut, *The Story of Chautauqua*, xiii.

60 Andrew Ward, *Dark Midnight When I Rise: The Story of the Jubilee Singers Who Introduced the World to the Music of Black America* (New York: Farrar, Straus, and Giroux, 2000), 110.

61 Toni Anderson, quoted in *Jubilee Singers: Sacrifice and Glory*, prod. and dir. Llewellyn Smith, PBS, WGBH Boston, with assistance from Nashville Public Television, 2000.

62 Ward, *Dark Midnight*, 100.

63 G. D. Pike, *The Jubilee Singers and Their Campaign for Twenty Thousand Dollars* (Boston: Lee and Shepard, 1873), 99.

64 Ward, *Dark Midnight*, 395.

65 John T. Flynn, "The Quaker Professor Entertains Millions of People," *American Magazine* 102 (September 1926): 142–143.

66 "The Beginning of Jubilee Singing," *Lyceum Magazine*, April 1920, 19.

67 Redpath-Vawter, season program, n.p., 1918. Iowa.

68 Ward, *Dark Midnight*, 395; Gustavus D. Pike, *The Singing Campaign for Ten Thousand Pounds; or, the Jubilee Singers in Great Britain* (New York: American Missionary Association, 1875), 205.

69 Cindy S. Aron, *Working at Play: A History of Vacations in the United States* (New York: Oxford University Press, 1999), 116.

70 The Piney Woods Country Life School still exists. It is the largest surviving histori-
    cally black boarding school in the United States. Its mission is "to provide that excel-
    lence in education within a Christian community through creation of an exceptional
    academic model which supports the tenet that all students can learn, develop a strong
    work ethic, and lead extraordinary lives through academic achievement and respon-
    sible citizenship." http://www.pineywoods.org. October 21, 2003.

71 Day, *The Little Professor*, 125.

72 Redpath-Vawter, season program, n.p., 1918.

73 Walls, *The Missionary Movement*, 235.

74 Redpath-Vawter, season program, n.p., 1915; Swarthmore Chautauqua, season pro-
    gram, n.p., 1921, Swarthmore; Redpath-Vawter, season program, Anamosa, Iowa,
    1922; Allerton Chautauqua, season program, Allerton, Iowa, 1929, Iowa; White and
    Myers, season program, Gage, Ok., 1922, Iowa; Ellison-White Chautauqua,
    Chautauqua Week, 1926, 1, Iowa.

75 Redpath-Vawter, season program, Burlington, Iowa, 1914. Iowa.

76 Rawei letterhead, 1913, Iowa; "The New Zealanders in Song, Story, and Picture from
    Cannibalism to Culture," publicity brochure, mid 1920s. Iowa; "Lyceum Events for
    the Week," clipping, n.d., Iowa; "From the Romantic Southern Seas," *Lyceumite and
    Talent*, September 1910, 28.

77 "Lyceum Events."

78 "From the Romantic," 27.

79 Eric D. Langer, "Preface," in *Historicizing Christian Encounters with the Other*, ed. John C.
    Lawley, xi (London: Macmillan, 1998).

80 Wherahiko Rawei to Ford Hicks, November 15, 1923. Iowa.

81 Ibid.

82 "Dr. Rawei Passed Away in New Zealand," clipping, n.d. Iowa.

83 Redpath-Vawter, season program, n.p., 1915.

84 Veit Erlmann, *Music, Modernity, and the Global Imagination: South Africa and the West*
    (Oxford: Oxford University Press, 1999), 14.

85 "From Africa," publicity brochure, n.d. Iowa.

86 "Thirty Years of Africa," publicity brochure, ca. 1916. Iowa.

87 Erlmann, *Music*, 102.

88 "Chautauqua Stars," *Everybody's Magazine* 33 (September 1915): 331.

89 J. B. T. Marsh, *The Story of the Jubilee Singers; with Their Songs* (Boston: Houghton and
    Osgood, 1880), 18.

90 Horner, *Strike the Tents*, 182.

91 S. J. Kleinberg, *Women in the United States, 1830–1945* (New Brunswick, N.J.: Rutgers
    University Press, 1999), 175.

92 U.S. Department of Commerce, Department of the Census, *Comparative Occupation
    Statistics for the United States, 1870–1940* (Washington D.C.: Government Printing
    Office, 1943), 91–92, 99.

93 Glenda Riley, *Inventing the American Woman: A Perspective on Women's History 1865 to the Present* (Arlington Heights, Ill.: Harlan Davidson, 1986), 61.

94 Sara M. Evans, *Born for Liberty: A History of Women in America* (New York: Free Press, 1989), 160.

95 Community Chautauqua, season program, Fennville, [no state], 1915. Iowa.

96 Midland Chautauqua Circuit, season program, Ackley, Iowa, 1914. Iowa.

97 Redpath-Vawter Service, *Twenty Years of Chautauqua Progress.*

98 Redpath-Vawter, season program, Belle Plaine, Iowa, 1909. Iowa.

99 Redpath-Vawter, season program, Canton, Mo., 1923. Iowa.

100 Quoted in Blanche Wiesen Cook, *Eleanor Roosevelt: The Defining Years*, vol. 2, *1933–1938* (New York: Penguin Books, 1999), 119.

101 Canton Chautauqua, season program, Canton, Mo., 1928. Iowa.

102 Independence Chautauqua, season program, Independence, Kans., 1906. Iowa.

103 Aron, *Working at Play*, 119.

104 Riley, *Inventing the American Woman*, 43.

105 "Miss Belle Kearney: One of America's Foremost Lecturers," publicity brochure, mid 1910s. Iowa.

106 Glenda Elizabeth Gilmore, *Gender and Jim Crow: Women and the Politics of White Supremacy in North Carolina, 1896–1920* (Chapel Hill: University of North Carolina Press, 1996), 53.

107 Quoted in Evans, *Born for Liberty*, 155.

108 Rieser, *The Chautauqua Moment*, 151.

109 Case and Case, *We Called It Culture*, 148.

110 Castle, "Chautauqua," 371. See also MacLaren, *Morally We Roll Along*; "The Uplift of Chautauqua Week," *Literary Digest*, October 18, 1913, 684–685; Tapia, *Circuit Chautauqua*; Harris Dickson, "Barnstorming with the Chautauqua," *Collier's*, August 12, 1916, 31, for similar versions of this tale. Bruce Bliven refers to "women from the farm—tired women in black with sunburnt faces" ("Nearest the Hearts of Ten Million," *Collier's*, September 8, 1923, 6).

111 Helen Knox, *Mrs. Percy V. Pennybacker: An Appreciation* (New York: Fleming H. Revell, 1916), 148.

112 Rebecca Richmond, *A Woman of Texas: Mrs. Percy V. Pennybacker* (San Antonio, Tex.: Naylor, 1941), 199.

113 Ibid., 196.

114 MacLaren, *Morally We Roll Along*, 121.

115 Ibid., 122.

116 Ibid., 123.

117 Ibid.

118 Charles Horner to Harry Harrison, November 26, 1919. Iowa.

119 Ibid.

120 Jacquelyn Dowd Hall, "O. Delight Smith's Progressive Era: Labor, Feminism, and Reform in the Urban South," in *Visible Women: New Essays on American Activism,*

ed. Nancy A. Hewitt and Suzanne Lebsock, 171 (Urbana and Chicago: University of Illinois Press, 1993).

121 Shannon Jackson, *Lines of Activity: Performance, Historiography, Hull House Domesticity* (Ann Arbor: University of Michigan Press, 2000), 136.

122 William A. Colledge to Selma Lenhart, November 17, 1922. Iowa. This letter appears in the files of several performers in the Redpath Collection. Lenhart was of sufficient status to merit a special postscript assuring her she was not being singled out and that the letter was sent "to all our attractions."

123 Ibid.

124 Horner, *Strike the Tents*, 182–183.

125 Harrison, *Culture under Canvas*, 173; Evelyn Bargelt, "The Young Girl in the Lyceum," *Lyceum Magazine*, (n.d.): 14. Iowa.

126 Adams, *Second Fiddle to Chautauqua*, 33.

127 Harry Harrison, undated memo draft to Crew Men, ca. 1918. Iowa.

128 Ibid.

129 Adams, *Second Fiddle to Chautauqua*, ix.

130 Ibid., 2.

131 "Mother made the momentous announcement that she wanted to join the Chautauqua. The word Chautauqua meant nothing to me but, I knew it was 'momentous' when I saw Dad's tight-lipped expression. Days of early morning and late night discussion followed between Mother and Dad. Although they thought they were protecting us by not disagreeing in front of us, we could overhear them in their bedroom. Dad sounded cross. 'But what will happen to the children? Who will take care of them?' Mother had easy answers: 'We can get a full-time housekeeper. . . . They won't even miss me.'" Handley's mother-in-law finally comes to take care of the household while she is on the road. Ibid., 19.

132 Ibid., 49.

133 "The Only Artist of Her Kind in the World," publicity brochure, n.d. Iowa.

134 Adams, *Second Fiddle to Chautauqua*, 33.

135 "Can a Woman Run a Home and a Job, Too?" *Literary Digest*, November 11, 1922, 54, 61.

136 Iris Marion Young, "The Ideal of Community and the Politics of Difference" in *Feminism/Postmodernism*, ed. Linda S. Nicholson, 301 (New York: Routledge 1990).

3. THE PLATFORM IN THE TENT

1 Neil Litchfield Trio, publicity brochure, 1908. Iowa.

2 It remains so today. Tourism has been continual since the publication of the book. Since the early 1920s people have been visiting the site of Bell's novel and enjoying a dramatization of the book. The production was professionalized in the 1950s, and in 1999 hundreds of former cast members returned to celebrate the fortieth anniversary of the current incarnation. By coincidence, it is near the live popular entertain-

ment mecca, Branson, Missouri, which ensures a steady stream of spectators. http://www.shepherdofthehills.com. October 21, 2003.

3 M. Beryl Buckley, publicity brochure, ca. 1915–1916. Iowa.

4 Tapia, *Circuit Chautauqua*, 164.

5 *The Shepherd of the Hills*, publicity brochure, 1920s. Iowa.

6 Day Keene and Dwight Vincent, *Chautauqua* (New York: G. P. Putnams' Sons, 1960), 310–311.

7 "Donald Bain: A Trip to the Farm," publicity brochure, 1927. Iowa.

8 Frank Preston Johnson, publicity brochure, 1920s. Iowa.

9 Llewellen MacGarr, publicity brochure, ca. 1925. Iowa.

10 "Hon. Otis Wingo, the 'Rural Credit Congressman,'" publicity brochure, ca. 1915. Iowa. He served for seventeen years in Congress, from 1913 to his death in 1930.

11 Neil Smith and Cindi Katz, "Grounding Metaphor: Towards a Spatialized Politics," in *Place and the Politics of Identity*, ed. Michael Keith and Steve Pile, 69 (London: Routledge, 1993).

12 James R. Shortridge, *The Middle West: Its Meaning in American Culture* (Lawrence: University Press of Kansas, 1989), 135–138.

13 Weibe, *The Search for Order*, 12.

14 Dickson, "Barnstorming," 12.

15 Harrison, *Culture under Canvas*, 96. The circus tent, by contrast, was always white, so the visual difference must have been quite clear. Janet Davis, phone conversation with author, September 23, 2003.

16 William Lawrence Slout, *Theatre in a Tent: The Development of a Provincial Entertainment* (Bowling Green, Ohio: Bowling Green University Popular Press, 1972), 40.

17 Ibid.

18 Ellerbee and Ellerbee, "The Most American Thing in America," 446.

19 Davis, *The Circus Age*, 2.

20 Brooks McNamara, "Popular Entertainment," in Wilmeth and Bigsby, *The Cambridge History of the American Theatre*, 2:385.

21 Ibid.

22 Davis, *The Circus Age*, 193.

23 Ibid., 208.

24 Ibid., 140.

25 Ida M. Tarbell, "A Little Look at the People," *Atlantic Monthly* 119 (May 1917): 608.

26 Tapia, *Circuit Chautauqua*, 68.

27 Orchard, *Fifty Years of Chautauqua*, 290–291.

28 Marvin Carlson, "The Development of the American Theatre Program," in *The American Stage: Social and Economic Issues from the Colonial Period to the Present*, ed. Ron Engle and Tice L. Miller, 102 (Cambridge: Cambridge University Press, 1993).

29 The exception to this is the programs offered by independent Chautauquas. Those tended to rely heavily on advertising (although usually not as heavily as the average

theater program), and this makes sense given that they were reaching those who could take advantage of local goods and services. It was also a way for businesses to declare their investments in the local community.

30 Davis, phone conversation.

31 "Theatre Playbills and Programs," http://memory.loc.gov/ammem/vshtml/vsprgbl. html. September 24, 2003.

32 Midland Chautauqua Assembly, season program, Midland, Iowa, 1909. Iowa. This program contains quite a few ads, all for businesses in the Midland area.

33 Redpath-Vawter, season program, Carson, Iowa, 1915. Iowa. This cover was signed by Fred Craft, one of the very few covers that actually indicates the artist.

34 A. B. MacDonald, "Tent Universities," *Country Gentleman*, August 12, 1922, 13.

35 Shortridge, *The Middle West*, 6–7.

36 Frieda Knobloch, *The Culture of Wilderness: Agriculture as Colonization in the American West* (Chapel Hill: University of North Carolina Press, 1996), 17.

37 Tapia, *Circuit Chautauqua*, 116.

38 William Jennings Bryan, "The Cross of Gold Speech [1896]," in *William Jennings Bryan: Selections*, ed. Ray Ginger, 46 (Indianapolis: Bobbs Merrill, 1967).

39 Colby, "A Chance for Cultivation," *Lyceumite and Talent*, May 1913, 24.

40 Ibid.

41 Knobloch, *The Culture of Wilderness*, 75.

42 Ned Woodman, "Our Town," *Lyceum Magazine*, May 1914, 24.

43 Knobloch, *The Culture of Wilderness*, 118.

44 Orchard, *Who Said Quit?*

45 Ned Woodman, "The Sower," *Lyceum Magazine*, June 1919, 15. Edwin Wright "Ned" Woodman, the cartoonist of both "Our Town" and "The Sower," also lectured on Chautauqua. His lectures were "built around those big crayon pictures he draws for you while you are listening to him" (publicity brochure, n.d. Iowa). In addition to his platform career, he did editorial cartoons for journals and newspapers. His work was billed: "Wholesome, instructive features are not omitted, for his appreciation of serious things is as deep as his sense of humor; but whatever he offers his audiences in the way of sober material is generally so pleasantly flavored as so to be 'easy to take'" ("Woodman the Cartoonist," publicity brochure, 1909. Iowa).

46 Redpath-Vawter, season program, Canton, Mo., 1923.

47 Simon Schama, *Landscape and Memory* (New York: Vintage, 1995), 10.

48 E. Bradford Burns, *Kinship with the Land: Regionalist Thought in Iowa, 1894–1942* (Iowa City: University of Iowa Press, 1996), 14.

49 John Edward Tapia, "Circuit Chautauquas Promotional Visions: A Study of Program Brochures, circa 1904–1932" (Ph.D. diss., University of Arizona, 1978), 132–133.

50 Frederick Jackson Turner, "Significance of the Frontier in American History," in Knobloch, *The Culture of Wilderness*, 147–148.

51 Knobloch, *The Culture of Wilderness*, 61.

52 Shortridge, *The Middle West*, 29.

53 Richard Hofstadter, *The Age of Reform: From Bryan to F. D. R.* (New York: Alfred A. Knopf, 1977), 35.

54 Lawrence Bacon Lee, *Kansas and the Homestead Act: 1862–1905* (New York: Arno Press, 1979), 2.

55 Roy M. Robbins, *Our Landed Heritage: The Public Domain, 1776–1936* (Princeton, N.J.: Princeton University Press, 1942), 209.

56 Knobloch, *The Culture of Wilderness*, 54–55.

57 Lee, *Kansas and the Homestead Act*, 20.

58 Ibid., 591.

59 Elizabeth Sanders, *Roots of Reform: Farmers, Workers, and the American State 1877–1917* (Chicago: University of Chicago Press, 1999), 101.

60 Ibid., 118.

61 Chambers, *The Tyranny of Change*, 42–43.

62 Deborah Fink, *Agrarian Women: Wives and Mothers in Rural Nebraska, 1880–1940* (Chapel Hill: University of North Carolina Press, 1992), 25.

63 Ibid., 2, 27.

64 *American Lumberman*, clipping, n.d. Iowa.

65 Keith Vawter, "Introductory remarks," Redpath-Vawter, season program, Belle Plaine, Iowa, 1909.

66 Ibid.

67 Ibid.

68 Kessinger, "What the Small Town Must Do," 12.

69 W. Frank McClure, "Under the Big Tent," *Independent* 82 (June 21, 1915): 504.

70 Burns, *Kinship with the Land*, xi.

71 Ibid., 66.

72 Danbom, *Born in the Country*, 92.

73 Burns, *Kinship with the Land*, 66.

74 Diner, *A Very Different Age*, 196.

75 Danbom, *Born in the Country*, 93.

76 Ibid., 164.

77 Burns, *Kinship with the Land*, 67.

78 "Chautauqua-Community Development Page," *Lyceumite Magazine*, June 1914, 17.

79 Charles F. Horner, "Introductory Remarks," Redpath-Horner, season program, n.p., 1909. Iowa.

80 Orchard, *Who Said Quit?*

81 Truman H. Talley, "The Chautauquas: An American Achievement," *World's Work* 42 (June 1921): 184.

82 Ibid., 172.

83 Frances D. C. McCaskill, "Chautauqua in a New England Community," *Lyceum Magazine*, June 1919, 16.

84 Schultz, *The Romance of Small-Town Chautauquas*, 41, 58, 77.

85 Oram, interview, February 16, 1996.

86 Ibid.

87 William L. Shirer, *Twentieth Century Journey, a Memoir of a Life and the Times: The Start 1904–1930* (Boston: Little, Brown, 1976), 156.

88 Ibid., 163.

4. PERFORMANCE ON THE PLATFORM: ORATORY

1 Harrison, *Culture under Canvas*, 158.

2 Case and Case, *We Called It Culture*, 87.

3 Richard T. Ely, *Ground under Our Feet: An Autobiography* (New York: Macmillan, 1938), 319.

4 Case and Case, *We Called It Culture*, 89.

5 William Jennings Bryan (as completed by Mary Baird Bryan), *The Memoirs of William Jennings Bryan* (Philadelphia: John C. Winston, 1925), 248–249.

6 Bryan, "The Cross of Gold Speech," 46.

7 Gretchen Ritter, *Goldbugs and Greenbacks: The Antimonopoly Tradition and the Politics of Finance in America* (Cambridge: Cambridge University Press, 1997), 61.

8 Sanders, *Roots of Reform*, 140.

9 Ibid., 156.

10 Kevin Phillips, *William McKinley* (New York: Times Books/Henry Holt, 2003), 74.

11 Charles Edward Russell, *Bare Hands and Stone Walls: Some Recollections of a Side-Line Reformer* (New York: Charles Scribner's Sons, 1933), 319.

12 Joe Mitchell Chapple, "On the Chautauqua System," clipping, n.d. Iowa.

13 Horner, *Strike the Tents*, 122.

14 Harrison, *Culture under Canvas*, 158.

15 Robert W. Cherny, *A Righteous Cause: The Life of William Jennings Bryan* (Norman: University of Oklahoma Press, 1994), 94.

16 Allen Albert, "The Tents of the Conservative," *Scribner's Magazine* 72 (July 1922): 57.

17 Harrison, *Culture under Canvas*, 159.

18 "R. H. Cunningham: 'The Prince of Peace,'" publicity brochure, n.d. Arizona.

19 Cherny, *A Righteous Cause*, 94.

20 Horner, *Strike the Tents*, 131.

21 Benjamin McArthur, *Actors and American Culture 1880–1920*, 2nd ed. (Iowa City: University of Iowa Press, 2000), 209.

22 Quoted in John P. Horshor, "American Contributions to Rhetorical Theory and Homiletics," in *A History of Speech Education in America*, ed. Karl Wallace, 132 (New York: Appleton-Century-Crofts, 1954).

23 Constance Rourke, *Trumpets of Jubilee* (New York: Harcourt, Brace, 1927), vii.

24 Redpath-Horner, season program, Lubbock, Texas, 1925. Iowa.

25 Mary Margaret Robb, "The Elocutionary Movement and Its Chief Figures," in Wallace, *A History of Speech Education in America*, 179.

26 Charles Horner to G. D. Roberts, January 10, 1923. Iowa.

27 McArthur, *Actors and American Culture*, 209.

28 Frank Bohn, "America Revealed in Its Chautauqua," *New York Times Magazine*, October 10, 1926, 18.

29 Frank, "The Parliament of the People," 415.

30 Frederick J. Antczak and Edith Seimers, "The Divergence of Purpose and Practice on the Chautauqua: Keith Vawter's Self-Defense," in *Oratorical Culture in Nineteenth-Century America: Transformations in the Theory and Practice of Rhetoric*, ed. Gregory Clark and S. Michael Halloran (Carbondale: Southern Illinois University Press, 1993), 212.

31 Michael Kammen, *American Culture, American Tastes: Social Change and the Twentieth Century* (New York: Alfred A. Knopf, 1999), 37.

32 Robert W. Snyder, *The Voice of the City: Vaudeville and Popular Culture in New York*, 2nd ed. (Chicago: Ivan R. Dee, 2000), 88.

33 Ibid., xix.

34 Richard Butsch, *The Making of American Audiences: From Stage to Television, 1750–1990* (New York: Cambridge University Press, 2000), 95.

35 "The Successful Entertainer: An Interview with Mr. S. T. Ford," *Werners Magazine* 22, no. 5 (January 1899): 419.

36 Richard Oram, interview by author, May 20, 1998.

37 M. Allison Kibler, *Rank Ladies: Gender and Cultural Hierarchy in American Vaudeville* (Chapel Hill: University of North Carolina Press, 1999), 7.

38 Butsch, *The Making of American Audiences*, 111, 100.

39 Ibid., 100.

40 Kathryn J. Oberdeck, *The Evangelist and the Impresario: Religion, Entertainment, and Cultural Politics in America, 1884–1914* (Baltimore: Johns Hopkins University Press, 1999), 322.

41 Ibid., 208.

42 Kibler, *Rank Ladies*, 7.

43 Albert, "The Tents of the Conservative," 55.

44 Kibler, *Rank Ladies*, 8.

45 Butsch, *The Making of American Audiences*, 118.

46 Oberdeck, *The Evangelist and the Impresario*, 91.

47 Gregory Mason, "Chautauqua: Its Technic," *American Mercury* 16 (January 1929): 277.

48 Star Chautauqua, season program, n.p., 1914. Iowa.

49 Bliven, "Nearest the Hearts," 7.

50 Rushed while out on the road, Pearson wrote his wife: "Do you want me to tell you my troubles? There is not time. Today . . . a member of the Romano Orchestra has been writing love letter to a little girl of 13 at Bellefonte [?], which has been forwarded to me" (Paul M. Pearson to Edna W. Pearson, July 18, 1914. Swarthmore). The Ben Greet Players provided their share of worries. George Seybolt, who played Antipholus of Ephesus in *Comedy of Errors* and Charles Marlowe in *She Stoops to Conquer*, left his room in Columbus, Georgia, "in very bad order." He was scolded, "The Chautauqua

institution is supposed to have the highest type of ladies and gentlemen and I am hoping it is a mistake" (Harry P. Harrison to George Seybolt, May 24, 1913. Iowa). When the players were reported to have been drinking heavily, Harry Harrison wrote Greet himself: "You certainly appreciate that it takes very little of this sort of criticism to give a black eye to the Ben Greet Players as well as to the Redpath Bureau. This must not be" (Harry P. Harrison to Sir Ben Greet, March 5, 1930. Iowa). Greet's reply is not preserved. Even as late as 1941 a club in Holland, Michigan, evaluated Gay MacLaren and was disappointed. "Found her very charming but surprised to see her smoking cigarettes after the program. Club comprised of men and women none of whom have ever smoked among the others during the social hour. Suppose in large cities nothing is thought of it" (Holland, Mich., club, General Report on Attractions, Chicago Redpath Bureau, October 20, 1941. Iowa). There was never, however, a nationally publicized scandal, suggesting that while performers may have fallen short both of Chautauqua rhetoric and audience expectations, they usually adhered (even if only loosely) to community standards of behavior, morality, and respectability.

51 Bruce Bliven, "Mother, Home, and Heaven," New Republic, January 9, 1924, 174.

52 Paul Pearson, "The Chautauqua Movement," Lippincotts 78 (August 1906): 192.

53 Harrison, Culture under Canvas, 136.

54 Bliven, "Mother," 174.

55 Robert A. Wauzzinski, Between God and Gold: Protestant Evangelism and the Industrial Revolution 1820–1914 (Cranbury, N.J.: Associate University Presses, 1993), 151–152.

56 Case and Case, We Called It Culture, 253.

57 Ibid., 255.

58 Dillavou, "The Swarthmore Chautauqua," 45.

59 Amos Elwood Reynolds, "Grandfather's Boy," unpublished manuscript, 1993. Swarthmore.

60 W. C. Crosby, "Acres of Diamonds," American Mercury 14 (May 1927): 107.

61 Evening Star, season program, Gorin, Mo., 1917 or 1918. Iowa.

62 Redpath-Vawter, season program, Belle Plaine, Iowa. 1909.

63 "Chautauqua Stars," 326.

64 Mason, "Chautauqua," 275.

65 Roland W. Baggott with Philip McKee, "Christian Culture, R.F.D.," Outlook and Independent 158 (August 1931): 429.

66 Crawford Peffer to Keith Vawter, April 1, 1929. Iowa.

67 "Chautauqua," Outlook, March 16, 1927, 326.

68 Woodrow Wilson, "Mere Literature," from Atlantic Monthly (1893), in The Origins of Literary Study in America, ed. Gerald Graff and Michael Warner (New York: Routledge, 1989), 89.

69 Kenneth Cmiel, Democratic Eloquence: The Fight over Popular Speech in Nineteenth-Century America (New York: William Morrow, 1990), 14.

70 Ibid., 47.

71 Ibid., 179.

72 Gerald Graff and Michael Warner, "Introduction to Woodrow Wilson," in Graff and Warner, *The Origins of Literary Study in America*, 82.

73 Mason, "Chautauqua," 279–280; Mary Austin, "The Town That Doesn't Want Chautauqua," *New Republic*, July 7, 1926, 195.

74 Paul Edwards, "Unstoried: Teaching Literature in the Age of Performance Studies," *Theatre Annual* 32 (Fall 1999): 59.

75 Nan Johnson, "The Popularization of Nineteenth Century Rhetoric: Elocution and the Private Learner," in Clark and Halloran, *Oratorical Culture in Nineteenth-Century America*, 148.

76 Ibid., 150.

77 Quoted in ibid., 150.

78 Warren Guthrie, "Rhetorical Theory in Colonial America," in Wallace, *A History of Speech Education in America*, 55.

79 Johnson, "The Popularization of Nineteenth Century Rhetoric," 141.

80 Gladys L. Borchers and Lillian R. Wagner, "Speech Education in Nineteenth Century Schools," in Wallace, *A History of Speech Education in America*, 281.

81 Cmiel, *Democratic Eloquence*, 146.

82 Johnson, "The Popularization of Nineteenth Century Rhetoric," 149.

83 Hanscom, *Pioneers in Grease Paint*, 21.

84 Ibid.

85 Marie Hochmuth and Richard Murphy, "Rhetorical and Elocutionary Training in Nineteenth Century Colleges," in Wallace, *A History of Speech Education in America*, 167.

86 Lynn Miller Rein, *Northwestern University School of Speech: A History* (Evanston, Ill.: Northwestern University, 1981), 1.

87 Margaret Prendergast McLean, "Oral Interpretation—A Re-creative Art," in *Studies in the Art of Interpretation*, ed. Gertrude E. Johnson (New York: Appleton-Century, 1940), 44.

88 Magdalene Kramer and Margaret M. McCarthy, "The Development of Personality," in Johnson, *Studies in the Art of Interpretation*, 192.

89 Reynolds, "A Historical Study," 116, 101.

90 Redpath-Vawter, season program, Canton, Mo. 1916. Iowa.

91 Lucille Adams, publicity brochure, n.d. Iowa.

92 Frank M. Rarig and Halbert S. Greaves, "National Organizations and Speech Education," in Wallace, *A History of Speech Education in America*, 491, 494.

93 Rein, *Northwestern University School of Speech*, 123–124.

94 Maud May Babcock, "Impersonation versus Imitation," in Johnson, *Studies in the Art of Interpretation*. This article was originally published in the *Quarterly Journal of Public Speaking* (October 1916), 105.

95 Eugene Bahn and Margaret L. Bahn, *A History of Oral Interpretation* (Minneapolis: Burgess, 1970) 162; Maud May Babcock, "Interpretative Presentation versus

Impersonative Presentation," in Johnson, *Studies in the Art of Interpretation*, 89. Babcock's essay was originally delivered as a paper at the National Association of Academic Teachers of Public Speaking conference in 1915 and published the next year in the *Quarterly Journal of Public Speaking*.

96 Bahn and Bahn, *A History*, 169.
97 Babcock, "Interpretative Presentation," 88.
98 Ibid., 89.
99 Ibid., 102.
100 Farmington, Iowa, Chautauqua Association, season program, 1905. Iowa.
101 Lincoln Chautauquas, season program, Harvard, Ill., 1916. Iowa.
102 Gentile, *Cast of One*, 84–85.
103 Redpath-Vawter, season program, Anthon, Iowa, 1917. Iowa.
104 Rein, *Northwestern University School of Speech*, 180.
105 MacLaren, *Morally We Roll Along*, 52.
106 Harrison, *Culture under Canvas*, 137. Harrison credits this to Keith Vawter.
107 Cherny, *A Righteous Cause*, 95.
108 "The Only Artist of Her Kind in the World."
109 Harrison, *Culture under Canvas*, 196.
110 "The Only Artist of Her Kind in the World," 12. Jimmy was a one-act play about businessmen that well-known comic actor Fran Craven had popularized between 1910 and 1930.
111 Waterloo, Iowa, Chautauqua and Bible Institute, season program, 1912. Iowa.
112 Slout, *Theater in a Tent*, 55.
113 Case and Case, *We Called It Culture*, 54–55.
114 Redpath-Vawter, season program, Canton, Ohio, 1921. Iowa.
115 Donald K. Springen, *William Jennings Bryan: Orator of Small-Town America* (New York: Greenwood Press, 1991), 81–82.
116 Ibid., 43.
117 Paolo Coletta, *William Jennings Bryan II: Progressive Politician and Moral Statesman 1909–1915* (Lincoln: University of Nebraska Press, 1969), 107.
118 Shirer, *Twentieth Century Journey*, 162–163.
119 Cmiel, *Democratic Eloquence*, 39.
120 Johnson, "The Popularization," 144.
121 Judy Baker Goss, "'Expression' in the Popular Culture of Dallas in the Early 1900s," in *Performance of Literature in Historical Perspectives*, ed. David W. Thompson (Lanham, Md.: University Press of America, 1983), 276.
122 Bahn and Bahn, *A History*, 157.
123 "The Only Artist of Her Kind in the World," 13.

5. PERFORMANCE ON THE PLATFORM: THEATER

1 Harry P. Harrison to Ben Greet, February 25, 1913. Iowa.
2 Harrison, *Culture under Canvas*, 199.

3   Ibid., 189.

4   Adams, *Second Fiddle to Chautauqua*, xi.

5   Paul Pearson claims to have introduced drama onto the Circuits as early as 1901, but there is nothing in surviving archival materials that supports this. Pearson did not start his own Circuit until 1912. Pearson, "A Chronology of the Paul M. Pearsons."

6   Harrison, *Culture under Canvas*, 189.

7   Morrison, *Chautauqua*, 125.

8   Ibid.

9   Ibid., 156.

10 Harrison to Greet, February 25, 1913.

11 Harrison, *Culture under Canvas*, 199–200.

12 Ibid., 200.

13 Charles F. Horner, *Strike the Tents*, 184–185.

14 Vincent, *The Chautauqua Movement*, 17.

15 Nathan O. Hatch, *The Democratization of American Christianity* (New Haven, Conn.: Yale University Press, 1989), 55.

16 Alessandro Portelli, *The Text and the Voice: Writing, Speaking, and Democracy in American Literature* (New York: Columbia University Press, 1994), 280.

17 Hatch, *The Democratization of American Christianity*, 193.

18 Morrison, *Chautauqua*, 31.

19 Hurlbut, *The Story of Chautauqua*, 23.

20 Rebecca Richmond, *Chautauqua: An American Place* (New York: Duell, Sloan, and Pearce, 1943), 59.

21 Jeanne Halgren Kilde, "The 'Predominance of the Feminine' at Chautauqua: Rethinking the Gender-Space Relationship in Victorian America," *Signs* 24, no. 2 (1999): 461.

22 Da Boll and Da Boll, *Recollections*, 33.

23 Noll, *A History of Christianity*, 243.

24 Case and Case, *We Called It Culture*, 51.

25 "The Church and the Theatre," *Harper's Weekly* 48 (June 11, 1904): 804.

26 Jonas Barish, *The Anti-theatrical Prejudice* (Berkeley: University of California Press, 1981), 81.

27 "Platform and Stage Do Not Mix," *Lyceum Magazine*, (February 1919), 10.

28 Richmond, *Chautauqua*, 120.

29 Case and Case, *We Called It Culture*, 51.

30 McArthur, *Actors and American Culture*, 130.

31 Rein, *Northwestern University School of Speech*, 13.

32 Richmond, *Chautauqua*, 120, 121; McArthur, *Actors and American Culture*, 132.

33 Susan Harris Smith, *American Drama: The Bastard Art* (Cambridge: Cambridge University Press, 1997), 20, 75.

34 Morrison, *Chautauqua*, 156.

35 Smith, *American Drama*, 75.

36 Hanscom, *Pioneers in Grease Paint*, 55.

37 Faye Dudden, *Women in the American Theatre: Actresses and Audiences 1790–1870* (New Haven, Conn.: Yale University Press, 1994), 5.

38 Faye Dudden reports that theater managers were proactive in reassuring prospective patrons that they would encounter nothing objectionable if they attended theater. One manager claimed in a newspaper article that a spectator would experience "the same decorum in the theatre which is observed in the drawing room" (ibid., 80).

39 John Frick, "A Changing Theater: New York and Beyond," in Wilmeth and Bigsby, *The Cambridge History of the American Theatre*, 2:201.

40 Nancy Brooking, "Charles M. Sheldon and the Social Gospel," http://spider.george towncollege.edu/htallant/courses/his338/students/nbrooking/CMS.htm. October 22, 2003.

41 Charles M. Sheldon, "Is a Christian Theatre Possible?" *Independent*, March 14, 1901, 616.

42 Ibid., 618.

43 Postlewait, "The Hieroglyphic Stage," 107.

44 "The Ben Greet Players of New York and London," publicity brochure, ca. 1911. Iowa.

45 Winifred F. E. C. Isaac, *Ben Greet and the Old Vic: A Biography of Sir Philip Ben Greet* (London: author, n.d.), 149.

46 Robert Speight, *William Poel and the Elizabethan Revival* (Cambridge: Harvard University Press, 1954), 43.

47 Ibid., 74.

48 Orchard, *Fifty Years of Chautauqua*, 182.

49 Hedges, "Actors under Canvas," 48.

50 Isaac, *Ben Greet*, 131–132.

51 James S. Smoot, "Platform Theatre: Theatrical Elements of the Lyceum-Chautauqua" (Ph.D. diss., University of Michigan, 1954), 79–81.

52 Ibid., 84.

53 Harrison, *Culture under Canvas*, 192.

54 "The Ben Greet Players of New York and London."

55 "The Ben Greet Players," Redpath publicity brochure, n.d. Iowa.

56 Redpath, season program, Savannah, Ga., 1913. Iowa.

57 "The Ben Greet Players of New York and London."

58 "The Ben Greet Players."

59 William Fulton, clipping, Redpath attraction report, Indianapolis, Ind., November 15, 1915. Iowa.

60 Hedges, "Actors under Canvas," 51.

61 Harrison, *Culture under Canvas*, 202. Emphasis mine.

62 Ibid., 191–192.

63 Arthur Row, "The Actor in Chautauqua," unpublished manuscript. New York.

64 Hanscom, *Pioneers in Grease Paint*, 57.

65 Ibid.

66 Harrison, *Culture under Canvas*, 202.

67 Charles Rann Kennedy, *The Servant in the House* (New York: Harper and Brothers, 1908), 113.

68 Ibid., 127.

69 Bliven, "Mother," 174.

70 Baggott with McKee, "Christian Culture," 446.

71 Redpath, season program, Savannah, Ga., 1913.

72 White and Myers, season program, Gage, Ok., 1922.

73 Redpath, season program, n.p., 1920. Iowa.

74 White and Myers, season program, Highmore, [no state]. 1921. Iowa.

75 Redpath-Horner, season program, Checotah, Ok., 1920. Iowa.

76 Evening Star, season program, Agen, S.D., 1922. Iowa.

77 Frick, "A Changing Theater," 201.

78 Robert Lee Wyatt III, *The History of the Haverstock Tent Show: "The Show with a Million Friends"* (Carbondale: Southern Illinois University Press, 1997), 7–8.

79 McNamara, "Popular Entertainment," 399.

80 Alfred C. Bernheim, *The Business of the Theatre: An Economic History of the American Theatre, 1750–1932* (New York: Bloom, 1964 [1932]), 107.

81 Quoted in Baggott with McKee, "Christian Culture," 446.

82 Harrison, *Culture under Canvas*, 202.

83 Crawford Peffer, "Outline History of the Redpath Lyceum Bureau," unpublished manuscript, 1956. Texas, HRC.

84 Harry P. Harrison to William Keighley, April 7, 1926. Iowa.

85 John F. Chambers to William Keighley, March 11, 1926. Iowa.

86 Ibid.

87 George E. Vincent, "University Extension Drama," *Chautauquan* 11 (1913): 120.

88 Case and Case, *We Called It Culture*, 52.

89 "Chautauquas Are Helping Better Drama Movement," *Lyceum Magazine*, April 1922, 21.

90 Smith, *American Drama*, 20.

91 Harrison, *Culture under Canvas*, 201–202.

92 Orchard, *Fifty Years of Chautauqua*, 275.

93 Crawford A. Peffer, "Why the Chautauqua Drama?" *Platform World*, April 1929, 19.

94 G. S. Chance, "The Lecture, Play, and Reader Wanted," *Lyceum Magazine*, June 1924, 21.

95 Redpath, season program, n.p., 1916. Iowa.

96 Case and Case, *We Called It Culture*, 51.

97 Walter Prichard Eaton, "The Real Revolt in Our Theatre," *Scribner's* 72 (November 1922): 598.

98 Ibid., 600.

99 Keith Vawter to *Scribner's*, October 31, 1922. Iowa.

100 Kenneth Macgowan, *Footlights Across America* (New York: Harcourt Brace, 1929), 74, 76.

101 Orchard, *Fifty Years of Chautauqua*, 275–276.

102 Bernheim, *The Business of the Theatre*, 107; L. Verne Slout, "The Chautauqua Drama," *Lyceum Magazine*, April 1923, 19.

103 Slout, "The Chautauqua Drama," 19.

104 Ibid., 20.

105 Horner, *Strike the Tents*, 187.

106 Bohn, "America Revealed," 3.

107 Oram, interview, May 20, 1998.

108 Case and Case, *We Called It Culture*, 52–55.

CONCLUSION

1 *The Trouble with Girls*, dir. Peter Tewksbury, MGM, 1969.

2 Peter Guralnick, *Careless Love: The Unmaking of Elvis Presley* (Boston: Little, Brown, 1999), 322.

3 Vawter to Harlan, April 10, 1935. *O Chautauqua* did not do well and was not a popular success. Duncan would have to wait twelve years, until 1947, when his book about the success and failure of a circus owner, *Gus the Great*, became a Book-of-the-Month Club selection and Universal bought the film rights. "Famous Iowans," *Des Moines Register*, http://desmoinesregister.com/extras/iowans/duncan.html. October 10, 2003.

4 "Chautauqua at 100," *Newsweek*, September 2, 1974, 73.

5 C. E. Backman to James S. Smoot, May 18, 1954, quoted in Smoot, "Platform Theater," 286. It would be interesting to know if Backman also included his wife Gay MacLaren's book on her Circuit Chautauqua experiences, *Morally We Roll Along*, in this category.

6 Keith Vawter to I. R. Rehm, December 18, 1926; Harry Harrison to W. S. Rupe, January 8, 1927; M. M. Davies to Harry Harrison, January 10, 1927; W. S. Rupe to Harry Harrison, February 18, 1929. Iowa.

7 Schultz, *The Romance of Small-Town Chautauquas*, 146.

8 Ibid., 148.

9 Ibid., 151.

10 Oram, interview with author, February 15, 1996. Oram remembers the year as 1938 or 1939, considerably after the end of the New York–New England Redpath. As far as I can tell, the Chautauqua he performed in was not part of a Circuit but was put on for single towns.

11 Frederic Babcock, "Among the Authors," *Chicago Sunday Tribune*, January 23, 1944, 14.

12 Harrison, *Culture under Canvas*, 270.

13 Horner, *Strike the Tents*, 189.

14 Keith Vawter, interview, July 13, 1934. Iowa.

15 E. B. Wilson to H. J. Thornton, October 10, 1936. Iowa.

16 C. J. Harlan to H. J. Thornton, October 12, 1936. Iowa.

17 Model T Ford Club of America, http://www.mtfca.com/index.htm. October 10, 2003.

18 Paul Pearson, "The Circuit Chautauqua: First Tentative Outline," unpublished manuscript, ca. 1931–1935. Swarthmore.

19 Ibid.

20 Ibid.

21 Ibid.

22 "Paul Pearson," *Lippincott's Magazine*, August 1906, 190.

23 New York–New England Redpath, season program, n.p., 1929. Iowa.

24 Michael McGerr, *A Fierce Discontent: The Rise and Fall of the Progressive Movement in America 1870–1920* (New York: Free Press, 2003), 315.

25 Without the part on Chautauqua, this is the case Loren Kruger makes for the FTP. The FTP argument was "for *federated* theaters whose national standing might no longer exclusively depend on the mass presence of the national audience in one place, but which might include a national federation of local audiences." Loren Kruger, *The National Stage: Theater and Cultural Legitimation in England, France and America* (Chicago: University of Chicago Press, 1992), 5.

26 Chautauqua Network, http://www.ciweb.org/chautauqua_network.html. October 13, 2003.

27 "CPS Being Revived in Waxahachie," *Chautauqua News* 1, no. 1 (2000): 1.

28 Rieser, *The Chautauqua Moment*, 291.

29 George Frein, "The American Renaissance: Summer Scholars in Residence," National Endowment for the Humanities General Program Division, 1990 application, 3.

30 Susan Savage, opening remarks, Chautauqua, Tulsa, Ok., June 1993.

31 Frein, "The American Renaissance," 4, 5.

32 Everett C. Albers, Introduction, "Reflections on Doing Chautauqua," in Frein, "The American Renaissance," 2.

33 Frein, "The American Renaissance," 4.

34 "Shall We Chautauqua?" http://www.jimhightower.com/tour/index.asp. July 22, 2004.

35 "A Little Chautauqua History," http://www.jimhightower.com/tour/history.asp. July 22, 2004.

36 Ibid.

37 *The Trouble with Girls.*

38 Chautauqua Network.

Index

MacGarr, Llewellen, 113
Macgowan, Kenneth, 207
MacLaren, Gay, 4, 92, 109, 165, 174, 175,
    176, 178, 185, 186, 220
Main Street, 16, 17, 18
"Mammy," 99
managers, 3, 9, 11, 13, 16, 26, 39, 52, 71,
    75, 81, 82, 85, 91, 93, 113, 118, 119, 163,
    165, 178, 187, 188, 191, 193, 194, 198,
    199, 200, 201, 203, 204, 206, 207, 208,
    209, 218, 219
Manchester, Iowa, 153
Maryville, Missouri, 180
Matthews, Anne Lauers, 220
Matthison, Edith Wynne, 200
Mayo, Margaret, 201
McCaskill, Frances D. C., 5
McClure, W. Frank, 72
McRaven, Mrs. John, 82, 99
Meanest Man in the World, The, 203
Melting-Pot, The, 6, 53–56, 68, 69, 87, 172,
    174
Mentone, Indiana, 66
Mentzer, Margaret, 66
Methodism, 6, 167, 190, 191, 192, 193
Methodist Amusement Ban, 192–93
middle class, 18, 37, 92, 100, 117, 163, 191,
    194, 223
Midland Chautauqua Assembly, 143
Midwest, 9, 10, 18, 76, 79, 120
Military Girls, 14
Miller, Alex, 77–78, 98
Miller, Lewis, 6–7, 190–191
Minakuchi, Yutaki, 86
minstrelsy, 79, 82, 164
missionaries, 73, 82–88, 164, 188, 204
mock weddings, 43, 46, 66, 134
Moore, Maureen, 224
Mooresville, Indiana, 59
morality, 14, 19, 20, 22, 34, 36, 39, 41, 43,
    52, 75, 92, 93, 94, 95, 97, 117, 126, 128,
    129, 130, 155, 161, 162, 163, 164, 165,
    166, 167, 168, 169, 171, 172, 174, 175,

176, 178, 188, 189, 191, 194, 195, 199,
    200, 202, 205, 206
morals. *See* morality
Mother Goose Festival, 64
Mother Goose Party, A, 43, 45, 47
Mount Sterling, Kentucky, 62
movies, 2, 23, 53, 200, 220, 221, 223, 227
music, 5, 14, 20, 23, 84, 87, 93, 95, 96,
    111, 156, 159, 171, 173, 190, 196, 200,
    209, 224

nation, 18, 21, 22, 23, 34, 36, 38, 39, 43,
    46, 49, 50, 51, 54, 56, 71, 73, 74, 75, 76,
    112, 114, 119, 122, 125, 126, 128, 160, 161,
    162, 168, 191, 201, 223, 225, 227, 228
Nation, Carrie, 89
National Endowment for the Humanities,
    224, 225
National Register of Historic Places, 230
Neil Litchfield Trio, 111
neo-Chautauqua, 224, 225, 228; Great
    Plains, 225
Next-best Man, The, 112
North End Women's Club, 107
nostalgia, 39, 85, 121, 159, 218, 222
Nothing But the Truth, 201

O' Chautauqua, 218
O'Neill, Eugene, 192, 202
O'Neill, James, 192–193
Oram, Richard, 20, 43, 46, 66, 134, 162,
    209, 215, 220, 228
oratory, 22, 155, 159, 160, 161, 167, 169,
    170, 171, 174, 177, 178, 198, 200, 209,
    217, 221, 227
Oregon Shakespeare Festival, 3
"Our Town," 152
Owen, Ruth Bryan, 90, 106

pageant, 34, 43, 44, 45, 59, 64, 193
parades, 62, 66, 67, 136
Parish Players, 206
Parlette, Ralph, 109

Wood, Fred Dale, 53
Wood, Grant, 3
Wood, Harrie, 121
woodsman-poet. *See* Lew Sarett
World War I, 10, 12, 21, 33, 34, 36, 41, 42, 49–57, 89

Zangwill, Israel, 53–56, 68, 173
Zen and the Art of Motorcycle Maintenance, 2, 227
Zilborg, Gregory, 86
Zueblin, Charles, 16, 30, 72

Studies in Theatre History & Culture